Home Away from Home

Home Away from Home

The Forgotten History of Orphanages

Richard B. McKenzie, *Editor*

Encounter Books
New York □ London

First American edition published in 2009 by Encounter Books,
an activity of Encounter for Culture and Education, Inc.,
a nonprofit, tax exempt corporation.
Encounter Books website address: www.encounterbooks.com

Manufactured in the United States and printed on
acid-free paper. The paper used in this publication meets
the minimum requirements of ANSI/NISO Z39.48—1992
(R 1997) (*Permanence of Paper*).

FIRST AMERICAN EDITION

LIBRARY OF CONGRESS CATALOGING-IN-PUBLICATION DATA

Home away from home : the forgotten history of orphanages /
Richard B. McKenzie, editor.
    p. cm.
Includes bibliographical references and index.
  ISBN-13: 978–1-59403-245-5 (hardcover : alk. paper)
  ISBN-10: 1-59403-245-9 (hardcover : alk. paper) 1. Orphanages—
United States—History. 2. Orphanages—History. I. McKenzie,
Richard B.
  HV978.H66 2009
  362.73'2—dc22

                              2009018131

Contents

Preface

□ Richard B. McKenzie

Home Away from Home has its genesis in the intense but unfortunately short-lived orphanage debate of late 1994. In early November of that year, just after the Republicans won a majority in the U.S. House, then-Representative Newt Gingrich was elected Speaker of the House. In a speech he gave shortly after his new post was assured, Representative Gingrich made an offhand comment to the effect that many children ensnared in bad families and neighborhoods and in the public welfare system would be better off in private orphanages. He proposed that states be allowed to use savings in welfare benefits to establish orphanages.[1]

Representative Gingrich's comments and proposal set off a media and political firestorm, with all the major news magazines running cover stories on the orphanages of the nation's past.[2] The covers typically depicted turn-of-the-century orphanage waifs. One memorable cover consisted entirely of a black-and-white photograph of young orphanage girls in dresses made from feed sacks, their hands stretched outward and upward as if they were pleading for more gruel.[3] These images, judged by both the living and childcare standards of the 1990s, were a none-too-subtle commentary on the widely believed sordid history of orphanages.

The syndicated columnist Ellen Goodman denounced the Gingrich proposal in no uncertain terms. "These orphanages [in the early part of this century and before]," she said, "were not only Dickensian institutions where children were literally lost, but they were expensive."[4] Then-First Lady

Hillary Rodham Clinton declared the Gingrich proposal "unbelievable and absurd."[5]

Virtually all child welfare experts interviewed for these orphanage stories in 1994 condemned the childcare records of orphanages throughout history, usually without qualifications.[6] Given the onslaught of negative media reaction to his initial comments, Representative Gingrich retreated, suggesting that he meant that the children of welfare mothers should be placed in modern-day "group homes," not in anything similar to the orphanages of the past, as imagined by the media and the general public.[7]

□

I took note of the childcare experts' reactions to Representative Gingrich's comments because I grew up in an orphanage, a place called Barium Springs Home for Children, in North Carolina in the 1950s. While I certainly could point to the care limitations of my upbringing there, I never thought I was as badly damaged as the experts claimed I must have been, with confidence and often *without* the qualifications generally found in scholarly pronouncements. No, many experts' policy recommendations were unequivocal: Bringing back orphanages was a bad idea, period—because of orphanages' uniformly poor historical record.

Throughout my life, I've heard the orphanage experience condemned by any number of people who knew it only from the way orphanages are portrayed in novels and movies. The experts' public testimonials in 1994 piqued my interest because I was then hard pressed to think of many, if any, of my orphanage peers who had been as badly and completely damaged as the quoted childcare experts suggested. Indeed, I could point only to alumni (aside for maybe one) who had done reasonably if not very well in life. But I also had to consider that perhaps my orphanage home was different. Perhaps it was unique within a sea of bad orphanages. Was the track record of my orphanage in my era (the 1950s) different from its record in earlier times? It was possible that most other orphanages in earlier times did indeed resemble the Dickensian hellholes portrayed in movies and literature.

Plenty of maybes went through my mind as I witnessed the one-sided media "debate" in 1994. Indeed, the only historical issue worthy of discussion seemed to be that of just how bad the childcare records of orphanages were. Few reporters seemed willing to entertain the possibility that there may have been some (or many) good orphanages throughout history, ones that did reasonably well by the children in their care.

In spite of these many maybes, I did something in the middle of the Gingrich-inspired orphanage debate that I had never done before. Writing in the *Wall Street Journal*, I went public with my orphanage upbringing.[8]

> At the start of the movie *Annie*, Miss Hannigan—the decadent, overbearing house mother of twenty or so little girls—wonders in obvious exasperation, "Why any kid would want to be an orphan is beyond me."
>
> The stark contrast between the movie version of life in the orphanage and the life Annie came to know with her adopted father, the extravagantly wealthy Daddy Warbucks, probably left many movie goers convinced that Miss Hannigan was right, no one in their right mind would ever want to be an orphan.
>
> I've spent a lifetime quietly listening to others disparage orphanages as cold and loveless institutions where every child longs to be adopted. I know that the popular description of homes for children is distressingly out of date and out of whack, and should have no bearing on the debate of how to help some of the least fortunate children among us. I grew up in a home with 150 or so other girls and boys in North Carolina in the 1950s—and I'm damn proud of it, and thankful.
>
> Life in my Home was no picnic. When we were young, we got two baths and changes of clothes a

week, regardless of whether we needed more. We worked hard for long hours on the farm and in the shops, and we lacked a lot, not the least of which were the daily hugs other children take for granted.

Critics of orphanages stress what the children there did not have. Those of us who were there have a different perspective. We were, and remain, able to draw comparisons between what we had at The Home with what we would have had. If any one of us had had a choice between growing up with Ozzie and Harriet or in The Home, each would surely have taken the former. However, we either didn't have parents or left parents behind who were not worthy of the roles they had assumed. Few of us would have entertained adoption, and virtually all of us today shudder at the foster-care option.

We understand that we have not always set the world on fire. At the same time, we realize that we would not be where we are today had we not had the opportunity to grow up the way we did. With all the current talk about "family values," critics must never forget that some families value very little.

With unforgettable pictures of Miss Hannigan, I know many people harbor fears about workers in homes for children. They, however, could not have known Mrs. Mac, one of the many house mothers with big hearts, who, after I left The Home, sent a birthday card every year until her death in the late 1980s.

The critics have never had the opportunity to sit in Francis Moore's seventh grade class. By her unbounded force of character, she made us believe what then was surely a myth that it was us, not our circumstances, that would ultimately determine how far we would go in life. Last year, she sent one of the best Christmas gifts I have ever received, a two-by-three-foot framed set of original verses in needlepoint on what it means to be successful—not the money kind, but the kind that affects the heart and soul. Square that with the likes of Miss Hannigan.

Most critics would like the public to believe that those of us who went through orphanages were throttled by the experience. No doubt, some were. However, most have charged on. In many ways, we represent the best of what this country is about, plumbers and nurses, ministers and managers, teachers and baggage handlers—in the main, good well-meaning Americans who have answered the call to rise above expectations.

Most might be surprised to learn that of the boys and girls who graduated from high school in the late 1950s more than 80 percent now have college and advanced degrees, no minor accomplishment for kids who supposedly grew up the "hard way."

Miss Hannigan, you should have asked a real orphan, not the ones cast in Hollywood or Washington. Life in a home for children cannot be perfect. However, people should understand that homes for children must remain a viable option for many children. Those of us who were there share an array of experiences that, when the balance is struck, children from many traditional families can only envy.

I was astounded by the volume of responses to that column. The morning it appeared, my phone truly did ring off the hook. My email inbox lit up with responses. Later, my university mailbox was jammed with letters. Publishers called to ask if I'd write a memoir, which, incidentally, I had finished the previous summer without intending to publish it; thanks to the column, it was published a year later (*The Home: A Memoir of Growing Up in an Orphanage*[9]). Much to my surprise, I even had a Hollywood producer drive out to my university to take me to lunch and to discuss the development of a sitcom based in an orphanage, an intriguing idea that went nowhere.

Through all the contacts made, I was mainly struck by the large number of orphanage alumni who emailed, called, or penned letters to tell me in some detail that they, too, had had a good, albeit imperfect, orphanage experience. I began to doubt whether the childcare experts who had been interviewed for the magazine cover stories in 1994 knew what they were talking about. With the help of about thirty childcare academics and practitioners, and people skilled in undertaking surveys (whom I enlisted to ensure that my personal views on orphanages did not color the way the survey was written and distributed and the data was evaluated), I undertook two separate surveys of orphanage alumni, with more than 2,500 taking the time to fill out the detailed nine-page questionnaire. The general conclusion of both surveys stood in marked contrast with the expert claims of 1994: As a group, the orphanage alumni, categorized by age, outpaced their counterparts in the U.S. general population on almost all social and economic measures, not least of which were education, income, and positive assessments of their life experiences, both during their upbringings and afterwards. I did indeed receive responses from orphanage alumni who had hard feelings about their orphanage days, and I do not want to bury such responses with any sweeping suggestion that *all* orphanages did well by *all* the children in their care. The negative assessments, however, were a tiny minority (less than 3 percent), and a major finding of my surveys defied conventional wisdom: A substantial majority of the alumni (upwards of 85 percent) recalled favorable or very favorable childhood experiences at their orphanages. The rest of the survey respondents (11 to 12 percent) had mixed experiences.[10]

As I began to talk about the orphanage issue around the country, I came to understand that there were a number of questions about orphanages that needed to be addressed, not the least of which are: Why did the orphanage system of yesteryear fade from the child welfare scene so rapidly after 1950? What happened to the cost of orphanage care over the decades? How sound were the findings of the academic child welfare articles and books cited so frequently during the 1994 debate?

These and a number of other questions were addressed in my first edited volume on orphanages, *Rethinking Orphanages for the 21st Century*.[11] For that volume, scholars from several disciplines were asked to address the types of questions raised above. *Rethinking Orphanages* has apparently proven useful to many students and academic researchers and to groups who have wanted to investigate the possibility of the development of modern-day orphanages in their communities.

Still, academic research can only reach so many people, and most people interested in the child welfare debate couldn't care less about dry statistics and specialized scholarly arguments.

When I gave talks in the mid-1990s on the orphanage issue, my audiences were often intrigued by the revelation that my home held a homecoming every year, with hundreds of alumni and their families attending. Indeed, orphanages all over the country hold homecomings, a fact of which I was reminded by the many alumni who contacted me—several of whom asked me to speak at their own homecomings. This was clearly an important lesson for my audiences, many of which were largely ignorant of the subject: If the orphanage alumni still gather for reunions, decades after their homes have closed or radically changed missions, maybe the orphanages of yesteryear weren't as bad (across the board, at least) as experts had claimed.

In 1996, hoping to reach a larger audience, I set out to develop a documentary film through which aging orphanage alumni could relate, with personal stories and in vivid color, the good, the bad, and the ugly of orphanage life in the 1950s and earlier. The film could convey what articles could not: the emotional content of personal childhood experiences. Because I had little knowledge of the complexities and expenses involved in filmmaking, the project took ten years to complete, but it would likely never have been completed at all without the help of Gary Byrne, a savvy businessman and good friend, and George Cawood, the film's director. Cawood assembled a group of Burbank-based filmmakers—including Sheila Moreland, the film editor; Adam Hauck, producer; and Jeffrey Hepker, composer and music director, along with many others who devoted more than 20,000 pro bono hours to the project—and produced a beautiful and emotionally powerful film: *Homecoming: The Forgotten World of America's Orphanages*. The film was selected for screenings in four film festivals and won "Best Documentary" in one festival in 2005. To date, it has aired on over 220 PBS stations.[12]

□

When I joined the orphanage debate with my *Wall Street Journal* column in 1994, I did not expect to spend the next dozen or more years working on the issue. I had a justified suspicion back then that the conventional, widely held (and parroted) view of orphanages—that they all matched the desperate conditions of the orphanage Charles Dickens described in *Oliver Twist*—was not likely to hold up under careful scrutiny. There were too many orphanages throughout history and across the country (San Francisco alone had over forty orphanages in the early part of the twentieth century) to not suspect that at least *some* of them did reasonably well by many of their charges. There were also too many alumni from different homes who had contacted me to explain why their homes were better than mine for me to accept the experts' broad-brush claims. Then, too, I had my own experience, which had been pretty good, all things considered, to fall back on. I knew my home did not fit the grim Dickensian mold.

But at every turn in the ongoing debate I had with various childcare experts from 1994 forward, it became clear that perceptions of the history of orphanages, constructed and purveyed by political interest groups, had a stranglehold on the contemporary debate over what to do with disadvantaged children in our society. The perceived history also had a grip on public consideration of any suggestion that modern-day orphanages (or "children's homes," "academies," or "boarding schools for disadvantaged youth," whatever they are called) be considered one of several childcare options. It became obvious that the history of orphanages needed to be reconsidered as an open academic question, with tentative conclusions drawn not from conventional wisdom, which had long escaped critical academic scrutiny, but from hard-nosed scholarly inquiry.

Fortunately, in the 1990s, without connections to the political debate ignited by Representative Gingrich, academics from the fields of history, political science, and economics began revisiting the history of various orphanages across the country, the history of the overall orphanage movement, both in its ascendancy and its decline, and the history of childcare alternatives to orphanages, such as "placing out" and "orphan trains." A number of academic researchers had by the mid-1990s published whole books on their respective subjects. In a number of cases, they began their research assuming that they would uncover Dickensian conditions in the orphanages studied. They often ended their research with a different perspective, however: that orphanages throughout history were all imperfect institutions but that they were often (or more frequently than conventional wisdom would have it) better than adequate childcare solutions given the living conditions of the times and the dire circumstances of the children in need of out-of-home care.

Several of these academic researchers have contributed to this volume. In developing *Home Away from Home*, I asked contributors to condense their larger scholarly works into manageable chapters both for the common reader and for those readers who, after reading the chapters in this volume, might want to turn to the contributors' longer histories for more information. I assured the contributors that I wanted them to relate their histories just as they found them, not in the way they or I might want them to be. But, then, the contributors to this volume and I understood that orphanages were real-world institutions, almost always struggling with difficult social problems under serious financial and resource constraints. Institutional imperfections were to be expected.

Chapter Summaries

In Chapter 1, "Orphanages in History and the Modern Child Welfare Setting," Duncan Lindsey and Paul Stuart have provided a review of the history of orphanages in the context of the development of social welfare in the United States. Orphanages played an important role in the development of the modern child welfare system but were largely rejected by expert opinion in the twentieth century. This chapter, and book, extends the Lindsey/Stuart review by providing a much broader examination of the history of orphanages and the evolution of the institutional model of childcare over the course of the last millennium.

In Chapter 2, Timothy Miller discusses the inception and early history of orphanages. Going back to the first century, "The Early History of Orphanages: From Constantinople to Venice" examines the development of Christian group homes and orphanages in Greco-Roman society. These institutions, which evolved from Jewish traditions preserved in the Torah, were established as a practice of faith, and served as the foundation of the orphanage concept as it evolved over a thousand years.

In Chapter 3, "Christian Charity and the Politics of Orphan Care in the Dutch Republic," Anne McCants provides an overview of orphanages as the product of the social-historical phenomenon known as "charity," which is as much a matter of conscience as it is of faith. She examines richly endowed charitable institutions which were a source of great pride during the "Golden Age" of the Dutch Republic, in the seventeenth and eighteenth centuries. These institutions, she argues, served as the genesis of social welfare as a manifestation of government policy.

The focus of Chapter 4, "Mooseheart: The Child City" by

David Beito, is the role of American fraternal organizations in the development of orphanages in the early part of the twentieth century. It is his contention that mutual aid was at the heart of social welfare, surpassing the efforts of both government and charitable organizations. Fully one-third of the adult American population belonged to lodges in the 1920s, and those fraternal orders built many of the orphanages of that period.

In Chapter 5, "A Home of Another Kind: An Orphanage in the Midst of Chicago's Elite," Anne Duggan interprets and summarizes the work of her late husband, Kenneth Cmiel, who examined the Chicago-based orphanage Chapin Hall, which was once a residential treatment center but now serves as a monitoring agency and major research center. Engaged in "building knowledge to improve the health and well being of children," Chapin Hall strives to provide "focus on meeting the real-world needs of those who are working directly with the programs and institutions that affect the daily lives of children."

In Chapter 6, "Fates of Orphans: Poor Children in Antebellum Charleston," John Murray discusses the different paths taken by children who had resided in America's first public orphanage in antebellum Charleston, the Charleston Orphan House. Murray focuses on the post-orphanage outcomes, economic and otherwise, of the alumni and the light those outcomes shed on society's attitudes towards its children. Placed in a historical context that dates back to the Civil War era, the chapter is most enlightening with regard to "harsh" verses "gentle" practices of childrearing.

In Chapter 7, "The Transformation of Catholic Orphanages: Cleveland, 1851–1996," Marian Morton reviews the transformation of St. Vincent's Orphanage in Cleveland. During its first 150 years, St. Vincent's went from a Catholic charitable institution serving an all-white population of impoverished boys to a publicly-funded family services center responding to the needs of children and families regardless of race or creed. Much of the chapter focuses on Catholic charities, which, in the nineteenth and twentieth centuries, were among the most used and least studied non-secular institutional responses to impoverished, homeless, and emotionally disabled children.

In Chapter 8, "Baltimore's Nineteenth-Century Orphanages," Nurith Zmora discusses three childcare institutions born of ethnic and religious communities, in contrast with the publicly-funded orphanages that existed at that time in other American cities. Zmora provides valuable context for the examination of the orphanage concept and its relationship to religious institutions. Interestingly, all of the Baltimore orphanages existing during the time period addressed were segregated according to religion or nationality.

One of the most important developments to affect the development of orphanages in the nineteenth century was the so-called "orphan train." In Chapter 9, "The Orphan Trains as an Alternative to Orphanages," Marilyn Holt examines this principal alternative to turn-of-the-century orphanages. Believing that home placement was the most desirable means to care for indigent and abandoned children, various religious organizations in the early nineteenth century took city-dwelling children and shipped them to the Midwest for placement, especially with religious families. "Child relocation," as it was often called, is one of the most interesting aspects of the history of child social welfare.

In the final chapter, "Orphanages as a National Institution: History and Its Lessons," Timothy Hacsi examines the rapid growth of orphanages during the several decades before the Civil War (1830s to 1850s). During the 1930s, more than a thousand orphanages were functioning and represented the major form of out-of-home care for children. With the growth of foster care, there has been a decline in the number of large orphanages coupled with increased use of residential institutions. But given heavy criticism of the foster care system, Hacsi demonstrates that the history of orphanages provides some important lessons about the options society has available to help disadvantaged children who lack stable homes.

Taken together, these chapters provide a compelling picture of the potential for orphanages to meet the needs of the many children who currently languish for years in the foster care system. Studying the history of this original model is essential to progress in child welfare.

Nonpartisan History of Orphanages

Readers hoping for a partisan history of the orphanage phenomenon will be sorely disappointed. Contributors were not chosen on the basis of ideological alignment; indeed, I've never even inquired into the politics of the contributors. After all, the core concern—the care of disadvantaged children—should not have partisan boundaries, contrary to the manner in which the orphanage issue was framed in Washington, D.C., in 1994.

The contributors and I agreed that the histories had to be *real*, warts and all, and that, where possible, they had to be set in the context of comparative data on living and child-care standards outside of orphanages for their time periods and geographical locations. The value of this volume will emerge ultimately from its academic intent and approach, its historical reviews of orphanages by academics concerned with true scholarship, not propaganda.

This book isn't the last word on orphanages. One reason for this is that it provides only a sample of the histories of orphanages. Innumerable orphanages have opened and closed in communities across this country (there were forty-four orphanages in San Francisco alone in the 1930s) and throughout the world, for reasons which this book will address. Many histories remain to be told. Sadly, some of those histories will go unrecognized and unrecorded. Another reason this book cannot hope to provide the last word is less obvious: Orphanages never really disappeared in this country or anywhere else in the world. Many have continued to serve disadvantaged children, admirably. They continue to create their own histories.

I have two favorite homes that have continued to serve disadvantaged children for either close to or more than a century: The Connie Maxwell Children's Home in Greenwood, South Carolina, and The Crossnore School in Crossnore, North Carolina (deep in the mountains). My third favorite home is Happy Hill Farm, Academy, and Home in Grundy, Texas, outside of Fort Worth, which was established in the 1970s. To those who say it can't be done today at reasonable cost, I say go to Connie Maxwell. Go to Crossnore. Go to Happy Hill. And be prepared to be amazed.

Communities around the country have begun to recognize that they need a menu of childcare options, including modern-day orphanages (not just treatment facilities for *troubled* children, but long-term care centers for *disadvantaged* children). Homes have emerged in San Diego County, California (San Pasqual Academy); Minneapolis, Minnesota (Mary's House); and Sonoma County, California (Sonoma County Children's Village). The World's Children Center, which plans eventually to care for eight hundred children, is being built outside of Atlanta, Georgia, and homes are being planned for Santa Barbara and Orange Counties, California, all as of this writing. Before I began my orphanage work, Heidi Goldsmith was hard at work developing public and media support for residential education for disadvantaged children. She now heads the Coalition for Residential Education (or CORE) with forty homes that are saving the lives of thousands of children throughout the country (and sending a higher percentage of the children in care on to college than is true of the general population).

At least once a month I hear from some group someplace that is planning the development of a modern-day orphanage. These homes' histories will be recorded one day, perhaps in a volume such as this one. I doubt that all homes now under development will be successful, but should we not expect any number of them to have histories no less impressive than the ones described in this volume?

□

For me, this volume completes a circle of sorts. I have written my own personal orphanage story. In *Rethinking Orphanages*, I asked academics to address a number of key academic issues on the operation of orphanages of the past and future. I have had the good fortune of enlisting George Cawood in the development of a film that conveys the emotional side of orphanage life. And I have been able to bring together in these pages a reconsidered history of the orphanages of our past. All of these projects have been completed with the hope that readers and viewers will have a more informed view of orphanages and a more informed reaction to widely and glibly made claims that orphanages have never been a solution to childcare problems and, hence, never can be in the future.

□

This book project could not possibly have been completed without the support and encouragement of others, including the contributors to this volume who firmly agreed on the value of making this book widely available. While I have edited several books over my career, I have never edited a volume that needed less editing, or criticisms and comments for improvement, than this one. Readers will find the chapters herein clearly written and informative.

In all of my orphanage-related projects, I have been indebted to the Lynde and Harry Bradley Foundation for its considerable financial support, which is acknowledged with tremendous gratitude. I am also thankful to Bill Podlich for his financial support, which has helped indirectly in this book's development. The UNTIL Foundation, headed by Mark Nix, was invaluable in helping me bring this project to fruition. Last, but hardly least, I am indebted to my wife, Karen McKenzie, who edited the following chapters.

□ *Irvine, California*
  July 2007

1 □ Orphanages in History and the Modern Child Welfare Setting:
An Overview

Duncan Lindsey and Paul H. Stuart

Since at least 1912, prevailing opinion in social welfare has been that under most conditions, children who cannot for whatever reason live with their own parents should be placed in homes or home-like environments. This opinion was almost universal during the twentieth century; it echoes the conclusion of the 1909 White House Conference on Dependent Children that "[h]ome life is the highest and finest product of civilization . . . Children should not be deprived of it except for urgent and compelling reasons."[1] Responding to a generation of child welfare reformers who had denounced institutional care for children, the conference favored keeping dependent children in their own homes if possible. If family care proved to be out of the question, the conference recommended out-of-home placement in foster homes. The conference recommended that in cases where institutional care seemed necessary, institutions use the cottage system rather than barracks or other congregate systems for housing children.

In favoring the home and home-like arrangements, the conferees reversed the trend of the previous century's social policy. Nineteenth-century reformers had promoted orphanages as the means to rescue children from bad conditions, including placement in undifferentiated or omnibus institutions that held poor persons of all ages. But in earlier times, care of children in homes or community settings was the norm.

The Poor Law

The English Poor Law of 1601, which was widely implemented in England's North American colonies, included provisions for building dwelling places for the poor. The emphasis, however, was on community placement. Children who were parentless or whose parents were found by local authorities to be unable to provide care were to be apprenticed "till such man-child shall come to the age of four and twenty years, and such woman-child to the age of one and twenty years, or until the time of her marriage."[2] Similarly, the act authorized local officials to provide relief for disabled or "impotent" poor persons in their own homes. Although the act is often cited as the origin of the English and American social welfare systems, expenditures for poor relief were insignificant in England and English North America until the early nineteenth century, in the judgment of the economic historian Peter Lindert.[3]

A New Role for Residential Institutions

The situation changed, in both England and the new nation called the United States, in the early nineteenth century. Spending for poor relief as a percentage of gross national product increased dramatically, making both countries world leaders in social spending.[4] At the same time, institutions were viewed for the first time as promising means of solving problems of charity and corrections, not only as places to care for unfortunate members of society. In England, the Poor Law Amendment Act of 1834 provided for the placement of all able-bodied applicants for poor relief in workhouses.[5] In Anglophone North America this law was widely imitated.

Beginning in the 1830s, American states as well as voluntary philanthropists turned to institutions as the solution for the problem of dependent children as well as a variety of other human problems.[6] States, local communities, and private organizations constructed almshouses and workhouses for the poor, prisons for felons, houses of refuge for youthful delinquents, asylums for mentally ill people, and residential schools for persons with a variety of disabilities. Orphanages provided a way to separate children from undifferentiated almshouse populations, which were supposed to have a deleterious effect on their development. Institution building in the United States responded in part to English exemplars. Much of the motivation for the new institutions, however, was homegrown, as "old" Americans confronted a society that was undergoing rapid social change in the early nineteenth century.

The population of the United States grew from nearly four million persons in 1790 to thirty-one million persons in 1860 as a result of immigration and a high rate of natural increase. International migration to the United States was no doubt fueled by a liberal land policy that facilitated land ownership for persons without substantial means. Since federal land was located in the West, land policy spurred western expansion, resulting in the creation of new states. By 1860, twenty new states, including California and Oregon on the Pacific Coast, had been admitted to the union, joining the original thirteen. Most of these states were west of the original thirteen and most adopted more democratic constitutions, creating, in the view of some historians, anxiety about the threat of disorder that would result from giving power to the poor. Residential institutions, along with such other eleemosynary institutions as Sunday Schools, provided a way to impose order on an increasingly disorderly society.

Although social planners envisioned a well-functioning system of institutions, the reality was often far from the ideal. Prisons and mental institutions were often overcrowded, as local officials dumped their criminal and dependent populations on the new state institutions. Institutions were expensive, and state governments found themselves unable to keep up with the demand for beds. Initially, this situation led to attempts to secure federal assistance to the states. In 1848, for example, Dorothea L. Dix, the advocate for asylum care for the mentally ill, asked Congress for five million acres of public land to provide a fund for the support of state mental hospitals.[7]

President Franklin Pierce's 1854 veto of the resulting bill to aid the states ended federal assistance to the states for social welfare until the 1920s. Beginning in 1862 in Massachusetts, states began to develop mechanisms to advise on the operation of state residential institutions. By 1900, most states had established boards of charities composed of prominent citizens to visit and make recommendations for the more efficient management of state prisons, hospitals, residential schools, and orphanages. The state boards, which usually had only advisory responsibilities, investigated state institutions and made recommendations for more efficient management. State boards aimed to promote humane care and economy in state institutions—insane asylums, prisons, orphanages, and other institutions—and sometimes in local government and voluntary institutions as well. In general, the boards promoted improved efficiency and effectiveness in making recommendations for the operation of state institutions.

During the nineteenth century, orphanages flourished as the preferred arrangement for caring for children whose parents were deceased or unable to care for them because of poverty or other reasons. Orphanage care would separate the children from the negative influences of the undifferentiated almshouse, providing a humane refuge for the dependent child. In some nineteenth-century orphanages, true orphans were a minority of the inmates, as parents turned to orphanage care as a means to weather difficult economic times or the stress of westward migration.[8]

Children's institutions for particular groups were intended to accomplish important national objectives as well. The children of newly freed slaves, and those of Native

Americans, were placed in boarding schools created by religious societies and the federal government after the Civil War. The number of Indian boarding schools increased after 1865 as education and cultural assimilation became the goals of federal Indian policy;[9] Freedmen's schools, like Indian schools, included a heavy dose of teaching intended to encourage assimilation. An interesting synergy developed between Indian and Negro education, as changes in one area affected the other.

The most important late-nineteenth-century Indian boarding school, Pennsylvania's Carlisle Indian School, was modeled after Hampton Institute, an institution for the children of freed slaves in Virginia. Booker T. Washington, the famous African-American educator and founder of Alabama's Tuskegee Institute, began his career as superintendent of the "Wigwam," the dormitory for Indian boys at Hampton. A large number of government and church Indian boarding schools enrolled thousands of children by the end of the nineteenth century.

Carlisle founder Richard Henry Pratt thought that the school's location in the East, far from the reservations, would be advantageous in that contact with Native American relatives would be minimal.[10] The school used an "outing system," which placed Native American students with white families in nearby communities "to learn English and the customs of civilized life."[11] Community placement would solidify the gains achieved in the boarding school environment, socializing the Native American child to white ways and assimilating him or her to European-American beliefs. Community placement was a supplement to group care; both furthered the goal of acculturating Native American and African-American children to European-American culture.

The Progressive Era

By 1900, most states had created state boards of charities. By the end of the nineteenth century, boards were promoting the adoption of civil service rules for the appointment of personnel in state institutions, bidding for contracts to supply institutions, aftercare for persons released from state institutions, and the development of community alternatives to institutional placement. Care in the home, board members believed, was more humane. It was also considerably cheaper than institutional care.[12]

The shift from institutional care to family care for dependent children was mirrored by a shift from institutional to community care for other previously institutionalized populations, at least in reformers' thinking. The Progressive Era saw the rise of a variety of community care programs for previously institutionalized populations, including probation and parole for adult and juvenile offenders, aftercare programs for the mentally ill, and mother's pensions for widows and other single women with children.[13] The turn to family and community placements for previously institutionalized populations was associated with the rise of new professions serving children, in particular social work, and a new understanding of childhood as a unique stage in human development.

Criticisms of Institutions

While Richard Henry Pratt had used the placement of children with families as a supplement to institutional care, Charles Loring Brace, a Protestant minister who devoted his career to work with dependent children in New York City, advocated family placement as an alternative to institutional care. Initially, Brace, who began his work with children in 1853, created new institutions for dependent children, including industrial schools for girls and boarding houses for homeless newsboys. Brace became convinced, however, that life in the city was harmful to children, and he devised the plan of placing children with Protestant farm families in the Midwest and West as a way of solving the problem of childhood dependency. The "orphan trains" conceived by Brace transported poor children to rural communities. Many of the children were not true orphans but the children of impoverished parents who had difficulty caring for them. Brace became a vocal opponent of institutional care for children. Ironically, the orphan trains may have stimulated the development of orphanages sponsored by the Catholic Church and Jewish organizations as a protective measure, as almost all of the orphan train placements were with Protestant families.

Brace and other "child saving" reformers promoted community placement as an alternative to institutional care that would be better for children. It was also less expensive, and states began to develop family placement programs that would develop into foster care in the early twentieth century. The Russell Sage Foundation (RSF), founded in 1907, was an important stimulant to the development of state child welfare programs. The RSF Child Helping Department, headed by Hastings H. Hart, a former Secretary of the Minnesota State Board of Corrections and Charities, promoted state child welfare programs and carried out studies on child welfare topics from 1907 to 1924, including studies of state child welfare programs.[14]

Two other developments in social welfare affected the debate about institutions versus family placement: changes in the prevailing scientific understanding of childhood, and the campaign against child labor. During the late nineteenth century, psychologists began to understand childhood and adolescence as distinct developmental stages that were qualitatively different from adulthood. Child welfare reformers took this insight to mean that children's needs differed in essential ways from those of adults. At the time, most poor children over the age of ten worked. Beginning in the 1890s, child welfare reformers were increasingly successful in getting state laws passed to limit the employment of children. Many state laws were only partially successful, as they reflected racial prejudices and beliefs about poor families' needs for income from their children's labor.[15]

The 1909 White House Conference on Dependent Children's statement on the importance of home life to child development summarized expert child welfare thinking of the first decade of the twentieth century. It represented a significant break from nineteenth-century thinking, which emphasized the benefits of institutional care. A national movement to codify state laws relating to children followed. The adoption of state children's codes would further the goal "to prolong the period of childhood . . . to shield and equip our boys and girls," in the words of one proponent.[16] Children's Code provisions typically tightened state regulation of child labor, increased the years of mandatory schooling, established or strengthened juvenile courts, and introduced widows' pension and foster care programs. By the 1920s, the changes were so pervasive that Robert W. Kelso, a former Massachusetts Commissioner of Public Welfare, could describe a "transition from charities and correction to public welfare" that had occurred during the previous half-century.[17]

The preference for family care rather than institutional care in professional and public opinion has been remarkably consistent throughout the twentieth century.[18] The Children's Bureau, established in 1912, promoted the development of mother's pensions and child labor legislation under its first two directors, Julia Lathrop and Grace Abbott. The number of children in orphanages did not decline, however, until the 1930s. Title IV of the Social Security Act (1935) established the Aid to Dependent Children (ADC) program, providing cash support to poor children in single-parent households. In Title V, the act provided funds to the states for child welfare programs. These funds could be used to support children in institutions, but the funds were initially limited and children's institutions began to emphasize care for children with special problems in the 1940s and 1950s.

The Golden Age of Research in Child Welfare

Beginning in the late 1950s, a new era of research on children's issues came into being. The most important study to signal this renaissance came from two researchers at the

School of Social Welfare at the University of California, Berkeley—Henry Maas and Richard Engler, one a social worker, the other a sociologist. Maas and Engler conducted an in-depth study of the public and voluntary child welfare system in the United States. After several years of exhaustive study and research, they published *Children in Need of Parents* (1959), the first large-scale examination of foster care as it operated in a representative sample of communities. Maas and Engler found that children removed from their biological parents and placed with foster families on a "temporary" basis often lingered in foster care for an indeterminate number of years. Further, most children even experienced multiple placements.

In the study's call for action, Joseph Reid, President of the Child Welfare League of America (CWLA), noted that of the 268,000 children in foster care, "roughly 168,000 children [were] in danger of staying in foster care throughout their childhood years. And, although in a third of the cases at least one parent did visit the child, approximately half the parents visited infrequently or not at all."[19] Since the early 1900s, the number of orphans had been steadily declining, so that by mid-century foster care was being provided to children with one or more living parent. Foster care had changed from serving orphaned children to serving neglected children. Maas and Engler reported neglect and abandonment as the most common reason for foster home placement, followed by death, illness, economic hardship, and marital conflict.

In reviewing the original data collected by Maas and Engler, Dwight Ferguson observed that "there was a direct relationship between the proportion of children who came into foster care because of economic hardship and the size of the AFDC (Aid to Families with Dependent Children) grant."[20] Those families who received a sufficient AFDC grant were able to care for their children adequately and thus were less likely to have their children removed. When the AFDC grant was too small, however, the families were in danger of losing their children," Ferguson complained. "[C]hildren are being separated from their parents where the primary problem in the family is economic hardship."[21]

Foster care was now commonly viewed as a temporary boarding arrangement for children while their parents could address severe personal, financial, or relationship problems (with orphaned children being placed through adoptive services). Although most child welfare experts believed that parents should be offered casework services in order to permit reunification with their child, few states provided such services. Maas and Engler found that children spent an average of three years in foster care.[22] Apparently child welfare agencies sought to aid distressed families by removing the children until the families could demonstrate an ability to provide for them adequately. In the absence of casework services, however, few biological families were able to show enough improvement to warrant the return of their children. Thus, the children lingered in "temporary" foster care for long periods of time, often extending over many years. Reid termed such children "orphans of the living."

Not only did Maas and Engler provide a critical analysis of the foster care system that had developed in the United States, but they also provided the first comprehensive scientific look at the nation's child welfare system. They investigated the system at eight broadly representative sites. With national statistics on the child welfare system lacking, their data permitted the first comprehensive understanding of how foster care was working across the country. The research revealed that foster care was no longer a service provided to orphaned children, but rather had been transformed into a holding service provided to living parents who, for a variety of reasons, were unable to care for their children. Further, foster care often became long-term substitute care.

In 1962, in a national survey of child welfare agencies, Helen Jeter of the Children's Bureau corroborated many of Maas and Engler's findings. Based on data collected from forty-two states, Jeter estimated that 115,168 children were in foster care and 63,391 children were living in institutions

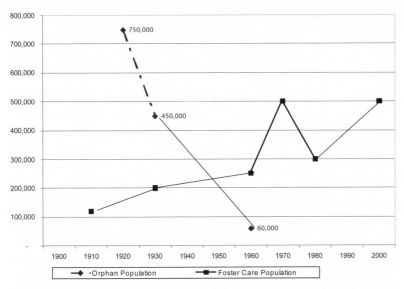

Figure 1: Children in Foster Care and Orphans in the United States.
Source: Pelton 1989, 6–7.

(51,000 in private voluntary institutions for dependent and neglected children). The data reported by Jeter represent the last national census of children in orphanages. They confirmed the essential replacement of orphanages by the foster care system (see Figure 1).

When Jeter compared the length of time in care for the national sample with the representative sample in the Maas and Engler study, she found them similar, with most children remaining in temporary foster care for more than four years. Moreover, few of the children in foster care were orphaned. Only 14 percent of the children had lost one or both parents (compared to 23 percent in 1945), while only 1 percent had lost both parents. Clearly, most of these children had been lingering in foster care for years, even though they had living parents. They were being treated by welfare agencies like orphans even though they were not.

In addition, Jeter found wide variations in the use of foster care, some states having foster care placement rates four times greater than other states'.[23] As did Maas and Engler,

Jeter examined children's "reason for placement." While children were entering foster care for a variety of reasons, little was being done to address the reasons themselves. As Maas and Engler had found, children were placed in foster care and simply left there.

Although problems with the foster care system were apparent by the early 1960s, few academic or professional social workers questioned the priority placed on home-like placements for children who could not remain in home placement for whatever reason. Martin Wolins, like Henry Maas a professor in the School of Social Welfare at the University of California, Berkeley, was an exception. Citing the examples of Israeli and Soviet boarding schools, Wolins argued that institutions provided "powerful environments" for achieving personal change. And, he argued, institutions need not be cold, heartless places devoid of human contact.[24] In a series of studies published over the next twenty years, Wolins, almost alone among child welfare scholars, argued for "rejuvenating the asylum" to allow a much broader use of institutional care.[25]

Attachment Theory

Shortly after Maas and Engler began their research on children in foster care, Harry Harlow, an experimental psychologist at the University of Wisconsin Primate Center in Madison, began a series of experiments with monkeys that would have profound implications for understanding the potential harm of long-term foster care.[26] Although Harlow was probably unaware of the Maas and Engler study and had little interest in foster care, his work had major implications for understanding the impact of foster care on children.

Harlow wanted to understand the importance of a mother's nurturing on human growth and development. He examined what happened to an infant monkey that was raised in a wire cage that provided necessary physical nourishment but did not permit any emotional interaction or attachment with other monkeys. The monkey's cage allowed it to see and hear other monkeys but did not allow any physical contact. Harlow observed that the infant raised in the isolated cage suffered from intense neurotic behavior when compared to an infant monkey raised with a cloth surrogate mother or to a monkey raised by its own mother. When placed with other monkeys, the isolated monkey would spend most of its time huddled in a corner, rocking and clasping itself. The monkey raised with the cloth surrogate did not develop the same problems. Further, the effects of social isolation continued for the experimental monkey into adulthood.

The implications of this were further drawn out by the research of John Bowlby.[27] Bowlby discovered that children who had been separated from their parents during the second or third year of life (because of war or other reasons) suffered severe distress. Most had been cared for in hospitals or residential nurseries without a mother or mother substitute. According to Bowlby, the "loss of the mother" during this early period of life generated "depression, hysteria, or psychopathic traits in adults."[28] From his extensive research, Bowlby concluded that disruption of the continuity of the emotional relationship with the parent seriously disrupts the normal development of a child.

Research suggested that children deprived of parental love and affection would suffer not only from stunted psychological development, but also would experience distorted and harmful developmental consequences. Their research was interpreted by developmental and child psychiatrists to mean that removing children from their parents, for whatever reason, was harmful to their development.[29]

Foster care could no longer be considered a harmless intervention undertaken for the benefit of the child. If used inappropriately, it could cause severe psychological harm. Further, the multiple placements many children experienced were especially harmful. Maas and Engler had observed that "[c]hildren who move through a series of families, reared without close and continuing ties to a responsible adult, have more than the usual problems in discovering who they are. These are the children who learn to develop shallow roots in relationships with others, who try to please but cannot trust, or who strike out before they can be let down. These are the children about whom we were most concerned."[30]

The research by Bowlby laid the foundation for the permanency planning movement to follow a decade later. Permanency planning emphasized the importance of ensuring that all children have a sense of permanency in their lives. Permanency planning advocates argued that children must not be left to drift in foster care because it would have a detrimental impact on their emotional and psychological development. In spite of this warning, caseworkers in child welfare agencies continued to believe that foster care was not, in and of itself, necessarily harmful to all children. Who was right? Was foster care, by its very nature, harmful or not? What exactly was the effect of foster care on children, and did it influence their development? To answer these questions, longitudinal research on the impact of foster care was necessary.

Longitudinal Study of Children in Foster Care

In 1963, the Child Welfare League of America and the National Association of Social Workers sponsored an Institute on Child Welfare Research in Amherst, Massachusetts.[31] The conference was a catalyst for basic research on foster care. David Fanshel and Eugene Shinn of the Hunter College School of Social Work published *Children in Foster Care: A Longitudinal Investigation*, based on research initiated in 1965.[32] Their study provided basic empirical research that laid the groundwork for subsequent demonstration programs in child welfare.

Fanshel and Shinn examined a sample of 659 children who entered foster care in New York City over a five-year period. They found a system that was not guided by any systematic scientific knowledge or principles. Although most children who came into foster care eventually left, they spent years in foster care before getting out. In most cases, the home situation they returned to had not improved. In fact, the economic situation had, in many of the families, actually deteriorated.

The study focused, using a battery of psychological, intellectual, and emotional measures, on the effects of foster care on the psychological and social development of children. Fanshel and his colleagues found little evidence that foster care had a detrimental effect on children in terms of personality, intellectual growth, or social development and behavior. In fact, most children appeared to improve slightly while in foster care.

The most important determinant of how well children did in foster care was parental visitation. Those children who were visited by their parent(s) while in foster care showed greater improvement and were most likely to be restored to their parent(s) than were children who were rarely visited. Like Maas, Engler, and Jeter, Fanshel and Shinn found that many children remained in foster care more than five years. In addition, many of the children had experienced multiple placements.

According to Fanshel and Shinn, "Behind these simple pieces of data lies a crucial issue about foster care, namely, *why so many children have become long-term wards of the system.* Why is the system, intended to offer *temporary* haven to children, incapable of restoring large numbers to their own families or in improving adoptive placements? The fact that 57 percent of the children still in care at the end of five years were unvisited by their parents, essentially abandoned, considerably colors our view of the situation."[33] Here again were the "orphans of the living" decried in the Maas and Engler study. Fanshel and others began to ask why, in the absence of contact with their parents, children were being kept in foster care. Foster care was not a treatment method; rather, it was viewed as the least restrictive form of out-of-home care, intended only for a temporary period.

Brace and his contemporaries had seen the practice of placing children out as a "permanent solution," even though the Children's Aid Society retained custody of the placed children. Many of the placed-out children were orphaned or abandoned and unlikely to return home, although some parents, as noted, relinquished custody to the Children's Aid Society. Current foster care, however, was different. Since the 1950s, central to the definition of foster care was the assumption that the child should be reunited with his or her family as soon as the parent could solve the problems that had led to placement.[34]

Child Welfare Services: From the 1970s to the Present

During the late 1960s, the issue of child maltreatment caught society's attention, thanks to medical professionals who pointed out the mysterious physical injuries they were coming across in children.[35] This eventually led to the 1955 publication of a report by Woolley and Evans implicating parents in these injuries. In 1962, Kempe elaborated on this report by conducting a survey that exposed 302 cases of children who had been hospitalized as a result of physical abuse by their guardians. Kempe's survey introduced a new terminology called the "battered child syndrome," which resonated with society and caused the issue of child abuse to become "an issue of national importance, stimulating legislation requiring the reporting of abusive incidents in every state."[36]

This attention on child abuse resulted in a preoccupation with protecting children from alleged abusers while ignoring the larger social ills affecting families. In essence, society traveled a full circle from protecting abused children, to improving inadequate social conditions affecting families, and back once more to protecting abused children. This time, however, the frenzy to protect abused children resulted in the creation of mandatory child abuse reporting legislation in virtually every state. All fifty states had passed new legislation mandating child abuse reporting by 1966. Additionally, in 1974, the Child Abuse Prevention and Treatment Act was passed for the purpose of providing direct federal assistance to states in the development of child abuse programs.

Such laws had a dramatic effect on the rate of child abuse reporting in the United States. In 1962, when Kempe and his colleagues published "The Battered Child Syndrome," there had been about 10,000 child abuse reports.[37] By 1976, the number of child abuse reports had risen to more than 669,900, and, by 1978, to 836,000. By 1992, according to the National Committee for the Prevention of Child Abuse, there were almost three million reports of child abuse nationwide.[38] During the past decade, the number of child abuse reports has remained stable at about three million per year.

The new mandatory reporting laws transformed not only the types of services provided by the child welfare system, but also the client base that the public child welfare agencies would serve. Child welfare resources were, as a result of mandatory reporting laws, redirected from providing services to needy children and families toward investigating and intervening in the increasing number of child abuse reports.

Kamerman and Kahn pointed out that

child protective services (CPS) (covering physical abuse, sexual abuse, and neglect reports, investigations, assessments, and resultant actions) have emerged as the dominant public child and family service, in effect "driving" the public agency and often taking over child welfare entirely. . . . Child protective services today constitute the core public child and family service, the fulcrum and sometimes, in some places, the totality of the system. Depending on the terms used, public social service agency administrators state either that "child protection is child welfare," or that "The increased demand for child protection has driven out all other child welfare services."[39]

In other words, the transformation of the child welfare system into a protective and investigative agency resulted in the narrowing of service eligibility criteria and consequently of the client base. By shifting its resources and energy to those children who allegedly had been mistreated by their parents, the system no longer had room to provide assistance for children with non-abuse-related needs. Consequently, the public child welfare agency has emerged as an agency of "last resort," where only those families suffering from the most extreme allegations of abuse are given attention by the system. Troubled families with non-abuse related problems (e.g., hunger, homelessness, health issues) therefore have become systematically left out of the system. Pringle outlined distinct disadvantages of this system by saying that it was "primarily concerned with the breakdown of the family as a functioning unit" and that it was "almost entirely a 'rescuing' service for a limited section of the child population."[40] These criticisms of the child welfare system made in the late 1960s are still relevant to today's system.

Summary and Conclusion

Concern for child welfare arose in the latter half of the nineteenth century as a societal response to the needs of children whose parents had died or abandoned them. It began with orphanages that provided food and shelter and limited instruction. Soon after, foster care emerged as a response to the high cost and limited public satisfaction with large state-operated orphanages. Foster care provided a more family-like setting, and was less restrictive and less expensive. Shifting the care of children from large custodial institutions into foster family boarding homes was viewed as progressive reform.

With the decline in the number of orphans, child welfare agencies expanded their focus to a broader concern for the welfare of impoverished and neglected children. They provided services to children who, it was believed, were not adequately cared for by their parent(s) and needed to be removed to substitute care. Over time these services evolved into a safety net to protect those children who were at greatest risk of harm through abandonment or neglect.

From 1850 to 1950 the debate had centered on how best to care for children who could not be properly cared for by their parents.[41] The choice was either institutional care (i.e., orphanages and residential facilities) or foster care. After World War II, foster care emerged as the major service public child welfare agencies provided.

Little effort was made, however, to understand foster care until the 1950s, when leaders in child welfare called for research and empirical studies that would examine its effects. One of the first studies, that by Maas and Engler in 1959, indicated that children temporarily placed in foster care underwent numerous placements and lingered in care for years. Nevertheless, other research found little evidence of a harmful effect on children. In fact, most seemed to benefit, however slightly, from foster care.[42]

In order to understand the current context of the public child welfare system within which special services and programs such as family preservation exist, it is important to consider the historical origins of providing social services to children and families in the United States. Modern landmark events that have affected public child welfare include the 1974 Child Abuse Prevention and Treatment Act and the 1980 Adoption Assistance and Child Welfare Act. Yet the concept of public assistance for the well-being of children and their families can be traced back as far as the seventeenth century. The Poor Law was enacted in 1601, at the start of the seventeenth century, and was widely imitated in the English North American colonies before 1700.

From the eighteenth century to the mid-nineteenth century, public services for children were targeted exclusively at those who had been orphaned or abandoned. Services for such children took the form of institutional custodial care with a great reliance on almshouses and infirmaries, where children were cared for "alongside the aged, infirm and insane." Although this kind of care provided some degree of assistance for children in need, it was eventually condemned as being a cruel and unhealthy environment for children.[43] Eventually, children were removed from almshouses and infirmaries and placed in asylums and orphanages created specifically for children.

Although these new asylums and orphanages were considered a more humane environment, many found them not much different from the earlier almshouses and infirmaries. They were regarded by some as "cold, people-processing institutions lacking the warm and loving care of family life."[44] Though there were many alternative views—see, for example, Francis LaFleche's *The Middle Five* (1900), a memoir of growing up in an Indian boarding school, which gives a generally favorable impression of boarding school life.

In the second half of the nineteenth century, the Children's Aid Society developed a radically different method of assisting orphaned and abandoned children. Charles Loring Brace, the society's founder, believed that a more family-oriented and "wholesome" environment for children was preferable to institutional care. Children, including children whose parents were poor, were "placed out" to Protestant farm families in the Midwest and West. This idea had great public appeal, since children would now be living in a home with a family instead of in large institutions packed with hundreds of other children. The appeal was also strong for the farm families, which could, in exchange of caring for an orphaned or abandoned child, gain an extra body to assist with farm labor.[45] Between the 1850s and the 1930s, the Children's Aid Society placed over 92,000 poor, orphaned, and abandoned children with farm families.

Although this system of caring for children marked an improvement on the asylums and institutions, it nonetheless received criticism for exploiting children for their labor on the farms. The religious issue was also a source of complaint on the part of Roman Catholic and Jewish authorities— Brace placed children almost exclusively with Protestant parents. Thurston characterized Brace's "placing out" system thusly: "It is the wolf of the old indenture philosophy of child labor in the sheepskin disguise of a so-called good or Christian home."[46] In the late nineteenth century as many as 25 percent of all children were employed.[47] Many others "helped out" on farms or in family businesses. So while the "orphans" who were placed out were in some ways similar to indentured servants, the expectation of work was not unusual or remarkable.

Today, the placing out of children started by Brace is still practiced, but with significant differences. Instead of "rescuing" children from dangerous streets and crowded institutions, children are removed from allegedly dangerous and abusive parents. From a form of indentured servitude where abandoned and orphaned children were provided a family in exchange for their labor on the farms, foster family care has evolved into a system where children are removed and protected from their families' abuse and/or neglect by placing them temporarily with substitute families.

Today, foster care represents the core service available to children through public child welfare, an evolved system of care without the kind of harsh demands of child labor that characterized Brace's original system of foster care in the nineteenth century. As the child welfare system entered the new millennium, the traditional orphanage essentially had been replaced by the child protection system and its subsidiary, the modern foster care system.

2 □ The Early History of Orphanages: From Constantinople to Venice

Timothy S. Miller

Historical note: Constantinople (modern Istanbul) was the capital of the Byzantine Empire for more than 1000 years until it was conquered by the Ottoman Turks in 1453. After the emperor Constantine's death in 337, the Roman Empire had separated into two states: the West Roman Empire centered on old Rome and the East Roman (or Byzantine) Empire centered on its capital Constantinople. These two empires differed in language: Latin in the Western Empire and Greek in the Byzantine Empire. Beginning in 405, the Western Empire was overrun by Germanic tribes. Here the Latin-speaking Catholic Church preserved the link with Greco-Roman civilization. In the Byzantine Empire, the Greek language and literature survived in close connection with the Orthodox Christian Church.

American orphanages—Catholic, Protestant, Jewish, as well as those with no religious affiliation—are the heirs of a tradition which began not in colonial America or eighteenth-century England, but much earlier in the cities of the Mediterranean. One can trace orphanages to Renaissance Italy—to Rome, Florence, and Venice, rich cities which opened elaborate institutions in the fifteenth century to shelter homeless boys and girls. These Italian cities, in turn, were influenced in building their orphanages by earlier institutions, established not in Western Europe, but in the cities of the Byzantine Empire—Antioch, Alexandria, Jerusalem, and the capital city Constantinople.

For 900 years, the Byzantine government maintained a vast orphanage on the citadel of Constantinople, an institution supported by estates scattered throughout the Balkan Peninsula and Asia Minor. This great Orphanotropheion (Greek for "orphanage") symbolized the government's commitment not only to assisting orphans but also to sponsoring many philanthropic programs.[1]

Unfortunately, no sources survive which provide a picture of how this imperial orphanage cared for its children. We know that it became a wealthy institution, and its director, called the *orphanotrophos* ("nurturer of orphans"), held a high place among top bureaucrats. Moreover, on at least one occasion, the orphanage director served as prime minister of the imperial government.[2] To understand how this orphanage functioned, however, one must begin by examining earlier Christian group homes for children and by studying smaller orphanages in provincial Byzantine towns before returning to the Orphanotropheion. The history of orphanages, in fact, begins not in Constantinople, officially dedicated in 330, but two hundred years earlier when Christian communities first developed institutional care for homeless children.

Classical Greece and Rome

Christian communities of the first and second centuries formed in the midst of Greco-Roman society, the source of many modern Western institutions, but the Classical civilization of the ancient Mediterranean world did not develop orphanages. Key centers of this civilization, such as ancient Athens, expected members of the extended family to care for the children of deceased relatives. In a similar fashion, the ancient Romans developed regulations to determine which family member had the responsibility of guardianship, a legal obligation to feed, clothe, and educate an orphaned relative.[3] The Romans also devised laws to protect orphans from family guardians who sometimes plotted to harm the children or their property.[4] Since Rome conquered the Mediterranean basin, its laws eventually supplanted local customs regarding guardianship.

Despite the interest that Greek and Roman legislators showed in providing guardians, Classical civilization never supported institutions to nurture and educate orphans who had no living relatives to care for them or who had been abandoned by parents too poor to support them. Many of these abandoned children were babies who died of exposure or ended up as slaves.[5]

Greco-Roman civilization believed that the gods especially loved children who had both a living mother and father. The Greeks called such fortunate boys and girls *amphithaleis*. In Athens, these *amphithaleis* participated in weddings, to bring new couples good fortune. In Rome, the emperor Augustus commissioned Horace to compose hymns for *amphithaleis* to sing on the Palatine Hill. Greco-Roman attitudes thus discouraged interest in the fate of orphans, children whom the gods themselves had rejected.[6]

Judaism and Christianity

Clearly, the concern of early Christian communities for orphans did not spring from the dominant Greco-Roman culture. Christians cared for orphans because their faith had inherited the Jewish traditions enshrined in the Torah and in the writings of the prophets. In Exodus (22:24) and Deuteronomy (10:15), the God of the Hebrews, the creator of the universe, swore to avenge crimes against strangers, widows, and orphans. Psalm 68 described the Lord of all as the father of the fatherless.

Despite these and other passages in the Old Testament emphasizing God's love for orphans, mainstream Jewish communities never supported orphanages. Historians credit this to the strength of Jewish extended families, which made guardianship laws unnecessary.[7] The Jewish sect of the Essenes, however, might have taken the first steps in creating orphanages. The historian Josephus mentions that some Essenes remained celibate and adopted the children of others so that they could convert these boys and girls to their sect. Josephus, however, does not clearly identify these children as true orphans.[8]

Early Christian sources definitely refer to orphans in the care of the community. *The Shepherd of Hermas*, a Christian text written at Rome ca. 110 A.D., describes a woman named Grapte who guarded orphans in the community and oversaw their instruction. Grapte's official position indicates some institutional structure to provide for homeless children.[9]

The first indisputable evidence of orphanages, however, comes from third-century Syria. A manual of Christian discipline which scholars call the *Didascalia Apostolorum* established guidelines for Christian communities and their local bishops. During the second century, the office of bishop had gained importance in churches throughout the Mediterranean, and thus the *Didascalia* assumed that these bishops would play the primary role in all Christian activities, including the care of orphans.

According to the *Didascalia*, the bishop bore the responsibility of maintaining care for the orphans of the community. He was to educate male orphans in a useful trade so that these boys could support themselves. The *Didascalia* assumed that the bishop would use the financial resources of the local church to support the orphan boys until they were old enough to practice their trade. The bishop was to care for orphan girls until they were old enough to be given in marriage. The *Didascalia* recommended that Christian couples without children adopt orphan boys and that families with eligible male children accept orphan girls as brides for their young men.[10]

The *Didascalia* had been prepared for the Christians living in Syria, a province of what would become the Byzantine Empire after 337. We cannot determine how many of these local churches actually followed the rules in the *Didascalia*, but one can assume that some of them did. Moreover, we have additional evidence from the fourth century that Christian communities supported orphanages. The historian Sokrates recorded that in 358 the Christians at Alexandria in Byzantine Egypt had purchased separate buildings to house both orphans and widows and stored supplies designated for their maintenance.[11]

Byzantine Orphanages

Sokrates's account provides no details of how the Alexandrian church actually organized its orphanage. A few years later, however, Basil, the bishop of Caesarea in Cappadocia (Byzantine Asia Minor), opened a school which also served as an orphanage. Fortunately, Basil wrote a set of rules which presents a detailed picture of how the school functioned.[12]

According to Basil's rule, his school was to accept first children who had lost their parents, and then children with living mothers and fathers. The school was to care for both girls and boys who were at least six years old. Basil stressed that the girls and boys were to be housed separately, but he adds no more details about the girls' training.

Basil separated the boys' school into a lower and an upper division and required that the older boys have no group contact with the younger children except during church services. The children in the lower school learned to read and write and studied the fundamentals of Greek grammar. The older boys read the Holy Scriptures, other Christian texts, and even some pagan literature, such as Homer's epic poems.[13] Basil adopted this two-tiered school system from pre-Christian schools maintained by Greek city-states during the Hellenistic period.[14]

Basil designed a system for selecting the best and most mature among the older students to lead groups of children from the lower school. These student monitors were to help the children with their studies and to discipline them when they misbehaved. Moreover, the monitors were occasionally to ask the younger boys what they were thinking about.

The younger children usually answered openly and thus revealed any silly or shameful thoughts they might be entertaining. Basil designed this practice to train the orphans and other students to control their thoughts.

Basil recommended that the students study the Bible, especially the Book of Proverbs, as a guide to proper behavior. He also suggested that the teachers frequently hold contests among the students to determine who had mastered the material. Basil emphasized that children loved contests and would study harder in order to win prizes.

In describing the punishments which student monitors were to assign, Basil never mentioned beatings. Rather, he recommended a system based on his study of ancient Greek medicine. Just as a physician prescribed a drug with a hot nature for a patient with a cold disease of the head or chest, the student monitor was to punish a student who stole food by requiring a day-long fast. One who yelled insults would have to remain silent for a prescribed period. Those who fought in anger would have to humbly serve one another.

In addition to the academic courses, Basil continued the older tradition of artisan training. For those boys who displayed special talent in a particular craft, the school located master craftsmen with whom the children worked as apprentices. The boys were to leave school each day to train with their instructors, but Basil required that they return in the evening to dine with the other students and to sleep within the institution.

Basil designed his school and orphanage to fulfill his obligation as bishop to care for orphans, but he also designed it to form part of a training program for a monastic community. During the third and fourth centuries, monasticism had become a major movement within Christianity. Initially, monks had sought to flee the world by living as hermits in the desert or in remote mountains; some also formed isolated communities of celibate men or women. Basil, however, belonged to a group of monastic leaders who stressed that monks who fled society could not serve the needy as Christ had commanded.[15] Therefore, Basil integrated his monks into the urban community by organizing monasteries that included hospitals for the sick, hospices for the homeless, and schools for orphans.[16] Basil's school thus formed an integral part of a monastic community he himself had founded. The school served both as a way for the monks to help the needy and as a method of training some of the boys to join the monastery.

According to Basil's instructions, the orphans remained in the school until they reached eighteen, the age at which youths became full citizens of the Greek city-states. At that time, the orphans could decide whether to join the monastery or to enter the secular world as adults. Basil stressed that the boys were to have a free choice in this decision, but evidence collected from Byzantine records stretching from 400 to 1453 suggests that the number of orphans among monks and nuns was higher than in the general population. Was this because, in fact, monastic schools such as Basil's put pressure on the orphans at the time they were to make their choice, or did the life of the world beyond the monastery's walls offer few opportunities for children without family connections?[17]

After the fourth century, we have many examples of monasteries that took in orphans. At the same time that Basil opened his school, his sister Makrina founded a community of female ascetics. These nuns collected infants abandoned along the roads of central Asia Minor; such abandoned babies were especially common during famines. Many of the girls among these infants eventually entered Makrina's monastery as professed nuns.[18]

From the end of the fourth century comes another description of an orphanage-school in the Syrian city of Melitene. This description appears in the biography or *vita* of Saint Euthymios, who became a monastic leader during the fifth century. Sometime around 400, Euthymios's father died, leaving his wife Dionysia and his son Euthymios, at the time only three years old. Instead of seeking appointment as the boy's guardian, Dionysia decided to entrust Euthymios to Otreios, the bishop of Melitene. Otreios accepted responsibility for the boy, and despite his young age, tonsured him and enrolled him among the lectors (low-ranking clerics) of his church.

According to his biography, when Euthymios was old enough, Otreios handed the boy over to the teachers of sacred scripture. In addition, the bishop appointed two older boys among the lectors, Akakios and Synodios, to help train Euthymios. The biography stresses that these two students played the primary role in educating Euthymios. They fulfilled a function similar to the monitors whom Basil had appointed at his school in Caesarea.

As Euthymios grew older, he rose through the higher ranks of the clergy until Bishop Otreios ordained him a priest and subsequently placed him in charge of the monasteries in and around Melitene. Some years later, Euthymios left his city to become a hermit in the desert. Later in life, however, he discovered that his student mentor, Akakios, had become the new bishop of Melitene.[19]

Euthymios's biography clearly describes a seminary at Melitene to train future deacons, priests, and even bishops for church service. At an early age (under seven), the boys were tonsured as lectors. When they were older, they learned to read and write and studied the sacred scriptures. Some no doubt left the seminary, but others, like Euthymios and Akakios, remained until they were ordained. Euthymios's *vita* also shows that such seminaries could function as orphanages. The *vita* of Saint Clement of Ankyra, a biography written at about the same time as Euthymios's, shows even more clearly how easily an orphanage could become a seminary.

Although some aspects of Clement's biography concerning his execution by the Roman emperor Diocletian (284–305) are fictitious, details about the orphanage no doubt reflect real institutions of the fourth century. According to the *vita*, Clement lost his parents early in life. A woman of Ankyra adopted Clement and raised him as her own. After Clement reached adulthood, he and his foster mother began to collect babies abandoned in and around Ankyra. Clement took in both Christian and non-Christian children and trained them all in the doctrines of his faith. Clement won such renown for charity that the Christians of Ankyra elected him bishop. When Clement assumed the administration of the church, he did not transfer the care of his orphans to others. Rather, he integrated the children of his orphanage, presumably all boys, into the various ranks of the clergy. Thus, what had begun as a private charitable institution quickly merged with the local church to become a seminary much like the one in Melitene where Euthymios had studied.[20]

Surviving Byzantine sources describe two other orphanage-seminaries in mainland Greece, but from a much later period. The first operated at Argos in the Peloponnesus during the tenth century and the second at Naupaktos in Western Greece during the thirteenth century.

According to his biography, Peter of Argos was born in Constantinople shortly before 900. He soon lost both parents; as a result he and his younger brother were raised in a monastery school similar to Basil's institution in Caesarea. When Peter reached adulthood, he joined a monastery in the Peloponnesus. Here he won such a reputation for holiness that the people of Argos selected him as their bishop. Once in office, Peter turned his attention to supporting charitable services for poor people and the sick. Probably because of his own childhood experience, however, Peter especially focused his philanthropic activity on assisting orphans.

He organized an orphan school at Argos which provided some of the children with training to become deacons and priests at Argos and other Greek towns. This seminary education obviously benefited some children, because the author of Peter's biography had been an orphan at the school and had managed to succeed Peter as bishop of Argos. In his introduction, the author states that he has written this *vita* as a gift of thanks to Peter for the care he received.

Peter's orphanage also trained boys in crafts. The school purchased tools that the children needed for apprenticeship in various trades. If the orphans had to leave Argos for training in other towns, the orphanage paid for their room and board while away. Peter's orphan school thus inherited the tradition of seminary training, which we first saw at fourth-century Melitene, as well as the more ancient practice of providing male orphans with useful skills to support themselves and their future families.[21]

John Apokaukos, bishop of Naupaktos in Western Greece from 1200 to 1232, described that city's orphanage in three detailed letters.[22] As at Argos, this orphanage trained boys for the clergy. Apokaukos stressed that this training included practice in singing. Like Peter, Apokaukos sent boys to other bishops for lessons not available at Naupaktos. Thus, he wrote to Bishop Nicholas of Vonditza asking him to teach accounting and calligraphy to an orphan named John. Apokaukos, however, admitted problems with the orphans. He felt blessed that God had entrusted many homeless children to his care, but he lamented that some hated him—a few even had fled his school.

In his letter supporting John, Apokaukos asked Bishop Nicholas to give the boy special care, which Apokaukos firmly believed required beatings. "I am confident that you will give him more care because of God, because of us . . . and because of the boy's orphanhood. . . . Let the training stick always be in your hands."[23] In another letter, he recommended that this same boy whom Apokaukos especially loved be beaten whenever he wandered away from his duties.[24]

Apokaukos's letters clearly reveal that the bishop considered physical punishment a sign of concern, even an act of love. Here Apokaukos was echoing a tradition of Christian thought which saw the rod of discipline as necessary for learning, granted fallen human nature. Physical punishment as a sign of love rested on ancient Jewish tradition expressed in Proverbs 3:12: "The Lord disciplines whom He loves and whips every son whom He accepts and cherishes." The New Testament writer of Hebrews (12:6) repeated these words, reinforcing their significance for Christians. Moreover, from early Byzantine times, teachers thought that the whip symbolized education.[25]

It seems obvious to a modern reader of Apokaukos's letters that the frequent beatings the bishop advocated might explain why some orphans hated him, but Apokaukos never made this connection. He unquestioningly accepted the Biblical norm and seems not to have considered Basil's more humane system of punishment, even though Basil ranked among Byzantine society's most influential spiritual writers.

This review of early Christian and Byzantine orphanages demonstrates that bishops and some monasteries maintained group homes for children and that these institutions had many features in common. Indeed, there developed a distinct orphanage tradition in Byzantine society. Having studied these smaller institutions, let us return to the great Orphanotropheion of Constantinople.

The Orphanotropheion of Constantinople

Although the Orphanotropheion functioned for almost 900 years, no single document describes *how* it functioned. The *Alexiad* of Anna Komnena, a historical narrative of the reign of her father, the emperor Alexios I (1081–1118), offers a fascinating view of the orphans studying ancient Greek language and literature, but no other details of the children's education.[26] An early reference to the Orphanotropheion in the fifth century, however, reveals a program in music. According to this source, the people of Constantinople enjoyed visiting the Orphanotropheion on Sundays to hear songs composed by Timokletos, the orphanage director's brother.[27] This source does not specify that Timokletos composed the songs for orphans to sing, but later descriptions of church liturgies and imperial court ceremonial in the ninth and tenth centuries suggest that orphan children did sing Timokletos's compositions.

By the ninth century, an orphan choir often sang at major liturgical services. On the Feast of the Presentation (2 February), an orphan choir greeted the emperor with songs as he entered Saint Sophia cathedral. On the Annunciation

(25 March), the orphans sang at an outdoor service in the forum of Constantinople. On the day after Easter, they participated in a service at the Church of the Holy Apostles.[28] On the Feast of the Epiphany (6 January), the orphans sang not in church, but at a state banquet in the imperial palace.[29] It is interesting to compare this orphan choir in Christian Constantinople with the chorus of *amphithaleis* singing on the Palatine Hill for the pagan Augustus.

These references to the orphan choir at imperial ceremonies do not state that the children came from the Orphanotropheion, but a contemporary ninth-century text describes choirs that sang "in the manner of the Orphanotropheion."[30] Such a statement indicates that the imperial orphanage maintained a choir with a distinctive style of singing. Conclusive proof that the Orphanotropheion in Constantinople provided choral training comes not from Byzantine territory in the East, but from the old Western capital of Rome.

After the emperor Constantine had moved the capital of the Roman Empire to his new city, Constantinople, the Western (Latin-speaking) provinces had become independent of the Byzantine East. After 405, much of Italy and Western Europe was occupied by Germanic tribes—Goths, Franks, Angles, and Saxons. During the seventh century, however, the Byzantine government regained a footing in Italy, and in 663 the Byzantine emperor Constans II even visited old Rome.

During these same years, one of the popes founded an orphanage in Rome which he named the Orphanotrophium, a Latin term which clearly derives from the Greek word *orphanotropheion* used in Constantinople. A few decades later, Pope Sergius I (687–701) refurbished this papal orphanage not only to provide good care for the city's orphans, but also to ensure "that the order of song not die out." One hundred and forty years later Pope Sergius II also refurbished the Orphanotrophium where he himself had grown up as an orphan, but by that time the people of Rome normally referred to this institution as the Schola Cantorum or the School of Songs.[31] As conclusive proof that the Roman orphanage was patterned on the Orphanotropheion in Constantinople, we have the words of a song the children continued to sing at the Schola Cantorum in Rome as late as the eleventh century; the lyrics of this song were written in the Greek of Constantinople, not the Medieval Latin of eleventh-century Italy.[32]

The singing programs at the orphanages in both Rome and Constantinople had their parallel in the smaller group homes of the Byzantine provinces. Apokaukos expected that orphans at his school would learn to sing the liturgical services in his cathedral.[33] As part of training for the clergy, Apokaukos also taught his orphans to read and write. So too the Orphanotropheion at Constantinople taught its children to read and write Greek. Little information survives, however, regarding Greek lessons at the Orphanotropheion before 1100. Shortly thereafter, the *Alexiad* provides the first detailed picture of language training at the institution; it describes students at the Orphanotropheion gathered about their instructor, busily copying *schede*, a form of word puzzle which involved recopying passages and correcting cleverly disguised errors in grammar and spelling.[34] The orphans practiced copying these *schede* and then participated in contests against pupils of other schools, contests which, on special occasions, took place before the emperor himself.[35]

During the twelfth century, some of Byzantium's best writers began their careers by teaching grammar and Greek literature at the Orphanotropheion. Theodore Prodromos, perhaps the leading creative writer of Byzantine literature, spent his entire life instructing children at Constantinople's orphanage and writing *schede* puzzles for them to solve.[36]

We have no idea how many orphans lived at the Orphanotropheion. Unfortunately, Apokaukos never mentioned how many orphans he cared for at Naupaktos, although he claimed that there were many. Fortunately, a ninth-century letter describes a private orphanage near the city of Prousa (modern Bursa in Western Turkey). This institution belonged neither to a monastery nor to a bishop, but was financed and supervised by a local aristocrat and his sisters. They fed, clothed, and educated forty boys and forty girls.[37] If a private orphanage in a provincial town had eighty children, surely the Orphanotropheion of Constantinople sheltered many more.

Western Orphanages

The orphanages of the Western Roman provinces (Italy, and the Latin-speaking provinces of Rome) have left fewer traces in the written sources. One of the first references to Christian care for orphans, however, appears in the previously mentioned *The Shepherd of Hermas*, written for the Church of Rome around 110. Latin bishops likely raised homeless children at their cathedral churches, as did Byzantine bishops in the East. Moreover, a tradition grew up in the Latin West, as it did in the East, of offering children to monasteries as oblates; many of these boys and girls were orphans.[38] Still, it is significant that the first large Western orphanage about which we have information was the Orphanotrophium at Rome, an institution modeled on the orphanage in Constantinople. Indeed, one medieval historian has claimed that orphanages did not exist in Western Europe until the late fourteenth century.[39]

Recent research, however, has revealed that Latin Christians definitely supported a major orphanage during the Middle Ages, not in Western Europe, but in Crusader Jerusalem, a city which had been ruled by the Byzantine Empire before Muslim armies conquered it in the 630s. Jerusalem remained under Muslim rule until the Crusaders seized the Holy City in 1099. There a new society of warrior monks (the Knights of Saint John) organized to protect Christian pilgrims and to assist them when they fell ill. To treat the sick, the Knights constructed a huge hospital in the Holy City, an institution that gave these warrior monks their second name, the Hospitallers.[40] Scholars have known that the Hospitallers hired physicians and surgeons to treat patients in their philanthropic institution, but a new document, first published in 1999, reveals that they also maintained an orphanage.[41]

This document, written by a monk visiting Jerusalem from Western Europe, mentions how the Hospitallers accepted unwanted babies from desperate mothers and also searched the streets of the Holy City to rescue exposed infants. The Hospitallers assigned the babies wet nurses, whom they carefully supervised. When the children were weaned, the Hospitallers educated them in the orphanage. This system was soon imitated in Western Europe, first in Montpelier in France and by 1220 in Rome.[42] The Hospitallers also founded an orphanage in Genoa, similar to their institution in Jerusalem. This Genoese orphanage clearly educated female orphans, since it provided dowries for older girls who wished to marry.[43]

These orphanages, inspired by the Knights of Saint John, provided the model for the famous Innocenti orphanage at Florence, which opened in 1445. Social historians consider this the first independent orphanage in Europe (i.e., not part of a cathedral school or monastery), but they have failed to connect it with earlier institutions of the Hospitaller tradition. To build the Innocenti, the Florentines hired the renowned architect Filippo Brunelleschi, who designed a graceful façade for the new institution—a series of rounded arches which represented a key development in Renaissance architecture. Like the Jerusalem orphanage, the Innocenti focused on caring for abandoned infants, though it also educated older children.

By the time Brunelleschi finished the Innocenti in 1445, other Italian cities had begun similar projects. In 1450, Bologna dedicated its Ospedale dei Bastardi, which even copied Brunelleschi's building design. In 1458, Milan opened an orphanage as part of its larger Ospedale Maggiore project. By 1465, the Pietà Orphanage in Venice was caring for 450 children. In the 1470s, Pope Sixtus IV expanded the Hospital of the Holy Spirit in Rome to take in many more children.[44]

These Western orphanages differed from Byzantine group

homes in that they focused specifically on saving unwanted babies. Byzantine orphanages had also accepted abandoned babies. Basil's sister Makrina sent out her nuns to rescue infants exposed along the roads of Asia Minor.[45] The Hospitallers, however, introduced a new aspect to this ministry. Not only did they rescue babies abandoned in the alleys of Jerusalem, but they also accepted the care of infants from all desperate women—unwed mothers as well as poor married women. The Innocenti and other Renaissance orphanages of Italy went further by inventing the *ruota*, a revolving compartment in the orphanage wall in which women could place their babies, ring a bell, and leave. The attendants on duty would turn the compartment from the inside so that infants passed through a narrow opening in the wall into their new home. There is no evidence that such a contrivance existed in Byzantine orphanages.[46]

Modern scholars and social workers criticize Renaissance orphanages because they made it easy to abandon babies. As a result of this ease, by the seventeenth century, Italian orphanages were severely overcrowded, a condition which led to high infant death rates; in some years more than 80 percent of the babies died. Critics charge that these institutions actually promoted infanticide behind the façade of Christian philanthropy.

Such negative views ignore serious efforts by orphanage officials to discover why so many babies were dying. Between 1657 and 1660, Papal supervisors at the Holy Spirit orphanage in Rome collected statistics concerning mortality rates among its infants and compared them with mortality rates among infants of a typical residential area in Rome. The researchers learned that a baby inside the orphanage was twice as likely to die in a year as one raised in a Roman family. The supervisors also compared their findings with infant mortality rates in hill towns around Rome and discovered that these babies had a better chance of surviving their first two years than did infants from Roman households. As a result of these statistical studies, the orphanage hired wet nurses living in these hillside towns to nurse orphan infants in their homes, instead of in the institution's nursery. This policy reduced mortality rates among orphans to 30 percent, the same rate as in the general population.[47]

By the seventeenth century, Italian physicians as well as the general public were aware of contagious diseases. In the fifteenth century, city state governments such as those in Milan, Venice, and Florence had enacted quarantine laws to retard the spread of bubonic plague. In the sixteenth century, a physician from Verona, Girolamo Fracastoro, had developed a theory of disease seeds, similar to our modern understanding of germs.[48] In pursuing their study of child mortality rates, however, the officials of the Holy Spirit orphanage in Rome were more concerned about environmental factors in illnesses, such as fresh air and the tranquility of a rural environment, than they were about contagion.

The major orphanage of Siena conducted a study in 1775 which compared mortality rates of orphan babies weaned early with those weaned later. The three physicians who conducted this study found that the longer babies nursed on human milk, the lower their mortality rate. As a result, the orphanage directors lengthened the time allotted for nursing and substantially increased the pay of wet nurses. This Sienese orphanage, thus, discovered in the eighteenth century that the consumption of human milk bolsters babies' immune systems, an important aspect of proper infant care which physicians in the United States only began to understand in the 1960s.[49]

Not all Italian orphanages, however, concentrated on abandoned babies. In 1543, a Spanish priest opened an orphanage, which he named the Conservatory of Saint Mary of Loreto, for homeless boys and girls found wandering the streets of Naples. In 1589, a Franciscan brother rented some houses in the same city to shelter boys aged seven to fifteen. His orphanage, the Conservatory of Christ's Poor, raised money by organizing the orphans into small choirs, which sang in the piazzas of Naples in return for small change. By 1632, the orphans not only performed in the streets, but also were paid for singing at funerals and other liturgical celebrations. The Conservatory also began instructing the boys in playing musical instruments. During the course of the seventeenth century, the Conservatory of Loreto also began to train its orphans to sing and play instruments. By 1700, four Neapolitan orphanages had evolved into famous music schools. Several well-known musicians and composers taught at these conservatories.[50]

At Venice, the Orphanage of the Pietà also organized an excellent music school for girls. By the eighteenth century, people came from all over Europe to hear the girls of the Pietà sing Sunday vespers. One of the best-known Baroque composers, Antonio Vivaldi, spent his entire professional life directing the girls' choir and orchestra at the Pietà and composing music for the orphans to perform.[51] In Italian orphanages of the Baroque period, music became so central to the teaching program that the word "conservatory," initially a synonym for orphanage, came to denote a school of music by the nineteenth century.

When Vivaldi composed music for his orphan choir in Venice, did he work in a tradition that went directly back to Timokletos, the composer at the fifth-century Orphanotropheion of Constantinople? As we saw above, the medieval Schola Cantorum at Rome had been directly patterned on the Byzantine Orphanotropheion. It is certainly possible to argue that later Italian orphan homes also evolved from Byzantine institutions through the agency of the Jerusalem orphanage of the Knights Hospitallers. One could also argue, however, that group homes for children in both the Latin West and the Greek East emerged from a common Christian tradition which early on included training in singing. With such instruction, the orphans were able to use their young voices to participate in liturgical celebrations, whether in the cathedral church of the bishop or in a monastery. It is also possible that orphan supervisors, both in Byzantine towns and in Italy, recognized the value of choral singing as a method both to teach the children discipline as well as to instill in them the importance of working together toward a common goal.

This brief survey of orphanages from early Christian institutions to the great Orphanotropheion of Constantinople and finally to the conservatories of eighteenth-century Italy reveals a remarkable continuity in the tradition of group homes for orphans. It is important to emphasize that music training, especially in choral singing, continually reappears as a central element in preparing homeless boys and girls for the tasks of life. The persistence of musical education raises the possibility that orphanage officials also found that music helped to soothe the sadness which surely, at times, overcame these children, deprived of parents by tragedy or abandoned because of poverty.

3 □ Christian Charity and the Politics of Orphan Care in the Dutch Republic

Anne E. C. McCants

> For the Lord your God is . . . the great God, mighty and awesome, who is not partial and takes no bribe, who executes justice for the orphan and the widow.
>
> Deut. 10:17–18 (NRSV)

> When you give a dinner or a banquet, do not invite your friends or your brothers or your kinsmen or rich neighbors, lest they also invite you in return, and you be repaid. But when you give a feast, invite the poor, the maimed, the lame, the blind, and you will be blessed, because they cannot repay you. You will be repaid at the resurrection of the just.
>
> Luke 14: 12–14 (NRSV)

Like the poor, who have indeed always been with us, the call for charity is a recurrent theme across all religious traditions. Certainly the biblical injunction to redistribute wealth from abundance to need has played a critical role in shaping Judeo-Christian, and hence European, social policy from antiquity. But despite the unambiguous description of the Jewish God's character in the Pentateuch, and the simple instructions left to the Christian West by the Gospel of Luke, the mode by which Europeans have seen fit to dispense charity is not now, nor has it been in the past, easily agreed upon, nor has the hope of eternal reward been their sole motivation for seeking the welfare of others. Indeed, the charitable impulse is not even always made manifest in the form of relief for the poor—presuming, of course, that we could so much as agree on what constitutes poverty. Thus, charity is as much a socio-historical phenomenon as it is an ethical or religious one. It is the aim of this essay to explore one particular manifestation of the charitable impulse, in the urban centers of the Dutch Republic of the seventeenth and eighteenth centuries, and to make sense of it in the context of contemporary economic, cultural, and especially political considerations.

Numerous and richly endowed charitable institutions form an important part of the lore associated with the "Golden Age" of the Dutch Republic. Contemporary reports suggest that the multitude of Dutch hospitals, orphanages, reformatories, and old age homes were not only the pride of the local population, but also the envy of all Europe. Dutch historiography has dedicated itself to the task of chronicling the establishment of these institutions since the seventeenth century. Histories of specific institutions have placed particular emphasis on the original benevolent testaments of godly individuals, both Catholic and Reformed, while general surveys have been more likely to focus on the precocity of the Dutch Republic in placing charitable services under the auspices of civic government. William Temple, the former English ambassador to the Dutch Republic, had this to say in 1673 on the occasion of his retirement about the social welfare policy of his adopted home:

> Charity seems to be very National among them,
> though it be regulated by Orders of the country, and
> not usually mov'd by the common Objects of Compassion. But it is seen in the admirable Provisions that
> are made out of it for all sorts of Persons that can
> want, or ought to be kept, in a Government.[1]

Temple's observations fit well with the dual historiography outlined above. That Dutch charities were among the richest and their institutions among the most beautiful in the world was beyond dispute for him. Yet they were also something of a puzzle to him, because these institutions were largely managed by civic governments. Moreover, they did not seem to find their inspiration in the visible display of what he expected to be the normal "objects of compassion." The destitute, the maimed, and the grieving were not publicly paraded about as they had been in the medieval past, or indeed as they still were in many other parts of Europe. This spared the rest of the population scenes of revulsion, but it also deprived them of what Temple assumed would be the most potent source of generous compassion. Yet generous they seemed to be regardless.

Despite Temple's hesitations, Dutch charity was nonetheless directed especially to those demographic categories of the needy that were already well-established as legitimately deserving in the Judeo-Christian tradition, including widows, the aged and infirm, and, most especially, orphans. Indeed, it would seem that demographic indicators of need were more important even than economic ones. For the Dutch did not target the majority of their collective charity to the economically destitute, as scholarship on the many civic orphanages, hospitals, and old men's and women's homes shows quite clearly.[2] Those who met the demographic qualifications but who were otherwise from the citizen middling ranks of society fared much better than did either of the overlapping categories of recent immigrants and the truly poor. Since the terms "poor relief" and "charity" are so often (and misleadingly) employed interchangeably by historians writing on issues of social welfare, this distinction requires some explanation. All orphans and widows need not, of course, be poor, although the condition of vulnerability occasioned by those two states could easily put someone on the path to poverty, given sufficient time. Nonetheless, if the alleviation of poverty were the primary impulse behind the provision of charitable assistance, a demographically organized distribution system would seem a less efficient solution than simple means testing. Clearly more was at stake than just the moral imperative to care for the destitute.

The "Logic of Charity"

Following upon a long tradition of writing about European charity largely as a manifestation of Christian virtue, scholars have more recently begun to assert the importance of self-interest, or at least collective self-interest, for explaining the shape and scope of competing relief schemes. In particular, they posit an implicit bargain between the rich (who can afford to contribute) and the poor (whose need is generally assumed to speak for itself). The terms of this negotiation are largely determined by the self-interest of the elites whose bargaining position is by definition the stronger one. This literature asserts that elites would have been unable to maintain their preferred mode of living if they had ignored the needs of the poor entirely. They would have been subject not only to the potential pangs of conscience, but also to the nuisance factor of unsightly and unsavory people roaming their communities. Even more threatening was the possibility of destruction of life and property by an angry mob or the invisible danger of epidemic disease bred in squalor and hunger—and spread far and wide, for that matter, by the mobility which so often accompanies poverty. Moreover, the provision of charity had the added benefit of eliciting from the poor a respect for the very social system in which their poverty was rooted. Marco van Leeuwen has identified this bargain most felicitously as the "logic of charity."[3] According to his model, elites used poor relief to elicit some specific social and economic benefits for their own class. These included 1) the maintenance of a reserve army of laborers; 2) the confirmation of the proper place of the poor in a static and hierarchical society; 3) the maintenance of public order; 4) the control of epidemic infections; and 5) the moral improvement, or "civilizing," of the poor.[4]

For their part, the poor had to cooperate in this system by accepting the charity of their social betters and with it the terms under which it had been offered.

It is worth noting that this particular characterization of the elite agenda is itself historically situated in what we have come to call the "early modern" world. It is not a valid characterization of elite motives good for all time, as even a cursory glance at the medieval practice of charity will quickly reveal. As John Bossy has so persuasively argued, "[C]alculations of public utility seem foreign to the ethos of medieval charity."[5] Rather, medieval charity resided more comfortably within the context of actual relationships, either between individuals directly or as mediated by religious institutions. Most often it took the form of payment for masses or indulgences for the deceased in one's family; sometimes it was manifested in small increments to the beggar in the street or to the pilgrim at the door—hence the frequent parading of its objects. Moreover, the primary concern of the medieval Christian doctrine of charity was "with the giver of charity, not with its object."[6] The distribution of alms was the antidote to avarice rather than to privation. If this had not been the case, it would have been impossible for alms to the voluntary poor (i.e., those renouncing wealth in favor of taking vows of religious poverty) to have been just as efficacious for the donor's soul as was the relief of the genuinely poor. Indeed, the rise of the mendicant orders to such prominence in the High Middle Ages could hardly be imagined otherwise.

When humanists and reformers alike railed against the begging orders at the dawn of the modern era, which they did with an incredible ferocity, they were doing much more than simply attacking traditional forms of Catholic piety. They were ushering in a new conception of charity, which was to be dominated by abstract benevolence, or what we might now call philanthropy. Their primary concern was no longer the salvation of the prosperous but the relief of the miserable and the control of the dangerous. If charity was to be efficacious it had to be properly directed; and neither the church nor individuals acting on their own initiative could be relied upon to probe adequately the true circumstances of the beggar before them. So it was to institutions under lay authority that they turned for both the proper investigation of the needy and the application of a suitable remedy, most often via the inculcation of diligent work habits. This was not only an attack on the authority of the Catholic Church, but also a reflection of a new general distrust of the ability of any religious authority to manage poor relief properly. It is only in the context of the period after this fundamental reworking of medieval charitable practice that we can begin to talk about the bargain between rich and poor as it is conceived of by van Leeuwen.

Yet even his move towards a rationalized understanding of charitable behavior does not take us far enough to fully explain the somewhat peculiar, if indeed generous, provision of relief in the Dutch Republic. For, as my research, along with that of others, has shown, the most amply endowed recipients of charitable assistance in the urban environment of the United Provinces were not the very poor, but the widows and orphans of the middling classes.[7] If the provision of charitable services was the result of a bargain, as van Leeuwen and others have suggested, the parties to this bargain were not simply the poor and the rich, but the middling as well. Indeed, the latter may have been the most important group of all, given their relatively large numbers in the urban centers of the western coastal provinces in particular, and their significant contribution to the tax base of both the local and national governments. Seen in this light, the provision of charity was critical to the process of building alliances and maintaining loyalties between the middling sorts and the relatively small cohort of their social and economic superiors. In particular, I want to argue that charitable assistance to them, perhaps best thought of as a form of risk management in response to demographic uncertainty, played a vital role in securing the acquiescence of an economically vital and largely literate citizenry for a system in which they were politically disenfranchised, heavily taxed, and truly vulnerable to downward social mobility. That system is worth exploring in greater detail.

The Political Context of the Dutch Republic

Shortly after coming into existence in the late sixteenth century (an existence which was defined more by what it was not than by what it was), the Dutch Republic acquired the dubious benefits of great-power status. This status was not a reflection of intrinsic resources, but rather resulted from the Republic's precocious commercial capitalism and the extensive reach of her trading empire in what was still the age of mercantilism.[8] The Republic was also the most urbanized state in Europe, the most literate, and the most heavily taxed.[9] Great-power status imposed a substantial financial burden on a per capita basis when carried by a state that had only between 7 and 12 percent of the population of its closest neighbors and rivals.

Were this not enough, the responsibilities concomitant with this status were shouldered by a state that had no fully coherent sense of itself as a unified political entity. Prior to 1650, Dutch political thought was deeply conservative, devoted to the ideal of the classical *regnum mixtum*. This model had, of course, been critical for legitimating the revolt against Philip II and Spanish hegemony in the first place. Yet if the Republic was to be some sort of a constitutional monarchy, it was missing its monarch. The Princes of Orange, even when safely in possession of the critical Stadholderates of Holland and Zeeland, were not monarchs, even by their own admission. And for two crucial periods in the Republic's history (1650–72 and 1702–47), the House of Orange was denied even the limited status of Stadholder. After 1650, when the tenor of political thought shifted to advance a purer form of republicanism à la Spinoza and the de la Court brothers, the Republic was faced with a contrary reality: namely an entrenched oligarchic rule by a merchant elite. Johan de Witt may have been the most articulate spokesperson the *States* party ever had, but he suffered no democratic leanings whatsoever. His conception of the "True Freedom" was one in which the urban elite governed at the expense of princely prerogative, and on behalf of both the propertied middle class and the unpropertied commons. He conceived of the Dutch Republic as properly an aristocracy, using the term "in its precise Greek meaning as the rule of the 'best' and therefore few, not as a synonym for nobility."[10] Moreover, his personal ties to the regent oligarchy of Holland's major cities were deep and close. His ultimate demise (both political and literal) in August of 1672 came at the hands not of the House of Orange, but of common rioters who believed their cause would be advanced by the restoration of Orange at the expense of regent power. Respectable burghers were either unable—or, more likely, unwilling—to rescue him. Indeed, the young men who had attacked de Witt in the streets of The Hague earlier that same summer were themselves "eminently respectable."[11] The tragedy of 1672, along with similar episodes such as the execution of the Grand Pensioner Johann Oldenbarneveld in 1619, and the riotous circumstances surrounding the restoration of Orange in 1747, all point to the fundamental fragility of political leadership in the Republic.[12]

The competing interests of the House of Orange, the regent oligarchy, burghers, and occasionally even commoners were layered on top of another fundamental struggle: that being waged between proponents of strict provincial sovereignty and those who wanted to create a unitary state under the sovereignty of the Estates General. In moments of crisis (almost always precipitated by foreign invasion) the Dutch even had at their disposal a quasi-legal institution which facilitated the fall of one government and its replacement by another. This so-called *wetsverzetting* (literally, the setting aside of the law) was essentially a rule for breaking the rules. That it existed at all, and had to be invoked from time to time, is indicative of the larger problem faced by the Republic. At no time in its over two centuries of existence did it fully come to terms with its own political configuration or its lack of a binding constitution.

The social environment of the Dutch Republic was likewise characterized by inherently unstable forces. The small citizenry (*kleine burgerij*) was by contemporary European standards unusually well educated and well integrated into the world of cultural production and consumption. Although actual upward mobility was severely limited, the households situated in the middle strata of Dutch society had by early modern standards ample opportunities to ape, on a smaller scale, the cultural and educational attainments of their social betters. This situation would have been conducive to a self-consciousness of social position on the part of ordinary burghers and a keen awareness of the quality of life of the elite. Both of these phenomena would have made downward social mobility particularly destabilizing. Cohesion in the urban environment was thus heavily dependent on shared notions of civic identity, and also on security for the middling groups against downward movement in the wake of either economic or demographic catastrophe.

Charity for Citizens

We should not be terribly surprised, then, that the most impressive of the Republic's charitable institutions were not open to the very poor, but were instead intended to succor unfortunate members of the middling classes. It was especially in the period of the Republic that the most ambitious building program commenced, with new homes established for aged citizens, both men and women, and for the orphaned children of burghers. In short, a situation existed not unlike the one that we see in the United States today, where the most benevolent, the most sacrosanct, and the easiest to access government programs are not those for the poor, but for the variously vulnerable members of the middle class. In the contemporary case, the two most expensive (and politically untouchable) programs are the home mortgage deduction (which only helps those who can first pass the down-payment barrier) and Social Security, which supports the aged in modified proportion to their income just prior to retirement. In the early modern world, relatively high rates of adult mortality put children at a much greater risk than they face today of the downward social mobility associated with the loss of parental income. Appropriately, then, charity for the middling classes was heavily tilted towards care for orphans. And despite the broadly inclusive Christian definition of one's neighbor, this provision for risk was most fully available to citizens, by either longevity or purchase, alone.

Thus, when a newcomer to the city of Amsterdam, for example, made the decision to buy citizenship rights, he not only paid into the system of charitable relief, but he also received access to certain potential benefits. Only the children of burghers could be taken into the Municipal Orphanage (*Burgerweeshuis*, hereafter) and the substantial care provided there made this a desirable option. That this exchange was clearly understood by the participants in the process is indicated by the effort on the part of the Regents of the *Burgerweeshuis* to convince the city to raise the cost of purchasing the *poorterrecht*. They argued that the poor were buying citizenship solely for the purpose of securing a place for their children in the Municipal Orphanage, should they come to die prematurely (*"alzo het door arme luiden veeltijds gekogt werdt eeniglijk opdat hunne kinderen na hun overlijden in 't Weeshuis zouden kunnen komen"*).[13]

In light of this contemporary opinion, it is reasonable to think of middling support for the Amsterdam *Burgerweeshuis*, and others just like it across the urban landscape of the Republic, as something akin to the purchase of middle-class social insurance against the deleterious consequences, for the next generation, of premature death. The support provided for the orphanage by the social and economic elite of the city, both in time and money, is further evidence of the effort made by those at the top of Republican society to preserve a sense of connectedness with those below them in status. The existence of such an institution guaranteed that the children of shopkeepers, craftsmen, and other petty burghers would not themselves end up as paupers through the accident of their parents' death. The social hierarchy was thereby protected from the potentially destabilizing effects of downward social mobility. Indeed, when the *Burgerweeshuis* did suffer from population pressure, as it did especially at several moments in the seventeenth century, the key criterion for allocating scarce spaces between competing citizen children was not based on need, but rather on the length of time that deceased parents had been members of the city corporation. This again reinforced the notion that the care provided by the orphanage was more a reward for long-standing participation in the civic life of the community than it was the straightforward relief of the most needy.

This distinction is very clearly delineated in the institutional history of another municipal orphanage, the *Burgerweeshuis* of Utrecht. This institution, the product of the efforts of the late-fifteenth-century Utrecht Bishop Evert Zoudenbalch, was the first such orphanage to be founded (in 1491) in the then-Hapsburg Netherlands. Zoudenbalch's initiative was grounded in the traditional Catholic teaching of the "seven works of mercy." In accordance with this, the orphanage welcomed all children, regardless of their parentage, *"oick van waen dat sij comen."*[14] Moreover, the Church controlled access to the financial assets of both the orphans and the institution, although even at this early date the city council required its consent for any major financial transaction. Another sign of the orphanage's medieval origins was the fact that the children were employed at begging whenever funds for the institution were running short. In 1531, Charles V, following the lead of both Catholic and Reformed humanist thought, outlawed begging in all imperial territories, but this rule was not fully imposed on the Utrecht *Burgerweeshuis* until 1565. In 1580, the city itself enacted a "reformation" and that changed the mission of the orphanage entirely.

It was at this time that the originally broad vision of God's needy was considerably narrowed. Not only was admittance now limited to children of Utrecht burghers, but also the Regents imposed a new health requirement. Deformed children were not to be admitted on the grounds that no amount of proper care would ever be able to make them into self-sufficient citizens. The new goal of the Utrecht *Burgerweeshuis* was quite simply to "guide their orphans into becoming useful burghers."[15] There was no point in providing special care for children who were doomed to a life of dependency regardless of their education and upbringing. The economic logic of this policy is clear enough, yet it is difficult to imagine anything further removed in its ideology from the "seven works of mercy" than this kind of civic charity. It was, however, entirely consistent with a policy geared to raising up future productive, tax-paying citizens and to promoting social stability within the ranks of the *burgerij*.

The Quality of Municipal Orphan Care

To be raised in a Municipal Orphanage was, as nearly as resources would permit, akin to being raised in a respectable laborer's household. To begin with, the Amsterdam *Burgerweeshuis* was managed exclusively by men from the most prestigious merchant and governing families. Regency was an unpaid position, unlike many other civic offices that carried either stipends (of widely varying amounts), the opportunity to make cash on the side, or both. The job was also onerous, requiring multiple long business meetings per week, supplemented by a variety of irregularly scheduled activities ranging from the collection of alms to the negotiation with local craftsmen for placement opportunities for the orphan boys. The Regents were also responsible for the maintenance and the management of the *Burgerweeshuis*'s extensive holdings of rental property as well as that of the many and varied financial assets associated with the institution. The day-to-day care of the children was attended to by a staff of approximately fifteen men and women, for whom the Regents were likewise responsible. The rewards for carrying out this difficult job were primarily social and political. An appointment to the *Burgerweeshuis* board was often a first step to higher (and lighter and better paid) public service or political office, a trajectory suggestive of the great value placed on the careful and successful administration of the orphanage itself.

The Amsterdam *Burgerweeshuis* typically housed between 400 and 500 children ranging in age from four to twenty-one, with population peaks topping off between 800 and 900 children.[16] The orphans were well-fed, well-clothed, and by all evidence well-reared. They were routinely served a diet of at least 2,500 calories per day (more than adequate to nourish a growing child today). Roughly one-third of these calories were derived from relatively expensive animal products such as milk, cheese, meat, and fish. Protein was more than adequate at all times. While cereals and legumes provided between 45 and 58 percent of this protein, keeping the institution squarely in the second tier of the conventional dietary hierarchy, they at no time faced the downward slide in protein quality which afflicted so many other communities in Early Modern Europe.[17] The only consistent deficiency in the orphan's diet was in the provision of vitamin C, a direct result of the very limited quantities of fresh fruits and vegetables available to the children. This widespread dietary deficiency was only remedied for the burgher orphans in the nineteenth century, when potatoes were added to the diet in increasing quantities. Ironically, the latter move towards regular potato consumption was generally regarded by contemporaries—and historians have followed suit—as clear evidence of deterioration in the standard of living of those in institutions and in poor and laboring households alike.

Although the orphan diet was remarkably stable over the two centuries of the Republican period, there were some minor trends which should be noted. The contribution of protein and fat in the provision of total calories was increased slightly over time, with a concomitant decrease in the importance of carbohydrates, bread in particular, and dark bread most of all. Interestingly enough, there was one category of carbohydrates which did experience significant growth over this period. Sugar in any form was a real luxury at the beginning of the seventeenth century, and it only appeared on the orphan's table in its cheapest form, treacle syrup. It contributed less than 1 percent of all calories. By the final decade of the eighteenth century, however, despite adverse price trends and increasingly constrained budgets, sugar accounted for over 4 percent of all calories, and treacle purchases had been supplemented by those for honey and even small amounts of refined sugar as well.[18] Perhaps more than any other feature of the orphan diet, the fourfold increase in the share of total calories derived from sugar is indicative of the increasing cultural importance attached to the consumption of sugar by respectable Dutch society. That the citizen orphans should partake in this social phenomenon seems to have been taken for granted.

The children's clothing allotment was likewise generous, even if distinctive in its pattern and coloration so that everyone would be able to recognize a burgher orphan at a glance. Even more important to the argument being made here than what the children wore while living in the institution was the bundle they were given upon graduating. It was this package upon which they had to rely when making their way in the world. Both boys and girls were supplied with several changes of everyday wear, undergarments, nightwear, and at least two heavy wool sweaters. They also received one outfit intended as Sunday best. High-quality English damask was the fabric used for the dress outfit until 1799, at which point the female governors (who were responsible for such things as clothing) substituted a cheaper serge. In addition to the clothing, the graduation bundle included twelve and ½ guilders in cash and craft tools as appropriate for the boys (the equivalent to approximately fourteen weeks in apprentice wages) and half of that cash for the girls. Finally, each child left the *Burgerweeshuis* with his or her very own Bible. The total cost of the graduation provisions (not including the local production cost of the clothing) was on average the equivalent of 3 percent of the total cost of caring for all of the children, not just those graduating in any given year.[19] In other words, it was a substantial expense, designed to smooth the passage of orphans back into the social milieu they had left.

All citizen orphans were taught to read, write and compute, certainly on a par with, if not better than, children of middling status reared in private homes. The extant records of the *Burgerweeshuis* suggest that a substantial amount of the children's time was devoted to education, despite the foregone income from the children's labor if it had been devoted more fully to paid employment. The fact that the Regents did not exploit the orphans' time indicates that they were committed to the long-term employment prospects of the children, not just to short-term gains from their unskilled labor. In short, they made possible a substantial investment in human capital of which the institution would not see the direct benefits. But this investment was nevertheless critical to the success of the orphans in maintaining the status of their erstwhile parents as members of the civic corporation.

Indeed, all of the children were trained for future employment in respectable (and, for the boys, often even well-paying) occupations. The artisanal trades were the primary destination for the boys, not highly lethal service in the East India Company. At no point in either the seventeenth or eighteenth centuries were VOC enlistments more than approximately 15 percent of all departures from the orphanage. Indeed, the Regents actively tried to discourage such enlistments, both by forbidding individual boys from signing up of their own volition, and eventually (after 1784) by fining any outsider a substantial fifty guilders for helping an orphan to enlist.[20]

The girls faced neither the same dangerous options nor the same opportunities to participate in guilded work. They were typically sent out into respectable domestic service, ideally to be followed by the practice of housewifery in their own abodes. Employment was secured before any young adult was permitted to leave the institution. This last guarantee was increasingly beneficial to the graduating orphans as the eighteenth century wore on and the Amsterdam labor market became ever more bifurcated between low-wage irregular employment and scarce, but stable, high-wage guild employment. The burgher orphans were moved to the head of the queue for these latter positions, giving them the full benefit of the Regents' capacity for extensive economic patronage.

All of this taken together made for a very high standard of care, one that was in fact relatively expensive by contemporary standards. Auditors working on behalf of the City of Amsterdam in the late eighteenth century concluded (with frustration, we might add) that the *Burgerweeshuis* required 150 guilders per year to care for each child. They further noted that the founding hospital, the *Aalmoezeniersweeshuis*, managed to get by with only 100 guilders. My own work on the orphanage budget during these years suggests that the city's estimate is reasonably accurate. The total expenditure on food, household items, clothing, and education between 1780 and 1812 suggests a per capital annual expenditure of 156 guilders. When the cost of the graduation bundle is added onto this, the average per capita expenditure rises to 161 guilders.[21]

A pauper family of four dependent on public relief received less than half of this amount. But it was not only pauper families that could not meet the level of care available in the orphanage. If we compare the annual expenditures of the *Burgerweeshuis* with local wage data, we find that the orphans must have been better provided for than even the children of working-class families that enjoyed steady employment. In 1783, the maximum annual earnings of unskilled laborers in Amsterdam's forestry service stood at 263.7 guilders. In subsequent years these workers enjoyed an annual bonus of twenty-five guilders, making for a total annual income of 288.7 guilders.[22] Although this wage was likely supplemented by the earnings of a wife, it alone could not support even two children at the rate of expense incurred on behalf of burgher orphans. Indeed, only a family solidly situated in the upper strata of the *burgerij*, above the level of even skilled craftsmen, could have afforded to spend the *Burgerweeshuis* per capita expenditure for multiple children of its own. Clearly, then, outlays of such a magnitude exceeded the children's material needs as defined in a rudimentary veterinary sense. As such, they demand explanations of a social and cultural nature.

The wealthy, politically powerful elite in Amsterdam (and in other cities of the Dutch maritime provinces especially) made a commitment to the tax-paying professionals, small traders, and artisans below them in the urban hierarchy, that their children would be secure in their middling status even if left prematurely bereft of their natal families. To the children of immigrants (often among the most destitute of the resident population), no such guarantee was made. Conditions in the *Aalmoezeniersweeshuis*, the repository of all non-citizen orphans and abandoned children, were markedly worse than in the *Burgerweeshuis*. No one, of course, honestly believed that the physiological needs of the two groups of children were fundamentally different. Yet the *Burgerweeshuis* consistently outspent the *Aalmoezeniersweeshuis* by 50 percent per capita. Not coincidently, this approximate differential reveals itself again in the mortality experience of the two populations. Childhood mortality was at a minimum 100 percent greater in the *Aalmoezeniersweeshuis* than in the city at large. Moreover, those orphan boys who did survive to their teen years there were routinely consigned to the Dutch East India Company as sailors upon departure. For many of them, this assignment was functionally a death sentence.

The two institutions not only differed in the material outlays made for their respective charges and in the future opportunities open to their graduates. They also purchased goods with very different cultural associations. Eighteenth-century menus from the two institutions suggest that at least some of the expenditure differential already noted was the consequence of a significant difference in the various components of the two diets. The children in the *Burgerweeshuis* were served meat at two noon meals per week and fish at two more. The remaining three days of the week, noon dinner was centered on a leguminous dish. In contrast, the Almoner's orphans were only served meat on Sundays, and they received no fish at all. They too had three leguminous dinners per week, but the remaining three days, their dinner consisted of the same grain porridge as their supper. Likewise, the citizen orphans enjoyed sugar with their evening porridge five nights per week and cheese with their bread on three other nights. The Almoner orphans had no cheese, and were served sugar only once per week. These menu differences are a reflection of the very different socially constructed "needs" of the two groups of children. The Regents of the *Burgerweeshuis* had to provide a level of care approximately equal with burgher parents if the graduating citizen orphans were to be rehabilitated back into the social milieus from which they came. It is in this context, then, that meat, cheese, and sugar were necessities in the orphan's diet. No such constraints were binding on the Regents of the *Aalmoezeniersweeshuis*.

This contrast can be seen even more graphically in the commitment made by the Regents of the *Burgerweeshuis* to provide each departing young man with a hat, despite the expense of doing so. While much of the children's clothing could be produced on the premises of the Orphanage using the labor of the older girls, the hats had to be purchased at considerable expense from a professional hatmaker. But it was the hat more than anything else that served as an outward sign of a young man's entry into middle-class respectability. Without it, he could not participate fully or comfortably with the members of his peer group raised in middling households. Thus it was that the hat became a standard part of the graduation bundle for over 200 years, in flush economic times as well as in lean.

Conclusion

The detailed example presented here of the high level of support allocated to citizen orphans in Golden Age Amsterdam is not an isolated one. Much of the charity dispensed by the various governmental bodies of the Dutch Republic was not specifically targeted at the already poor. Rather, it was designed by the regent oligarchy to prevent a slide into poverty by citizen families facing the financial fallout associated with illness and premature death. It served to moderate at least some of the economic risks faced by the middle strata of urban society, a group which was reasonably prosperous as long as adults were able-bodied and working, but which did not have household reserves capable of weathering a major loss of income, such as that which accompanied the death of a parent. Those groups which had been disenfranchised by the sixteenth-century prohibition against begging were not particularly well co-opted into the replacement system of civic and institutional charity. They were also not the political allies of the urban patriciate. The true champion of the poor (according to the popular pamphlet literature, anyway) was the House of Orange. In this, as in so many other things, these would-be princes were in keeping with the medieval and aristocratic origins of their house. So it is not surprising that much of the popular agitation for William IV in 1747 was in fact a response to high unemployment in the textile and other traditional industries and to the rapid increase in the prices of basic foodstuffs. Nonetheless, once William was safely restored to power, this kind of popular economic agitation was quickly suppressed with the able assistance of the various burgher civic guard units of the Holland and Zeeland cities. It was not until the last decades of the eighteenth century that charity for the truly poor had become an issue of widespread public concern or a noticeable financial burden on the public fisc. It was only under the worsening circumstances of the French Revolution and subsequent Napoleonic Wars that a new political agenda for charity emerged, which under the guise of the rationalization and centralization of poor relief dismantled much of the former largesse for the middle classes. The deterioration of the Republic's privileged economic position and her gradual loss of great power status, along with the diminution of regent political power vis-à-vis the Princes of Orange, provided the impetus for the development of yet another mode of charitable redistribution. But that is the story of another century, for another essay.

4 □ Mooseheart: "The Child City"

David T. Beito

Mutual aid was a cornerstone of social welfare in the United States in the early twentieth century. It probably surpassed the combined efforts of both governments and hierarchical organized charities. Fraternal societies were especially impressive as engines of mutual aid. A conservative estimate is that one-third of adult American males belonged to lodges in 1920.[1] These organizations provided an analogue to virtually every major service of the modern welfare state, including hospitals, job exchanges, homes for the elderly, and scholarship programs.

Many fraternal orders also built orphanages. They founded seventy-one such institutions between 1890 and 1922, almost all without governmental subsidy. The array of fraternal sponsors included the Masons, the Odd Fellows, the Independent Order of Foresters, the Knights of Pythias, B'nai B'rith, and the Sons of Italy.[2] But the single largest fraternal institution was Mooseheart, the national orphanage of the Loyal Order of Moose. Long after most other orphanages, both fraternal and nonfraternal, had closed down, Mooseheart stayed open and prospered. Mooseheart's formative years were in the golden age of American orphanages. During the first three decades of the twentieth century, all manner of groups stepped forward as sponsors. Among these were religious orders, immigrant organizations, and county and state governments.[3] The orphanage population increased from 50,579 in 1880 to an all-time high of 142,971 in 1923.[4]

The Loyal Order of Moose had started in 1888 with quite different goals. The founders had aspired to create an organization that would combine the best of the convivial and benefit features of the Elks and the Knights of Pythias. They made little headway. By 1906, when James J. Davis joined, the Loyal Order of Moose had fewer than 300 members and teetered on the verge of bankruptcy.[5] Davis, an immigrant from Wales who had settled in Pennsylvania and worked as an iron puddler, was a key figure in transforming the nearly moribund order by expanding and diversifying its services.

In 1910, the national convention of the organization, at Davis's prodding, authorized the building of a "Moose National Industrial School for the orphans and children of members of the Order" and delegated a board of trustees to carry out the task. From the outset, the founders hoped to create an exemplar of vocational training and pedagogical innovation. Edward J. Henning, a board member and federal judge from Pennsylvania, anticipated a Mooseheart slogan when he wrote that the public schools had made a great mistake by "training the boys and girls for the university instead of training them for life." The early promotional literature promised to "give a thorough practical training in any one of the many trades; to graduate pupils as skilled craftsmen who can earn a competence. Agriculture will be taught in all its branches."[6]

The board, after a two-year search, purchased 1,014 acres just outside of Aurora, Illinois. The location allowed for expansion. Financing for the purchase and early construction came through a mixture of voluntary contributions and the proceeds of a weekly "tax" of two cents on each member. To underscore the centrality of the orphanage to the fraternal members, the board named the enterprise Mooseheart.[7]

The opening ceremony in 1913 took place under less than ideal conditions. The organizers had hastily thrown up a circus tent to shield the guests from the blazing July sun.

Present were the eleven children who would be the first residents.[8] Thomas R. Marshall, the Vice President of the United States, delivered the dedication address. He had been reluctant to come. When first asked, he exclaimed, "I detest orphanages . . . I won't help you to lay the cornerstone of another one of them." Marshall relented, but only after a long-time friend, one of the trustees, promised that Mooseheart would not "be an orphanage at all. Technically, legally, yes, it will be an orphanage. Actually, it will be a home, a home and school for the dependent children of our deceased members."[9]

By the end of the first year, the Supreme Council of the Moose had selected a Board of Governors to administer Mooseheart and to appoint a superintendent. Although the members included several prominent politicians, those from the fraternal leadership, most notably Davis, exercised working control.[10] Davis continued to shape Mooseheart's development while serving as U.S. Secretary of Labor from 1921 to 1930 and then as a U.S. Senator from Pennsylvania. Another board member who played an important role in the pedagogical philosophy and character of the institution was Albert Bushnell Hart, a prominent historian from Harvard University.

Early Development

Mooseheart grew rapidly. The student body increased six-fold by the end of 1914. Many of the children continued to live in circus tents until the 1920s. The tents had stoves and wooden floors, but the conditions were embarrassingly primitive. An employee remembered that "pranksters among the boys would get up at night sometimes and jerk the tents down or open the flaps so that the snow could get in."[11] By 1919, Mooseheart had 720 children; seventeen arrived during one day in March alone.[12] The number passed the 1000 mark in 1921 and did not begin to ebb until the 1940s.[13] Mooseheart was truly a "child city."[14]

It was akin to a "city" in other ways as well. The physical

infrastructure was vast. Mooseheart had a power plant, a separate water supply, a small stream and lake, a twenty-eight-bed hospital, a baby nursery, a large assembly hall, several buildings of classrooms, a department store, a post office, a bank, a radio station, and miles of storm and sanitary sewers. The farm, which consisted of 800 acres, had eighty-five cows, 185 hogs, 1,000 chickens, and an apple orchard.[15]

Because Mooseheart had a school year of forty-eight weeks, it could offer an intense and varied curriculum. The academic portion eschewed esoteric subjects such as Latin and Greek in favor of civics, American history, English composition, and commercial history. Students who could not fulfill the academic requirements graduated with vocational degrees. The vocational component started in the eighth grade with optional "try out" courses of three months each. The choices for boys included animal husbandry, carpentry, automobile repair, and electrical work. Try out courses for girls were shorthand, typing, sewing, printing, and music. Then, in the tenth grade, the boys and girls selected a specialty. The fraternal membership appreciated this pedagogical approach. As Davis pointed out, the "Moose are mostly working men, and so they equip their wards for industrial life." The Mooseheart vision was: "Industry first and literature afterward."[16]

Events soon proved that the initial reliance on voluntary contributions, while sufficient to start the project, was no longer adequate. In 1914, the Supreme Lodge instituted a compulsory annual membership fee of one dollar to support Mooseheart.[17] It encouraged lodges to sponsor special projects; more than one residence hall bears the name of the lodge that endowed it.[18] A lodge in Philadelphia raised the funds for the hospital, which cost $125,000.[19]

An important innovation was the establishment of the Mooseheart Laboratory for Child Research in 1930 under the leadership of Dr. Martin L. Reymert, a child psychologist and former graduate student of G. Stanley Hall of Columbia University. Reymert was attracted by the "limitless possibilities for Research" offered by an environment of "about thirteen hundred normal children" in "a complete and self-contained . . . community-embracing experimental laboratory."[20] During the next two decades, the Laboratory made itself available to psychologists, anthropologists, sociologists, and other academics. Researchers studied topics such as anorexia, bed-wetting, childhood slang, and the effect of environment on IQs.[21]

Admission Policies

The admission procedure for children was fairly straightforward. The local lodge helped fill out the paperwork. Each application required confirmation that the father had been a member for five years before his death, a certificate of the child's good health from a doctor, a statement by a schoolteacher, and details about the family's economic condition. A final stipulation was that the guardian sign a contract ceding day-to-day control of the child. In exchange, the Board of Governors provided free room and board, medical care, and education. This was a conditional promise. Mooseheart did not make a formal adoption, reserving the right to return the child at any time to the legal guardian.[22]

The children who lived at Mooseheart came overwhelmingly from working-class backgrounds. This reflected the claim that the Loyal Order of Moose represented "common people, the average American, men who largely work with their hands." Between 45 and 55 percent of the fathers were unskilled or semiskilled.[23] The children probably came disproportionately from families on the lower-income rungs of the membership.

The ever-expanding number of applications pressured the board to act as gatekeeper against the "unworthy." For example, it often denied admission to children with criminal records, even if they were guilty of minor infractions, for fear that they would be carriers of antisocial behavior.[24] It refused to admit children who were fourteen or older on the theory that they were less adaptable and more capable of self-support. The superintendent referred to the biographies of two board members who at age fourteen had been "thrown on their own resources and improved their minds between working hours. . . . It is hard to make such men believe that a fourteen-year-old boy or girl is a dependent child."[25]

The standards of worthiness applied to the guardians as well as the children. A consistent concern was that guardians would exploit Mooseheart as a free boarding school, withdrawing and readmitting children for short-term convenience. The board warned that "Mooseheart is not intended to be a charity to relieve comfortable people from their responsibilities."[26] This attitude was not surprising. Officials of many orphanages, fraternal or otherwise, expressed this concern.[27]

Despite the formal rules, the Board of Governors's final disposition of each application depended on individual circumstances. Special situations and ambiguities demanded a measure of discernment and flexibility. Between 1922 and 1924, the board considered applications for 472 children. It admitted 70 percent without imposing further requirements, accepted 15 percent conditionally, and rejected 15 percent outright.[28] One measure of the board's flexibility was that it repeatedly set aside the rule that the father must have been a member in good standing for five years prior to his death. Davis explained these exceptions as the result of the "utter destitution of the cases."[29]

The board's most radical departure from the original standard of worthiness involved the admission of children who had one parent living. The founders had conceived Mooseheart as a haven for full orphans. By 1919, the annual report indicated a change stating that if a mother was "ill or for any reason, not capable of taking care of her children, the Governors go beyond the letter to the spirit of the votes of the Order, the main issue being, are these children of a loyal Moose . . . who without Mooseheart would be thrown upon charity?"[30] Between 1922 and 1924, half-orphans accounted for 75 percent (Table 4–3) of admissions while full orphans were 22.3 percent.[31]

The vast majority of the half-orphans had mothers. As a matter of course, the board discouraged widowed fathers from applying. When it made exceptions, it usually required the father to send contributions for the children's upkeep.[32] This practice never really worked; the board's annual report complained that payments from fathers "are often slow or even cease."[33]

The board followed the opposite course with mothers, allowing them to come and live with their children. Indeed, it increasingly required them to do so. The board described the mothers as a key "factor in Mooseheart life."[34] By 1929, 110 mothers lived and worked there along with 1,274 children.[35] They provided a cheap source of labor as cooks, secretaries, nurses, laundresses, and, most importantly, dormitory house mothers. An obvious advantage of this policy was that indigent widows could be near their children. Just as importantly, the expectation that mothers would work deterred those who looked upon Mooseheart as a free boarding school or a place to abandon unwanted children.[36]

Other admission requirements had little to do with moral worth. Most notably, the rules barred children who needed constant medical attention, carried communicable diseases, or were "mentally subnormal." The underlying premise for the last was that "the child shall have the mental ability to tell right from wrong, and to guide his own character."[37] The board relied on IQ tests to make this judgment, admitting those too young for testing on a probationary basis. The Mooseheart Laboratory for Child Research administered the tests.[38]

Early criticism of Mooseheart centered on its use of the IQ test to exclude children. Neva R. Deardorff caustically stated that a policy "which classes dull children with imbeciles is not scientifically defensible. But before a man joins the Moose, as a means of obtaining insurance, he would be prudent to find out the IQ of his offspring."[39] Even some officials of Mooseheart privately expressed discomfort. Writing to James J. Davis, Hart agreed that Deardorff was "perfectly right in criticizing our present method of excluding children solely on an unfavorable IQ. It does not seem fair to the father."[40] Although officials were generally sincere in following the slogan "Stop Separating Families," the rules sometimes had that effect. Between 1922 and 1924, the board considered applications for 122 families. More than 85 percent came with all the siblings but for 14.9 percent only some of the children were admitted.[41]

In response to criticisms, the Loyal Order of Moose lowered the minimum IQ (Stanford-Binet Test) for admission from eighty-five to seventy. Another reform was the creation of the Mooseheart Extension Service in 1925.[42] The name was somewhat misleading because it was organizationally separate from Mooseheart. Financial support for the Extension Service came from a portion of the membership dues levied by the Supreme Lodge. The goal was to help lodges care for those children who were otherwise ineligible for Mooseheart. The local lodges, which received funds, worked in cooperation with the child's church and school and sought additional support from charities and government.[43]

In 1929 alone, the Mooseheart Extension Service helped 1190 children at a per capita cost of $130.[44] This amount compared favorably with that spent on mothers' pensions, the leading governmental aid program at the state level. In 1931, annual per capita spending on mothers' pensions was $136. Neither the Mooseheart Extension service nor state mothers' pensions, however, approximated Mooseheart's per child outlay. Mooseheart spent more than $800 (including the cost of room, board, extracurricular offerings, education, and medical care) per child.[45]

Financing

The tremendous expense of maintaining Mooseheart, the Mooseheart Extension Service, and other activities spurred the Supreme Lodge to approve a dramatic overhaul in fundraising methods in 1927. The system, dubbed the ABC Dollar (A Big Charity Dollar), included the following allocation from membership dues: two dollars for Mooseheart, one dollar to the Supreme Lodge, one dollar divided between Moosehaven (the home for the elderly in Florida) and the Extension Service, and ten dollars or so paid for services provided by the local lodge.[46]

The Supreme Lodge had also started to amass an endowment for Mooseheart. The money was raised primarily through the "Nine O'Clock" ceremony. The ceremony began at 9:00 p.m. to coincide with the nightly prayers at Mooseheart. As it proceeded, the head of the lodge appealed for contributions. Henning's description gives the flavor of the proceedings: "Here drama mounts almost to religious fervor. Here His words, 'Suffer the little children to come unto Me,' are employed and supplication is made for the blessing of the Almighty on our endeavors. 'God bless Mooseheart' is our fervent prayer."[47] By 1930, the accumulated endowment was half a million dollars.[48]

The Women of the Moose also contributed. The group came into its own after 1925 when Katherine Smith, a professional organizer, became Grand Recorder. She had risen to prominence as the campaign manager of the women's division of the Republican National Committee for the 1924 election. Her talents so impressed James J. Davis, then the Secretary of Labor, that he asked her to organize a ladies' auxiliary. Under Smith's leadership, the Women of the Moose established scholarships, paid the salary of the librarian, purchased thousands of books, and raised money for the Mooseheart Hospital.[49]

A "National School Home"

Throughout its history, Mooseheart represented a self-conscious rejection of the orphanage stereotype as popularized by the writings of Charles Dickens. It banished, or radically modified, such obvious badges of institutional life as uniforms, factory-like dormitories, corporal punishment, and military regimentation. In this way, Mooseheart followed the model of the "anti-institution institution."[50] Matthew P. Adams, the superintendent from 1916 to 1927, drew a contrast between Mooseheart and the "cruel old-fashioned institution." In his view, Mooseheart more closely approximated a loving family, or "National School Home," than an orphanage. Similarly, another official declared that "[r]eal homes, the genuine affection and the spirit of a home, can be found all over our Child City."[51]

The publicity for Mooseheart sometimes drew direct analogies to the extended fraternal family. An article in *Mooseheart Magazine*, written by a student, recounted the life of two siblings, Mable Stone, age nine, and Charles Stone, age nine. Their father had been a machinist in Syracuse, New York, and a Moose. The outbreak of influenza claimed both their parents but because of the father's fraternal membership, they could go to Mooseheart. Mable's playmates predicted a dire fate at this "school," which "would be a place with a high wall, where they whipped you with a paddle so hard that you had to eat your meals standing up, and fed you nothing but beans, milk, and mush." To Mable's surprise, Mooseheart was like a comfortable home. Not only was she able to play in an orchestra but she also found that the "eats are great." Mable summed it up: "Best of all, I'm not alone. I've got six hundred thousand daddies, all Moose. I'm glad my daddy was a Moose!"[52]

Mooseheart tried to find the middle way. Adams readily conceded that a "loving father and mother" is better than "any institution or school no matter how good," but he cautioned that "a good school home is better for children than some unfortunate homes." Officials made sincere efforts to foster a homelike atmosphere. When newcomers arrived, a "motherly woman" met them at the bus station. The entire family stayed for two weeks in a reception cottage. The goal was to ease the transition and to guard against communicable diseases. Then, the arrivals began daily life in a dorm or in the "baby village." Each residence hall was under the authority of a house parent charged with providing "real home love."[53] The house parents for the younger children were female; for the teenage boys, married couples often served. Three adults—a house mother, an assistant house mother, and a cook—lived in each hall.[54]

The home motif informed the design of the living quarters. Mooseheart was part of a nationwide trend to replace large barracks with a cottage, or modified cottage, arrangement. Each cottage had a kitchen, dining room, and living room. The goal was to foster a "normal home atmosphere" with "no central dining halls, no separate dormitories, in short, no institutional living."[55] There was, however, crowding. It was common to have six children to a room and thirty to a hall. In some rooms, up to nine slept on cots.[56]

The early practice was to mix old and young in the same residence hall, sometimes in the same room. This arrangement fostered "big brother and big sister" relationships. The older child had the duty of helping the younger to dress in the morning and to be on time to class. The authorities reasoned that since an "ordinary family" usually had children from different age groups, "Why not in a large family such as we have at Mooseheart?" A related goal was to encourage the older children to act as guides and role models.[57]

Two former residents of Mooseheart, Vivienne Cottingham and Suzanne Kelly, speak highly of the arrangement. It helped accustom them to an unfamiliar environment and to teach responsibility. "I had two sisters I had to keep track of," Cottingham recalls, "and they kept me on the straight road." Her greatest challenge was teaching English to a little Italian girl.[58]

Although age mixing served a useful purpose, it had lost its appeal by the early 1930s. Officials complained that it had become too unwieldy and did not allow them to cater to the individual emotional, educational, and physical needs of the children. Another charge against age mixing was that "seniority or size may permit 'one cock to rule the roost.'"[59] The board, therefore, instituted an arrangement based on age cohorts. Henceforth, children moved from hall to hall along with their peers.[60]

Christmas presented a visible opportunity to display Mooseheart's dedication to the family spirit. Gala events were staged, topped off by a lighting ceremony at a giant tree. Cottingham remembers that the children "would go out and sing carols under the stars. I must have been easy to please or something, but I loved every bit of it."[61] Each of the halls had separate celebrations with presents under a tree. Christmas was the only time when mothers and siblings came together for a meal. Adams wrote that "we agree on some hall where they are to eat and all of the brothers and sisters of that family, even including the babies in the nursery, are there to eat as one family."[62]

The holiday season brought a deluge of gifts. In 1922 alone, Mooseheart's post office delivered 4,000 packages and several thousand dollars. There was no guarantee, however, of gifts for all the children. Some who no longer had relatives or active home lodges received little or nothing. To ensure at least two gifts per child, the Loyal Order of Moose established a special Christmas fund. By the early 1920s, annual spending from the fund was about $4,000.[63]

By contrast, birthday celebrations received short shrift. They were not completely ignored. The rules set aside one day per month to observe the birthdays of children born in that month. These group celebrations included an exchange of gifts and sharing of birthday cake.[64] But enforcement by house mothers was spotty and some ignored birthdays entirely.[65]

Finding substitutes for the lost parental role in a large institutional context was difficult. The problem did not stem from a lack of adults per se. There were hundreds of teachers, house parents, deans, and support personnel on campus. In 1940, the ratio of adults to children was 1:1.8, larger than the "average private home." But an adult worker in the course of a career might encounter hundreds, even thousands, of children. Giving individual attention was a difficult task.[66]

The adults who mattered the most in the lives of the children were the house parents and cooks. Even the most critical generally give them high marks. A former resident credits them with providing "a nice clean home for us. I can't say that I always liked them, but I think that they were always pretty fair."[67] But because some residence halls had as many as forty children, the house parents had difficulty keeping tabs on everyone. As a teenager, Kari Reymert Morlock, a daughter of Martin Reymert, spent time with seven-year-olds. Although most children were "very peaceful," they usually included "one or two clingers" who craved attention.[68]

To their credit, authorities at Mooseheart tried to find substitutes for the parental role or at least to promote active involvement by adults. One solution was a program of "sunshine parents." The basic idea was for a lodge member to serve as a kind of surrogate parent by "sponsoring" a child. The results were mixed. The system did enable children to establish ties based on affection. By all accounts, sunshine parents regarded Christmas and birthdays as opportunities to shower children with presents. But the structure of the program did not encourage emotional intimacy.[69] The rules generally limited contact to a few hours on weekends and did not permit trips away from campus. Some children viewed their sunshine parents as primarily "a sugar daddy type of thing. . . . I know that I must have had one of the best sunshine fathers in the whole place, but you just never did really get close."[70]

Another source of adult emotional support was the Mooseheart Laboratory for Child Research. The staff compiled psychological profiles of the children and monitored employees. Reymert's prized innovation was "play therapy." Preschool children were allowed free reign to act out their feelings under the supervision of a nonjudgmental therapist.[71] Because of the small size of the staff, however, only the "problem children" could receive services. Most children encountered the Laboratory as the "bug house" or as a place where they went to take tests.[72]

Ultimately, it was the children who established among themselves the most durable and emotionally satisfying relationships. They, rather than the adults, came closest to achieving the ideal of "real home love." The family analogy shows up repeatedly in the comments of former residents. "Everybody was your sister," remembers Cottingham.[73] "You learned to function as a family," states Marie Smejkal, a student between 1937 and 1954. "[E]verybody depended on everybody else."[74]

The environment of Mooseheart greatly intensified normal peer loyalties. As Cottingham states: "[W]e had a moral attitude of our own. You just didn't snitch no matter what even if you got in trouble. You trusted them. You didn't tell on them and you didn't lie."[75] One measure of group cohesiveness was that the children coined their own "Mooseheart slang." Popular terms included "aggie" (to gossip), "walking tree" (night watchman), and "smutch" (to slip out without being noticed). Even a distinct accent took hold. Tellingly, the speech patterns of the mothers at Mooseheart and their offspring diverged sharply. The accents of the mothers retained their regional flavor, but those of the children were "unusually homogeneous . . . even in the case of the youngsters who [came] very little before high school age."[76]

The children with the greatest likelihood to establish loving relationships with adults were those with mothers at Mooseheart. One alumnus who lost his mother during the 1930s describes these children as "really the fortunate ones." They "had some place to go, a sanctuary, and just get away from it all. The mothers supported them in their accomplishments and encouraged them in school."[77] Mother and child could see each other every day and even leave the campus as long as they returned by curfew.[78]

In return, mothers gave up a great deal, including virtually all control in matters of discipline and education. The authorities did not permit them to live in the same residence halls as their children, lest they show favoritism. Rules prevented mothers from leaving the campus for more than one day, except under special circumstances, such as to attend a funeral. The weekly salary was $15.50 in 1924 and $75 by the 1950s. A Mooseheart mother faced obstacles in establishing romantic (much less marital) relationships. She could not keep a car or stay out past a "reasonable hour."[79] She was free to date, but not to have male visitors. "There was kind of a disapproval," comments Ralph Meister, who worked under Martin Reymert, "of those women who went into town and tried to have a personal post-widowhood life of their own."[80]

Some mothers chafed under these restrictions. In 1923, Adams reported to the Board of Governors on the subject. He cautioned that his comments applied to "a very few, perhaps five, six or seven out of the one hundred" mothers, and that most were "efficient, loyal, and fine in every way." Still, he recorded complaints by, and about, mothers guilty of such infractions as slackness, gossiping about "love affairs," and accepting gifts from men they had "only known for a few months." Some mothers complained of low pay. Others resented having to work in the laundry. One mother wrote an angry anonymous letter to a house mother: "You give the kids beans and mush and make them help with the work. . . . I hope they throw it in your face and don't forget, they didn't come to this dump for work." Another regarded it as unfair that she was compelled to come to Mooseheart because "there are so many children here who do not have any mothers and many whose mothers have never been here."[81]

There were also more serious incidents. The authorities transferred one house mother to the laundry because she had slapped a boy "on the shoulder, the mark of which was on for a day or two." Another mother had a reputation for making her hall "hell on earth," yelling "until she can be heard a thousand feet away. She is very vile mouthed." Pointing to such incidents, Adams asked the board to reconsider the requirement that mothers come to Mooseheart against their wishes. He concluded that if "they are the marrying kind, they will get married much quicker away from Mooseheart," thus relieving the institution of an additional financial burden. These words fell on deaf ears. The board did not relax its expectations.[82]

Even with these problems, there were compensations for a Mooseheart mother. She had free food, medical care, lodging, and, if she wished, job security after her children graduated. Her free time off campus was her own, and a bus service to Chicago and nearby communities opened access to the outside. While some felt socially deprived, others thrived. Helen Koepp, a house mother during the 1950s, says that the mothers "had a ball" playing bingo, dancing, and drinking beer at the Moose lodge in nearby Batavia. In addition, many developed loving relationships with the children they looked after.[83]

Although mothers gave up much parental authority, there were ways to exercise indirect influence. Many built relationships of trust with other mothers to share information and exchange advice about childrearing. In a limited way, these arrangements resembled an Israeli kibbutz. Koepp appreciated the discipline enforced by the house mothers who looked after her children. "I was agreeable," she declares, "to anything [the house mothers] did. I wanted [her children] to mind."[84]

Preserving Individuality

Officials of Mooseheart pointed with pride to their efforts to cultivate freedom of choice and the flowering of the individual personality. As Adams put it, "children are not numbered and are not 'cases'" and Mooseheart attempted to "conserve their precious individuality." He contrasted Mooseheart and the "cruel old-fashioned institution" where children were "sheep."[85] Sympathetic observers echoed these views, declaring that Mooseheart promoted "social responsibility, individual initiative, and individual responsibility" and that the children had freedom "to express themselves, in speech, in dress, and in occupation."[86]

Mooseheart was exceptional in not censoring the older children's mail, except upon specific request of a guardian. According to the promotional literature, they had "the right to communicate to outside people anything that takes place in the institution." Within limits, the children were free to decorate their rooms and to select their clothes.[87] For Rudolph Binder, a sociologist at Columbia University, it was a "pleasure to go through the cottages and note the color schemes of the different rooms, each presenting a different but always pleasant ensemble." The commitment to individualism even found application in the toys and other possessions which children owned as individual private property.[88]

Mooseheart offered many choices in extracurricular activities. It had a student newspaper, two debate teams, three theatrical organizations, and a small radio station. Two bands and an orchestra took part in state, regional, and national tours. The Camp Fire Girls and the Boy Scouts established several chapters.[89] The Junior Order of the Moose, with a campus membership of 153 children in 1933, served as a feeder organization into the Loyal Order of Moose.[90] In 1931, John C. Meikle, a veteran of the Junior Order, became the first graduate of Mooseheart to win election to the Board of Governors.[91]

Mooseheart's team sports included football, swimming, basketball, and volleyball. During the 1920s and 1930s, the track team won several state championships.[92] Between 1919 and 1926, the football team scored fifty-one victories and suffered four loses, a record that favorably impressed the celebrated Notre Dame football coach Knute Rockne, himself a member of the Loyal Order of Moose. (In the movie *Knute Rockne, All-American*, the Rockne character postpones a vacation to stop at Mooseheart "to talk to my boys.") The girls participated in intramural sports, including tennis, track, baseball, and swimming.[93]

Finding a Balance Between Freedom and Control

The authorities sometimes had to walk a fine line between freedom and regulation. One example was an imbroglio over hair bobbing, which Mooseheart prohibited for girls as well as adult employees. Adams fought a rear-guard action against this policy, castigating the ban as unfair and an incitement to disorder. The girls flouted the rule and nearly all who graduated "bobbed their hair the day after they left." The board backed down and legalized bobbing after an assurance from Adams that "the hair is not to be curled by any means." It also reiterated that the board, not the mothers, exercised ultimate authority.[94]

Mooseheart's policies toward gender further illustrated the tensions between freedom and control. It emphasized separation, requiring that boys and girls live on their own campuses and sit apart at assemblies, church services, and movies.[95] All the same, officials tempered separation by creating opportunities for teenagers to socialize. They acknowledged that complete segregation led to an "unhealthy atmosphere." Measures taken to prevent such an atmosphere included weekly dances for the sophomores.[96]

The board even showed willingness to compromise on the thorny question of whether to tolerate kissing and holding hands. During the 1920s, it partially lifted an earlier ban. Adams persuaded the board to compromise, arguing that it was entirely natural for teenagers to show physical affection and warning against the "danger in our fighting things at Mooseheart which are accepted by the general public outside."[97] By the 1930s, the board permitted the boys to visit the girls' campus on Sunday afternoons. Nevertheless, it made sure that chaperones were ubiquitous. By one measure, Mooseheart's approach to gender relations was a success. Neither the available minutes of the board nor the recollections of former staff and alumni imply that any girl became pregnant, though it stands to reason that it happened at some point.[98]

In matters of contact with the outside world, Mooseheart was less protective than the typical orphanage. Children were free to visit town on weekends, though overnight stays were forbidden. The outings were usually in small groups supervised by an adult. The reins of control gradually loosened with age. Teenagers, if they showed good behavior, could visit town unchaperoned on Saturdays or Sundays as long as they returned by 5:00 p.m. Many students, however, did not bother to leave. There was plenty to do on campus, including going to movies and dances. Mooseheart kids seemed to keep busy. Another factor that lessened the urge for shopping trips was the presence of stores on campus.[99]

Officials boasted that Mooseheart was receptive to visitors. Outsiders freely wandered the campus and struck up conversations with the children.[100] "We could talk to anybody who came along," Cottingham declares matter-of-factly. "No one told us that you couldn't say this and couldn't say that."[101] Binder said that "[e]very visitor is impressed by the cheerful, courteous behavior of these children." The authorities obviously took pride in the institution and staged special "state days" for members from particular states to visit.[102]

At the same time, the board was vigilant, sometimes overly so, against outside contagion. It prohibited female visitors from wearing knickers on campus because of "considerable excitement" among the boys who "sort of hung around them, watched them and made comments on them."[103] Mooseheart was equally protective of its public image. The authorities enforced a ban on the crew-cut hairstyle, possibly because it made the boys look uncomfortably like prisoners rather than members of a happy family.[104]

Character-Building Efforts

Character-building found a valued place in Mooseheart's pedagogical philosophy. The basic agenda included an emphasis on such virtues as politeness, thriftiness, religiosity, and proficiency in the arts of self-government. Mooseheart hoped to make children "independent, self-respecting, self-supporting, self-directing, God-fearing, law-abiding, country-loving and cheerful citizens." Not coincidentally, the Loyal Order of Moose had long embraced these values.[105]

The fraternal ideas of Mooseheart's founders clearly shaped its approach to religion. Like many societies, the Moose had followed a live-and-let-live rule of banishing organized religion from the lodge room. In 1915, Rodney Brandon, a member of the Board of Governors, had argued that this was the proper model for Mooseheart. "When you join the Loyal Order of Moose," he confidently declared, "you have to admit belief in a Supreme Being, and that is just the amount of religious practice there is at Mooseheart. Mooseheart is not in the religion business." Brandon's recommendation was to turn religious instruction over to the relevant local denomination. If, for example, the child came from a Brahman family, an official of Mooseheart would write to "the nearest Brahman church, and explain to the head of that church that it is up to him."[106]

Brandon's vision proved unrealistic over time, but Mooseheart achieved a fairly close approximation. A key requirement was that children be brought up in the faith of their fathers. This rule applied even if the mother or guardian objected. Mooseheart hired Catholic and Protestant chaplains to live on campus and conduct services. Attendance was compulsory. Older children from Mooseheart and volunteers from nearby communities served as Sunday school teachers.[107]

Mooseheart took care to respect sectarian differences. Local ministers from various denominations visited on Saturday mornings to give special lessons and to oversee Baptism and Confirmation. During the week, children attended fifteen minutes of mandatory Bible or catechism study in their halls. The authorities transported the few Mormon and Jewish children to Chicago for services and lessons.[108] One touchstone of this policy was that "[n]o arguments or discussions of religious questions are allowed."[109] Mooseheart prohibited any behavior which might lead to religious conflict. A particularly hot issue was the format of Bible or catechism study. During the first decade, the house mother of each hall had enjoyed considerable discretion concerning the details, but this system sparked controversy. Adams told of a Protestant house mother who had tried "to give instruction in the Catholic Catechism," a matter which could "only lead to trouble." Searching for a balance, he rejected as impractical proposals to separate the children for their daily religious instructions. Instead, he persuaded the board to accept a compromise: silent study. According to the new requirement, "No one is to give any instruction or help any of the students with their religious study. In case a younger student should need someone to find the Bible lesson . . . an older student of the same religious faith is to look after the matter."[110]

At times, the commitment to religious toleration and harmony led to almost comical results. In 1923, the Church of Latter-day Saints offered to send books on Mormonism to the library. The board accepted the gift but required that these books, and all other sectarian publications, be shelved in closed stacks. Furthermore, when loaned to a student of the particular faith, "the book MUST be in the student's locker. This book is not to be put in the Hall library or left on Hall tables. It is NOT to be loaned to or borrowed by other students."[111]

Mooseheart had much in common with another set of experiments during this period, the George Junior Republics. Beginning in the 1890s, William R. George organized self-contained communities for dependent and delinquent youth in New York, Michigan, Illinois, and other states. Many of these institutions featured alternatives to corporal punishment, a greater element of personal choice, student-run banks, and some degree of self-government.[112]

Like the George Junior Republics, Mooseheart endeavored to promote economic self-reliance and thrift. The children were paid small regular allowances to cultivate habits of "giving money, saving money, and spending money." Each boy was allocated a small plot of land on which to raise and sell produce. Jobs for pay were available to the older children on campus for between fifteen and twenty-five cents per hour. Through these opportunities, the board hoped to impart the "moral effect" of honest labor and the "glow of satisfaction" of "doing of work for a useful purpose."[113]

To teach thrift, Mooseheart followed the lead of the George Junior Republics by establishing a student bank.

Half the money earned by students went automatically into their checking accounts. From this, students could "draw checks for candy, baseballs, baseball bats, and the hundred and one things a boy or girl wants." Here, again, the authorities tempered freedom with control. They required a house parent to countersign each check and set a limit of three dollars at a time. The bank rested on the theory that children "are more apt to be spendthrifts or misers than adults. Unless they actually save money and get into the habit of doing it as children they never will as adults." The authorities deposited the remainder of the student's earnings into a "savings account" in a bank in Aurora. It earned interest, but the students could not make withdrawals until graduation.[114]

As in so much else, Mooseheart strove to maintain a balanced approach in matters of money. Its urgings in favor of thrift rested alongside others promoting good works. Each Sunday the staff encouraged children to donate a penny to their church.[115] The board's annual report urged that students be taught "to give and to 'give til it hurts' in a worthy cause" and reminded them that "The Gift Without the Giver Is Bare." If penury was a danger, so too was excessive altruism. The key was to steer clear of extremes.[116]

Mooseheart Weekly, the newspaper published by the students, underscored this point. A story, aptly titled "Self-Sacrifice," appeared in 1920. The main character was a hardworking man "who lived for his family." He spent little on himself and devoted his energy to making his family happy. After years of self-sacrifice, he grew resentful; he "began to feel that the burden he had imposed on himself had been imposed by them." The next step was fear and paranoia. The man began to misinterpret innocent conversations as plots against him. Here was the moral: "If he hadn't tried so hard to do it all himself, they would all have been happier still. Self-Sacrifice is as bad as selfishness when it becomes a fixed idea."[117]

One of the best known policies of Mooseheart was its prohibition of corporal punishment. Any employee who slapped a child was dismissed or transferred to another job away from children.[118] Suzanne Kelly, who was a student during the 1920s and 1930s, reflects the consensus of former staff and alumni when she insists that employees "knew they would be fired if they ever hit you." The authorities "wouldn't allow that for one minute."[119]

Instead, punishment involved a schedule of demerits that could be assigned by house parents, teachers, or deans. The following infractions carried penalties of two demerits each: disobedience, lying, impertinence, disorder, fighting, and missing short assignments.[120] A maximum of five demerits was levied for more serious offenses: possession of tobacco, truancy, bullying, destruction of property, or being "a little too demonstrative" with members of the opposite sex. The accumulation of demerits led to a gradual loss of privileges. Five or more demerits resulted in an assignment on the Student Work Line. Students who were "SWL" had to spend one hour per day for twenty days working in such tasks as weeding gardens and picking up rubbish.[121]

The authorities sent repeat offenders among the boys to one of several "punishment farms" on the outskirts of Mooseheart.[122] The most onerous was Fez Hall. It was characterized by long hours of work, near total isolation from the rest of the community, and a simple diet. Because the children said that the meals were mainly bean sandwiches, it became known as the "beanery." A boy on the farm could gradually work his way back to a clean record.[123]

For the most part, even troublesome boys committed relatively minor offenses. A list exists of nine boys in the vocational program who spent time on the farm between 1 July 1921 and 1 July 1922. Three had been sent to the farm for smoking, one for stealing popcorn, two for accumulating excessive demerits, two for fighting (a boy had a knife, in one case), one for general disobedience and impudence, and one for possession of cigarettes and for visiting North Aurora without a permit.[124] The girls had a gentler system. They did not have a punishment farm but worked off demerits in their residence halls.[125]

A theme in the publicity for Mooseheart was its system of "self-government." Until the 1920s, a junior and senior assembly met daily at 5 p.m. Each student over age eleven had voting rights. The assembly was compared to an "old town meeting." The names of students with five or more demerits were read as a means to shame them into good behavior.[126] "It was kind of humiliating," Cottingham recalls, "to stand up there and report that you were this sassy." The assembly heard appeals from children to reduce demerits, and could make recommendations for leniency, although this did not happen often.[127]

While the children may have learned useful parliamentary skills, the assembly never exercised real power. Its decisions were subject to the veto of the superintendent. The board noted that the "Mooseheart Assembly is not a self-governing body in the same sense that the George Junior Republic is, but is instead what might be called a supervised self-government."[128] For reasons that are somewhat obscure, the assembly fell into disuse and disappeared by the 1930s.[129]

The demerit system survived but underwent revisions. Reforms came after withering criticism by Albert Bushnell Hart, who noted that demerits (often for very minor offenses) tended to pile up quickly. Between 1922 and 1924, more than 200 students, or one-fourth of the children (not including preschoolers), were under some form of punishment at any given time. More than forty were on the farms. For Hart, these numbers indicated a flaw in the system. He expressed disbelief that "there is any state of things at Mooseheart that justifies such a number of continuing punishments."[130]

The board enacted reforms in punishment methods during the 1920s and 1930s. It increased the number of demerits necessary for a trip to the farm and placed much less reliance on the Student Work Line. It took steps to ensure that more boys served their punishments in the residence halls rather than on the farms.[131] Lastly, the board established incentives to counterbalance the punitive features:

It instituted "merits" that could be earned for proficiency in twenty categories including "Self Control in word and deed" and "Neatness and good taste in dress." Each merit resulted in extra privileges.[132]

The most serious discipline, of course, was expulsion (or "demission"). Between 1922 and 1924, (see Table 4–4) the board approved demissions for 167 children. Most demissions did not relate to a breach of discipline. More than 44 percent of the children were demitted by a relative (usually the mother) because the family had become able to provide support. Only 13.7 percent of the demissions entailed a specific breach of discipline, most commonly running away.[133] . As a former student recalls, "[Y]ou had to be a pretty bad actor in order to get it [demission for breach of discipline]. The average guy who was trying to obey the rules and stuff like that wouldn't be expelled."[134]

Mooseheart continued to flourish during a period when orphanages began to fall into disfavor. Childcare experiments increasingly gravitated toward solutions such as mothers' aid and foster homes. Many experts regarded orphanages as cruel, regimented, and harmful to the future success of the children. This view still holds sway among scholars who contend that orphanages "create children who tend to be behind other children in skills, achievement, and social adaptation."[135]

This characterization does not seem to apply to Mooseheart graduates. To be sure, the transition from a sheltered and well-regulated campus was not easy. Many graduates had to learn such mundane activities as paying bills and filling a car with gas. Others suffered homesickness for Mooseheart and lingered in nearby communities before venturing out. Some home lodges found jobs and housing for graduates, but others neglected this duty. More than a few graduates could not count on help because their home lodges had disbanded during the Depression.[136]

But the picture was far from bleak. Alumni established an association to help graduates obtain "a start in life." By 1931, it had loaned $20,000 through a special revolving fund. More significantly, graduates entered the market-place with vocational and academic skills and access to a network of alumni.[137] The letters they wrote to Ralph Meister showed that although graduates underwent "a period of readjustment . . . they seemed to have managed it rather well on the whole."[138]

The most compelling evidence was a study conducted by Martin Reymert of 402 graduates between 1919 and 1929. The response rate, 77.6 percent, was unusually high. The results point to a record of achievement. The male respondents (Table 4–5) earned weekly wages that exceeded the national average by 70.9 percent; the wages of the females were 62.5 percent higher than those of other American women.[139]

The gap was even wider when measured by standards of educational progress. Ironically, an institution founded to demonstrate the superiority of manual education turned out a bumper-crop of college students. Mooseheart alumni were four times more likely than other Americans (ages eighteen to twenty-four) to have attended institutions of higher learning. More than 34 percent of the graduates (female and male) went to college, compared to a U.S. average in 1930 of 7.6 percent for males and 4.8 percent for females.[140]

Mooseheart Since the Depression

In the decades after World War II, Mooseheart remained open while the orphanages of other groups, such as those of the Masons and the Odd Fellows, gradually closed their doors. The continuing commitment of the Loyal Order of Moose (now Moose International) to a social service such as an orphanage ran contrary to this general fraternal trend. It responded quite differently to the same set of economic and social conditions. Like other societies, the Loyal Order of Moose came under severe stress during the Depression and membership, which was 541,463 in 1930, plunged to 265,664 in 1936.[141] Massive unemployment put a tremendous strain on retention and recruitment efforts. The response, however, was not to eliminate or prune services to members. While the membership base fell, the population of Mooseheart (over 1,000 children) was maintained at pre-Depression levels.[142]

The leaders weathered this storm by finding creative ways to adapt. For example, they persuaded the Women of the Moose to assume the funding for the Mooseheart Laboratory for Child Research, as well as for Moosehaven.[143] On a more fundamental level, the Supreme Council addressed the problem of reduced membership. Working through thousands of subcommittees at the local level, it launched a vigorous campaign to help members pay arrears and to remain in good standing. These measures bore fruit. Membership began to recover and, by the middle of the 1940s, actually surpassed the levels of the 1920s.[144]

At the same time, the Loyal Order of Moose jealously preserved and, in many ways, expanded Mooseheart. In 1941, the Supreme Council voted to lower the admission requirements by allowing in more children with fathers who were alive and "children and their mothers who did not show complete dependence." This took place in tandem with efforts to improve the quality of the service by expanding the physical plant and increasing the size and variety of scholarships. The Loyal Order of Moose raised much of the money by strengthening the fraternal tie through the establishment of state Moose associations.[145]

Despite the liberalization of admission requirements and increased spending on services, the population of Mooseheart continued to fall for most of the postwar period. By 1950, it was down to 766 and, despite a comfortable endowment of $150 million, fewer than 300 were left in 2007.[146]

Even though mothers still had the opportunity to work and live at Mooseheart, declining numbers exercised this option.[147] According to Kurt Wehrmeister, the head of media relations for Mooseheart, "[W]e'd like to encourage a bit more of that. We think we have too many mothers who are too likely to say, 'No thanks. You look after them for awhile.'" In 1994, the Board of Governors responded to the declining numbers by admitting children in need who had no family connection with the fraternal organization.[148]

Significantly, the trend toward fewer children did not seem to correspond to changes in the size of the overall fraternal organization. In 2007, Moose International had nearly one million members, higher than when Mooseheart had its largest population in the 1920s, 1930s, and 1940s.[149] The children received a full college scholarship in 2007 as long as they maintained a B- average for four years at Mooseheart.[150]

At least two factors have contributed to the falling numbers at Mooseheart. The changing membership base of Moose International provides one possible explanation. Like the memberships of other fraternal orders, it is probable that it no longer draws significant elements of the very poor (who most need childcare services) to its ranks. A second explanation can be traced to the rise of alternatives such as foster homes and Aid to Families with Dependent Children (now Temporary Assistance for Needy Families). In short, Mooseheart, like other mutual aid services, arose from conditions of necessity. Without a return to the incentives created by these conditions, any prospects for future growth will remain limited.

Unfortunately, those in charge at Mooseheart did not give me permission to send a detailed questionnaire to alumni. Had they done so, I could have made a direct comparison to a more comprehensive survey of orphanage alumni by Richard McKenzie.[151] I relied on McKenzie's questionnaire for my survey of alumni of the children's home of the Security Benefit Association, another fraternal society.[152] My results largely duplicated those of McKenzie. They indicatedthat orphanage alumni outperformed the general population in such measures as income, political engagement, and positive attitudes about life.

Despite the lack of survey data for Mooseheart, the available evidence, pieced together from alumni interviews and statistical studies, indicates a similar pattern. It attests to the many advantages of a Mooseheart childhood, especially when compared to the probable alternatives: disadvantaged or abusive families or foster homes. The children were well-fed and -clothed, obtained superior health care, and received an excellent education. Their possession of a high school diploma gave them a crucial edge. Despite certain missteps by officials, Mooseheart taught the children less tangible, but perhaps more important, skills, such as a sense of right and wrong, tolerance of others, good manners, and self-restraint. The financial cost of Mooseheart may have been high, but it was money well spent.[153]

5 □ A Home of Another Kind: An Orphanage in the Midst of Chicago's Elite

Kenneth Cmiel, with Anne Duggan

Chapin Hall closed as a residential treatment center in June 1984, after 124 years in service to families in need. It reopened the next year as a children's issues research center affiliated with the University of Chicago. Chapin Hall Center for Children no longer provides direct services to children and their families, but in many ways its current incarnation is the logical next step in its story. Chapin Hall has, in fact, transformed itself into one of the monitoring agencies that the orphanage sparred with over the years. The research now conducted at Chapin Hall is part of local and national efforts to manage child welfare services.

Chapin Hall's mission is rooted in the twenty-first century in other more subtle ways. On its website, it describes its work as having one overarching concern, "building knowledge to improve the health and well-being of children." Chapin Hall's "focus on meeting the real-world needs of those who are working directly with the programs and institutions that affect the daily lives of children" guides the efforts of local, state, and federal agencies, as well as funders and service providers. Here is a very new managerial task, absolutely unimaginable for most of the twentieth century. And by addressing one of the key realities of contemporary bureaucratic life—that collection of information does not necessarily guarantee informed decisions—Chapin

Hall has moved into what might be called a "postmodern" phase of thinking about how to manage the data strewn about us and trying to make sure we are able to digest it instead of choking on it.[1]

A few remarks about the use of names in the text: The official name of the orphanage, from 1860 to 1984, was the Chicago Nursery and Half-Orphan Asylum. It started to be called Chapin Hall in the 1930s. In the context of the nineteenth-century orphanage, it is herein called the Chicago Nursery and Half-Orphan Asylum. In the context of the 1930s and beyond, it is called Chapin Hall. Similarly, the Chicago Council of Social Agencies (founded in 1914) became the Welfare Council of Metropolitan Chicago in the 1940s, and is referred to thusly herein.

A Nineteenth-Century Asylum

Sometime between fall 1859 and spring of 1860, three women organized a day nursery for children whose mothers had to work. They rented a cabin that had been a "ragged school" (a charity school for paupers) located "on the sands" (the Near North lakefront where the opulent Gold Coast stands today). By opening their nursery on the sands in 1859, the women who founded the Half-Orphan Asylum were entering a neighborhood that the *Chicago Tribune* had only recently called "the vilest and most wicked place in Chicago."[2] The nursery's founding was also part of a concerted effort by businessmen, city officials, and charity women to clean up that neighborhood.

The Chicago Nursery and Half-Orphan Asylum was in many ways a typical home for dependent children, one of dozens of sectarian orphanages opened in the mid-nineteenth century as part of a response to the dislocation of a bewilderingly mobile commercial society. It was a Protestant institution for Protestant children, at times housing close to 180 children at once. It served a working-class population and was run by a volunteer Board of Managers made up exclusively of women. The Chicago Nursery and Half-Orphan

Asylum was graced with a string of energetic and more than capable managers, from Helen Goudy in the 1870s to Clarissa Haffner in the 1950s, none of whom was ever considered part of the work force.

In 1868, as a first step toward a more financially secure asylum, the women managers sent invitations to "a number of gentlemen to invite them to form an advisory committee" to plan the asylum's future.[3] This was not unusual in the mid-nineteenth century. It was common in all sorts of charitable institutions to have a female board that managed operations (including day-to-day finances) and a male board that managed investments. By bringing in men to solve their financial problems, the women wound up creating an organizational structure that survived until the end of the 1970s.

Nineteenth-century welfare reformers used the categories of "dependent" and "delinquent" to differentiate needy children. The former were children who, through no fault of their own, could not be cared for by their parent or parents. Adult poverty, illness, or death brought dependent children to outside care. A delinquent child, however, came into contact with a welfare agency precisely because he or she had caused some sort of trouble.

The Nursery and Half-Orphan Asylum was just one of the many private institutions created in mid-nineteenth-century Chicago to care for the needy. The Chicago Orphan Asylum and Catholic Orphan Asylum were founded in 1849 (during the cholera epidemic), the Chicago Relief Society the next year, the Home for the Friendless in 1858, the United Hebrew Relief Organization in 1859, the Old Ladies Home in 1861, and the Uhlich Evangelical Lutheran Orphan Asylum in 1869, to name just a few.

As in other cities, Chicagoans copied institutional models from established urban areas. In the decades before the Civil War, there was tremendous growth throughout the United States of orphanages for abandoned children. The war only intensified the trend.[4] Philanthropists, guided by environmental theories of childrearing, wanted to remove children from poorhouses, where they might be corrupted by paupers, drunkards, idlers, and other undesirable adults.[5] Between 1830 and 1850, fifty-six orphanages were founded in the United States.[6] Even more were established after the war.

An overwhelming majority of these were private institutions. Robert Bremner has estimated that through the second half of the nineteenth century, fully nine out of ten institutionalized dependent children in the United States were cared for in private institutions like the Chicago Nursery and Half-Orphan Asylum.[7]

The creation of the Chicago Nursery and Half-Orphan Asylum was part of a large-scale private response to problems that could not be addressed by a notoriously weak public sector. Apart from these structural considerations, there were also more personal reasons guiding the founders. A religious commitment and a sense of noblesse oblige informed these women, as had been the case with many other mid-nineteenth-century philanthropists.[8]

Chicago's landscape may also have contributed. There were neighborhoods defined by income prior to the fire of 1871, especially south of the Loop. But the chaotic growth of the 1850s and 1860s meant that often the rich and poor lived practically side-by-side. Wealthy and poor areas were frequently just a couple of blocks apart from each other. Consequently, if one lived in the city, one *saw* its problems. There was no visual escape. The women who founded the asylum saw these children regularly.[9]

The asylum filled a need, and it grew rapidly. In the first winter the nursery population jumped from six to twenty-five children. By 1869, seventy-five children were under care.[10] From the original three volunteers, the asylum grew to twenty in 1865. By the late 1860s there was a small paid staff that worked and lived at the home. Crowding was a constant problem, and the asylum moved five times in its first five years.[11]

While there were exceptions, the orphanage primarily aided the working poor, families with an adult jobholder but without enough income to keep a home together. It tried to give such families the breathing space needed to get back on their feet.

The great majority of the children were brought in by a parent. That most children had a parent still living appears to have been the norm for late-nineteenth-century children's homes, regardless of whether they were called "orphan" or "half-orphan" asylums. In December 1878, for instance, fully 145 of 199 children at the Chicago Orphan Asylum were either half-orphans or were from destitute families.

That children with one or two living parents were admitted was reflected in the contract parents were expected to sign with the Half-Orphan Asylum. Unlike other Protestant orphanages in nineteenth-century Chicago, the asylum had no legal authority over a child's future. It assumed that the family would reassemble as quickly as possible. But the contract also stated that parents had to visit their children at least once every two weeks. Parents who regularly neglected this stipulation indicated that their family meant little to them and that their child did not belong in the Half-Orphan Asylum.

Most children had a short stay. Just under 40 percent of the children stayed fewer than three months; 57 percent stayed fewer than six months. A full 74 percent of the children spent less than one year in the asylum; 86 percent spent fewer than two years. Few children actually grew up in the Half-Orphan Asylum.[12]

While at the asylum, the children slept in large dormitories that could accommodate up to sixty at once, though at times there were more. Children were divided into three basic groups: those under six, who went to the nursery; the older boys; and the older girls. As described by a *Chicago Tribune* reporter in 1933, the youngest children were awoken at 7 a.m., "washed, and taken to their breakfasts, after which they take a romp until they want to sit down."[13] Then a short nap was in order, lunch, and more playtime in the afternoon. There was an afternoon nap, then dinner, and the nursery children were put to bed at 6 p.m. Once a child reached six years, he or she attended school, which, until the 1890s, was held on the premises. There were minor variations for boys and girls. In 1873, an "industrial school" was started for the girls. The boys were allowed to find part-time work. American culture as a whole was far more lax about school attendance in the nineteenth century. So long as the child learned responsibility, there was no rigid rationale for attending school during the day. Chapin Hall's school conformed to the child's schedule, not the other way around.[14]

That the goal of much late-nineteenth-century welfare was to help the working poor is certainly worth some notice, in part because they are probably the single most neglected group of the twenty-first-century American welfare state.[15] In the nineteenth century, however, helping the "worthy" poor was done to the effective exclusion of many others, including children, leaving huge holes in the welfare system. In the late nineteenth century, the Half-Orphan Asylum was *always* filled to capacity. Practically every week for decades on end it turned away children who qualified for aid. And it also turned away hundreds of children who didn't qualify for help because of the behavior of their parents. Throughout the city, there was never enough room in places like the Half-Orphan Asylum for all the children in need.

A Traditional Asylum: 1890–1910

In the years after 1890, welfare reformers appeared in Chicago with a seemingly bewildering array of new ideas about the care of dependent children. These reformers, including people as famous as Jane Addams and Florence Kelley, were often key figures in the national movement for progressive reform. While their influence may have been national, they rapidly created an interlocking network of local welfare institutions, becoming a "counter-establishment" to the older and more conservative philanthropic elite that included the leaders of the Chicago Nursery and Half-Orphan Asylum.

Between 1890 and 1910, as Chicago's charitable world continued to grow, it also became infinitely more complicated.

The new situation created a number of specific issues for the Chicago Nursery and Half-Orphan Asylum to confront. Managers had to adjust to the new welfare initiatives of state and local governments, some of which seemed threatening. And the managers were forced to respond to reformers, who attacked the asylum as "old-fashioned" or even "cruel."

There were tremendous changes afoot in the city's welfare efforts at the turn of the century. In 1885, there were twenty-three asylums in Chicago; by 1900 there were fifty-eight; by 1910 there were eighty-seven. Just about half of these catered to dependent children.[16] The Chicago Nursery and Half-Orphan Asylum was, as late as 1890, one of only twelve orphanages in the city. By 1905, there were twenty-two.[17] It was in these years that the Half-Orphan Asylum shifted from being one of Chicago's premier orphanages to being just one of the city's many welfare agencies.

The Child Welfare Exhibit that progressives put on at Chicago's Coliseum for two weeks in May 1911 gives some sense of how the meaning of "child saving" had broadened. In the nineteenth century, the term generally referred to placing children in some sort of beneficent institution or placing them out to a farm family in the West. But the Child Welfare Exhibit displayed far more. There were exhibits on food, toys, playgrounds, and model homes. Here were exhibits on the public library, on settlement houses, on children's hospitals and dispensaries, on summer camps, on nurseries, on preventive health measures such as those of the infant welfare stations. Of the sixteen major exhibits, only the one on "philanthropy" even mentioned orphanages.

Two things were happening. More and more institutions were being built at the same time as progressive reformers were downplaying the place of institutions in child welfare. Most of the private orphanages and asylums created after 1885 were built on patterns developed in the mid-nineteenth century, a fact usually missed by historians concentrating on "cutting-edge" progressive institutions like Hull House.[18]

Progressives roundly attacked the nineteenth-century asylum ideal, arguing that the asylum was unhealthy, that it was a warehouse, and that it emotionally stunted its residents. Children in particular, they claimed, were hurt by asylum living. Children needed a home. Locking children in large dormitories (or "barracks," as the progressives called them) deprived youngsters of needed warmth and succor. Instead of saving children from the ravages of the city, as the Half-Orphan Asylum managers had thought, progressives claimed that asylums in reality were creating the social misfits of the next generation.[19]

The mission of the asylum—family stability—was no different than that of the progressive reformers. The difference lay in their deeply different assumptions about how stability was best maintained. The asylum ideal was predicated on the belief that single parents, including mothers, should be in the work force. An orphanage like the Half-Orphan Asylum was there to care for children through times of crisis, to make sure children did not fall prey to the corrupting influences of the city while a parent was looking for work or at work but without the resources to care adequately for his or her children. Early nineteenth-century reformers, however, stressed the need to have children at home at every possible moment. All other alternatives were second best. This "need" was tempered by deeply ideological notions of what a "good" home was. By 1920, welfare reformers would try to accomplish this goal by reducing women's participation in the labor market via mothers' pensions, stipends paid by the state to single mothers.[20]

Behind the progressives' hostility to the asylum was another fundamental difference between the progressive and conservative camps, this time over the nature of charity. Progressives argued that relief, as commonly understood by people like the Half-Orphan Asylum's managers, was both insulting and inadequate. It was insulting because it demeaned the client. Jane Addams, for example, argued that friendly visiting did not create sympathy between the social classes. Wealthy women visitors rarely understood working-class needs or habits, and such visits only reinforced the visitors' sense of superiority and the recipients' sense of dependence.[21]

Nineteenth-century charity was inadequate precisely because it was only designed to provide relief. It did not get at the root of the problem; it only treated symptoms. Progressives saw themselves as more systematic, more thorough, and more effective than the conservatives. The smorgasbord of welfare activities on exhibit in 1911 at Chicago's Coliseum reflected the progressive sense that child saving was far more than relief, far more than keeping a boy or girl safe when a parent died. It was everything that could shape a child.

These attacks were troubling to the managers of the Half-Orphan Asylum. The asylum's managers, like Mary Richmond, sometimes worried that they were becoming old-fashioned.[22] While they resented the new progressives, there was no stony anger. Both sides listened to each other and were willing to compromise, although neither forgot that their respective priorities and values remained far apart. Chicago philanthropy did not acquiesce overnight to the progressive system, but neither did the old guard respond with dim-witted animosity. Rather, in the years after 1890, the two groups fell into an uneasy dance. The history of the Half-Orphan Asylum during those years reflects this as well.

One area in which the two groups were in accord was public health. Urban progressives spent a large amount of time worrying about the water, sewage, and garbage pickup of the city. This progressive concern for health rendered the number of deaths common in the nineteenth-century asylums simply unacceptable.

The worst mortality statistics in the entire history of the Half-Orphan Asylum came in 1892. Through that summer and fall, the managers watched in horror while the doctors worked unsuccessfully. Most of the nineteen deaths occurred among children under one year old and who were ill either from disease or malnutrition when they entered the asylum. Nevertheless, such a death rate, not uncommon at the time, now horrified the managers. Later that year, a separate small hospital building was erected on the grounds, designed to handle only contagious cases. Two years later, the managers began to consider a new quarantine ward. It took several years to raise the necessary funding, but it was finally built when the asylum underwent extensive repairs in the spring of 1896. In 1873, mortality of children under five accounted for 59 percent of all deaths in Chicago; by 1893, it was still at 45 percent.[23]

The managers also hoped to reassert the asylum ideal by removing the whole orphanage from the city. During the late 1870s and 1880s, the asylum's neighborhood had become a slum. By the 1890s, instead of single-lot homes with spacious yards, many owners had put up second or even third homes on the same lot. No longer a calm, suburban-like setting, Chicago's Near North side was, as the United Charities annual report stated in 1910, a "city wilderness."[24]

Still another element in the fight against disease was the introduction of preventive care for the children. In 1897, at the house physician's suggestion, it was decided that all entering children would have a complete physical examination. The next year, county physicians for the first time administered free diphtheria antitoxin. In 1900, the City Health Department notified the asylum that it would distribute free health supplies to dependent children. In the same year, arrangements for regular dental care in the asylum were made for the first time. In 1901, Northwestern University made its dental school available for free care. During the first years of the century, regular medical checkups became routine at the Half-Orphan Asylum.[25]

After 1892, the death rate at the institution dropped. Never again did ten children die in one year, which had been common in the 1880s. Between 1894 and 1906, the asylum averaged three deaths a year. But two other changes virtually eliminated all deaths in the asylum. In 1905, children ill with contagious diseases were for the first time sent to a community hospital. According to the asylum's own annual report, the health of the orphanage became better than that of the city at large.[26]

A few years later, there was a final change, spurred on by the city. An ordinance requiring strict quarantining of ill children was passed, and the Half-Orphan Asylum had to reduce its population to comply. Until that time the managers had let the institution's population slowly rise. Between 1885 and 1890, the first six years after the 1884 expansion of the facility, the average population was 160. During the 1890s, it slowly increased. In 1898, for the first time, 200 children and staff lived at the Half-Orphan Asylum.[27]

In 1910, "the increased strictness of quarantine regulations enforced by the City Health Department" immediately reduced the number of children in the asylum.[28] In the first nine years of the century there were on average 158 children and twenty-eight staff members living in the building. The city's strict enforcement cut down those numbers by about twenty.[29]

The managers of the asylum were not hesitant about looking for new ways to improve the health of their children. Once reformers raised the issue, it became a primary goal of the asylum. Yet it should be underlined that they succeeded by reinforcing the asylum ideal and by adopting the progressive public health agenda, not by accepting progressive notions of welfare reform. Welfare reformers, like the University of Chicago professor Charles Henderson, claimed that illness was unavoidable in "large, barrack-like edifices" such as the Half-Orphan Asylum. The solution to the health threat was to deinstitutionalize children or to move them into smaller "cottage" homes.[30] Instead, however, the asylum's managers used the older notion of the asylum-as-refuge to dramatically reduce contact between children and the unhealthy environment. The managers also fixed the water pipes, began using hospitals, secured regular check-ups for the children, and kept closer watch over the physicians. By quickly adopting many public health measures, the managers were able to insulate themselves from the progressive attacks upon the asylum.

In the years around the turn of the century, the asylum managers developed a passion for control. It was not so much that this was a change in outlook; the women had always wanted to run their institution. The new assertiveness was part of a changing of the guard. Many key nineteenth-century leaders retired or died at the turn of the century. In their place came younger women, all handpicked by the older generation to continue the asylum's work. The new generation came from the same social background as the Victorian leaders. Their husbands were all part of the city's commercial leadership. Nearly every manager in 1910 was listed in Chicago's social register. A number of the women were the second generation of their families to serve the Half-Orphan Asylum. They entered with a strong sense of tradition.

This broadened into more grandiose civic themes. In the 1907 annual report, the managers described their mission as the "physical, mental and moral training" of youngsters of "impressionable ages" whose parents, the "worthy poor," were facing financial crises. The work of the asylum was not described as it had been in the nineteenth century—that is, as religiously motivated and for those poor from similar religious backgrounds.

The manual training and civic ethos provide other examples of how the managers used the larger currents of urban progressivism to fend off the more specific demands of welfare reform. If the latter called for the end of the asylum, and either the deinstitutionalization of children or the creation of the more home-like "cottage" system, the managers focused on the broader, more diffuse progressive goals of citizenship.[31] Wherever progressivism did not threaten the Half-Orphan Asylum, it was easily adapted to, but wherever the progressive message told the managers that they should give up control, they resisted. That led to sustained resistance by the Board of Managers to progressive efforts to reshape Chicago's system for care of dependent children.

Control of the Asylum: The Issue of Autonomy

Progressive welfare reformers created an array of institutions designed to bring order to Chicago's relief system. They hoped to create a formal, but essentially private, system of charitable relief. New organizations like the Chicago Bureau of Charities (founded in 1894) or the Juvenile Court (1899) were supposed to set standards of care for the whole city. The managers of the Half-Orphan Asylum, like most conservative Chicago philanthropies, resisted. The Board of Managers did not want to become enmeshed in a system that would take their asylum away from them.

The Half-Orphan Asylum turned down repeated offers to collaborate with the Chicago Bureau of Charities. The leaders of "Associated Charities," as it was known, wanted to have all case investigations made by professionals. This was a progressive response to criticisms, made by people such as Jane Addams, of nineteenth-century "friendly visiting." If the Bureau of Charities had its way, case investigations would no longer be done by wealthy volunteer women but by a paid expert staff.

Similarly, the managers were very wary of any contact with the new Juvenile Court of Cook County. The first such court in the nation, it was a project dear to progressive reformers. This was an institution designed to make both a more humane system (taking children away from cruel environments) and a more efficient system (by linking together all welfare organizations through a single channeling mechanism). The Half-Orphan Asylum managers would cooperate, but only on their own terms. On various occasions during the next ten years, the asylum refused to accept children the court wanted them to take.

The managers' distrust had varied sources. One was probably defensiveness. They thought they were doing a good job and resented attacks upon the asylum ideal. And it was not as if Juvenile Court was uncontroversial. Loud, if not influential, voices in the city complained about the lack of due process children got at the court.[32]

Formal alliance with the new organizations meant new obligations but no new income. It meant accepting outside decisions about whom to care for. Relying on public authorities for intake had radically altered at least one of Chicago's welfare institutions.[33] Progressives saw the new system as rationalizing the delivery of welfare; the managers of the Half-Orphan Asylum saw it as a power grab. Both were right, explaining both the progressives' doggedness over the years and the conservatives' wary resistance.

The asylum quite willingly used resources offered with no strings attached, such as the new medical services. Similarly, the asylum called in city probation officers when needed. Finally, neglected children were sent to Dependent Court (started in 1898). Previously, such children had been sent to the Home for the Friendless, a private institution.[34]

Reformers had neither the power nor the money to force a system-wide change in the delivery of services to Chicago's dependent children. Still, if progressives did not have legal coercive power, and if they did not control purse strings, they artfully waged the battle of ideas even while political and financial struggles remained uncertain. Progressives mounted an intense ideological campaign against the asylum model.

This often put the managers of the Half-Orphan Asylum on the defensive. In 1901, *Chicago Charities*, a progressive organ published by Graham Taylor's Chicago Commons, published an article critical of the Half-Orphan Asylum's handling of a particular case. In 1903, the managers were informed that the Illinois Bureau of Justice was dissatisfied with their treatment of a child. In 1904, a court order forced asylum managers to allow a father visitation rights to his children. At the same time, the Bureau of Charities began to monitor the activities of all private charities in order to make sure that they met standards—meaning progressive standards. Unsuitable charities were put on a "bad" list, which was made available to donors and newspapers. For the first time in its history, the Half-Orphan Asylum was being monitored in the name of the public interest. For the first time in its history, the asylum had to worry about public embarrassment.[35]

Reforming the Orphanage: 1910–1930

By 1900, Chicago's Near North was crowded, decrepit, and unhealthy. Children at the asylum had little room to play. As early as 1902, the managers expressed hope of building a new asylum outside the city. Reflecting progressive thinking, they wanted a "modern and sanitary home further from town where the children can have more freedom in out-of-door life and work."[36]

The urge for a country home reflected an accommodation of progressive thinking, but it also reinforced other commitments. Managers may have wanted to remove children from the city, but until 1912 they saw this as a means of maintaining the asylum ideal. The managers suggested moving to the country but not giving up the congregate living arrangements so disliked by progressives. The interest in a country asylum reflected the changing lifestyles of the managers themselves. In the 1890s, the managers began moving from the city to wealthy North Shore suburbs. By 1910, 30 percent no longer lived in the city of Chicago.

For years, funds proved elusive. In 1909, the managers were able to convince the directors that a new asylum was needed. By October 1911, enough money was raised to buy a partially wooded ten-acre tract on Foster Avenue and California Street, in the far northwest corner of the city. In the next few years, inflation kept the directors focused on maintaining the current asylum instead of building a new one. Once the war in Europe started in 1914, it seemed that all philanthropy for local projects had dried up. Less than half of the $150,000 needed to begin the project had materialized.[37]

The difficulty in raising money was a direct reflection of the increased size of Chicago's philanthropic world and of the changing place of the Half-Orphan Asylum within it. In the late nineteenth-century, the Half-Orphan Asylum had relied on its contacts in the managers' "home" neighborhood of the Near North Side and within the business community at large. Downtown contacts no longer generated the money they had in the late nineteenth century. There were now more fashionable charities to give to. In the early years of the century, the Commercial Club, the Women's Club, and benefactors like Julius Rosenwald and Cyrus McCormick gave hundreds of thousands of dollars to "child saving" agencies, most of the funds going to build cottages at institutions outside the city. After 1900, with little public profile, no connections to welfare progressives, and no track record of progressive reform, the asylum was locked out of the considerable amount of money donated to children's institutions.[38]

What saved the campaign at a key moment was the asylum's carefully nurtured traditionalism. In October 1914, Mrs. Charles Chapin gave $70,000 for the new building. The Chapin family had long-standing ties to the asylum. Mrs. Chapin's late husband had served on its Board of Directors. His mother had been a charter member of the asylum in 1865, and Mrs. Chapin's mother had served on its Board of Managers.

The gift changed everything. Overnight, pledged donations jumped from $55,000 to $125,000. By September 1915, $150,000 had been raised and the Board of Directors voted to break ground.[39] A year later the new building was ready, and in honor of the Chapin donation it was named Chapin Hall. At this point, the building was known as "Chapin Hall," the institution itself as the Chicago Nursery and Half-Orphan Asylum. It wasn't until 1930 that the managers decided to begin referring to the entire institution as Chapin Hall.

Even before construction began, Chapin Hall's managers decided to adopt the cottage system. It was a dramatic indication of the increasingly progressive spirit among the managing board after 1910. In the new buildings, the children would not be housed in large congregate barracks; there would be no dormitories. The nineteenth-century asylum system would be abandoned. Instead, the managers planned a large administration building surrounded by four separate home-like cottages, in which the children would live supervised by house mothers.[40]

Yet, to commit to the cottage system was not to adopt it. Even with Mrs. Chapin's gift, the funds were not there. In 1916, the money available only allowed the managers to build a single building—Chapin Hall. When the children moved to Foster Avenue, they moved into the same sort of large dormitories they had lived in on Halsted Street. By 1917, "one step" had been taken "by grouping ten of the older girls in the lower floor of one detached building under the care of a matron." Except for their meals, which were taken in the congregate cafeteria in Chapin Hall, the girls had most of the amenities of a private home.[41]

Into the mid-1920s, the managers were not unduly worried about the slow pace of development. While they were in principle committed to the cottage ideal, they did not see the congregate asylum as dramatically inferior.[42]

That is not to say that agitation for the cottage system had ceased. The city and the nation were filled with calls for more foster care, more mothers' aid pensions, more cottages, and fewer asylums. Progressive reformers, by the 1920s often ensconced somewhere in some new welfare bureaucracy, knew that there was only so much progress.[43] But they bided their time. Partisans of "modern" philanthropy devoted their energy to solidifying the citywide welfare system they had begun to create before the war. And they did this with the carrot instead of the stick. No pressure was put on an agency like the Half-Orphan Asylum to change its practices. Rather, the managers were gently told, over and over and over again, how they might improve the asylum.

In 1928, the managers began raising funds for a cottage

for the older boys. This decision, like so many others, was part of a wave of cottage construction in Chicago institutions. Angel Guardian, for example, decided in 1928 to add ten new cottages to its plant.[44] This time, the drive was undertaken at the height of 1920s prosperity. The Donnelley family gave several thousand dollars. The names of Cyrus McCormick, William Wrigley, Jr., and other wealthy suburban Lake Forest residents turned up as donors.[45] On 27 September 1928, the Board of Directors voted to start construction. Work began in December and the building was dedicated on 6 October 1930. In 1929, the existing girls' cottage was also remodeled so they could cook and eat by themselves; such facilities had been built into the boys' cottage. To complete the home-like settings, husband and wife teams were hired to manage each cottage.[46]

This sense of renewal and change at Chapin Hall was part of a wave of reform going on around the city between 1927 and 1932. Many were convinced that the old system was on the way out. Not only was the Catholic orphanage Angel Guardian building new cottages, but also the Chicago Home for the Friendless and the Chicago Orphan Asylum both decided to devote themselves entirely to foster home programs. Jewish charities were expanding their foster care programs in these years as well—one of a number of reforms that eventually put the Orthodox (and old-fashioned) Marks Nathan Orphanage out of business. In 1929, Father William Cummings, head of Catholic Charities, announced that a primary goal of the organization was to keep poor women and children out of institutions.[47]

Very few of Chapin Hall's children ever lived in cottages. In 1930, only forty of the orphanage's 130 children did so.[48] The new cottage, rather than standing for a new beginning, actually stood as the apotheosis of the progressive agenda. In many ways, the cottage marked an end rather than a new beginning, but that was unclear at the time. There were many other changes in the air.

Progressives had attempted to create an urban welfare system, large but not entirely outside the public sector, to rationalize and upgrade the delivery of services to Chicago's needy. Beginning around 1910, the rancor dissipated; managers and directors were soon advertising the asylum's ties to other agencies. By 1913, the orphanage had established a working relationship with the Cook County Juvenile Court and actively pursued the endorsement of the Chicago Association of Commerce. Within a few years regular business was conducted with the Illinois Department of Welfare, the Juvenile Protection Association of Chicago, the Immigrants' Protective League, the Illinois Children's Home and Aid Society, the City of Chicago Department of Health, and the Chicago Council of Social Agencies—all progressive creations. By 1930, services were also provided to the orphanage by the Court of Domestic Relations, the Institute for Juvenile Research, Allendale Farm, the Joint Services Bureau, the University of Chicago School of Social Service Administration, and the United Charities of Chicago—again, all outgrowths of the progressive movement. By 1920, the Illinois Department of Public Welfare regularly performed psychiatric evaluations of children for the asylum, as did the Juvenile Protective Association of Chicago.

Another early sign of the new dependence on outside expertise was the decision to join the Chicago Council of Social Agencies in 1919. It was not council policy to censure any particular institution; the council simply provided the most "up-to-date" information on poverty, welfare, and social work. It functioned as a subtle propaganda machine for the progressive cause.[49]

One key way in which the Half-Orphan Asylum changed was by coordinating its intake with other agencies. As late as 1910, all of the Half-Orphan Asylum's referrals were private. By 1913, however, the orphanage's literature touted the "spirit of cooperation" that existed between the asylum and the Juvenile Court. By the 1920s, the managers' wariness of the progressive institution was forgotten.[50] Even at the end of the 1920s, the number of referrals from Juvenile Court remained small, not reaching above ten percent of the orphanage's population.[51] By the middle of the decade, the Half-Orphan Asylum also relied on private agencies to refer needy children. Most important was the Joint Service Bureau, a centralized intake and referral service created by the Council of Social Agencies in 1922 to coordinate Protestant institutions for dependent children.[52]

By the 1920s, institutions such as Juvenile Court and the Joint Service Bureau institutionalized a critical progressive goal. They were citywide clearinghouses (both public and private) that directed child placement throughout the metropolitan area. Poor parents in need of help were directed to the Joint Service Bureau, the Social Service Exchange, or one of several other referral agencies.[53]

By the mid-1920s, Half-Orphan Asylum managers also used numerous outside agencies either to look after children who had left the orphanage or to help find other institutional homes for those children no longer suited for the asylum. By 1930, children coming to the Half-Orphan Asylum no longer entered a single institution; they entered a complex urban welfare system.

In 1928, after years of prompting by the council, the managers made a decision that ensured that the standardized forms really would include standardized information. The Half-Orphan Asylum hired its first professional social worker. This innovation, like so much else in these years, was part of a massive change in institutions around the city in the early 1920s and 1930s.[54]

Relying on outside expertise put the orphanage under the experts' tutelage. The changes that made the Half-Orphan Asylum part of a complex urban welfare system also undermined the orphanage's carefully wrought autonomy. The asylum found itself enmeshed in a large bureaucratic web. Moreover, it developed the need for expert guidance in negotiating the system. When Chapin Hall and like-minded service agencies became involved with the new coordinating institutions, there was little sense that dependency would result. Yet, by agreeing to let central agencies define intake, or train staff, or set agendas, that is what eventually happened. The modern Board of Managers increasingly relied upon outside judgment. Divorcing policymaking from the provision of care was still another change that had enormous consequences for the whole urban welfare system into the 1980s.

It would be wrong to say a "regulatory" system emerged in the 1920s. The umbrella agencies had to depend upon cultivating good relations with the Chapin Halls of the city, gently prodding them to make changes. It is not at all surprising that the Council of Social Agencies and the School of Social Service Administration primarily tried to build a coordinated child welfare system in the 1920s instead of trying to force changes in the actual services provided to children. You can't manage agencies that don't belong to your system.

As a consequence, the orphanage continued to thrive. In 1930, there were still forty-five orphanages and industrial schools in the Chicago area. Eleven orphanages still housed more than 300 children. Another eleven, including Chapin Hall, accommodated between 100 and 200 children. While there was some decline in the number of children institutionalized, the orphanage still lived on.[55]

The End of the Nineteenth Century: 1920–1945

By the late 1920s, the managers saw the children in their care as individuals separate from their parents. The nineteenth-century managers saw themselves as running a place where the working poor facing a crisis could leave their children for a short period of time. By the late 1920s and 1930s, the managers increasingly saw Chapin Hall as providing a substitute home.

During the 1920s and early 1930s, the number of children in Chapin Hall slowly declined. Even the Depression did not occasion any increase. In 1918, 165 children lived at Chapin Hall. By 1934, the average was 132, the number hovering there through the 1940s.[56]

One important change was the increasing number of children living in foster homes. As late as 1923, Illinois had fewer children in foster homes than any other major industrial state. The ratio was 5:1 in favor of institutions. By 1933, Illinois's institution to foster care ratio was 2:1.[57] Through the 1930s, the number of children in foster homes continued to grow, while the number of children in institutions continued to drop.

While the number of children in Chapin Hall fell only slightly after 1920, and not at all after the early 1930s, the children in the institution were very different from those of the nineteenth century. They were older. They stayed at Chapin Hall a longer time. While they were still predominantly working-class, there were more lower-middle-class and middle-class children among them. There were fewer half-orphans and probably fewer children whose parents were physically ill. Illegitimate children were accepted for the first time.[58] At the heart of the change was one major difference—fewer children came to Chapin Hall because their families were destitute. More arrived because their parents had troubles of their own.

Behind the change were simple demographics—the number of orphans and half-orphans dropped dramatically after 1920. In that year, it is estimated, one of every six children in the United States under the age of eighteen had lost at least one parent. By the mid-1950s, only one in twenty had. The drop in full orphans alone was even more dramatic. They had become a statistical blip by mid-century.[59]

Public policy reinforced the demographics. Mothers' aid legislation did not empty out Chapin Hall, but it did help change the kind of child that came to the institution. In the nineteenth-century asylum, children came because their families had collapsed financially. In the 1920s, divorce, separation, and desertion became the leading causes of entry into Chapin Hall. While the clientele of the institution remained overwhelmingly working-class, the managers regularly commented that poverty no longer brought many children to the home.[60] Parents looked for help because they just could not get on. Increasingly, the children came from very unsettled homes, where love and nurturance had largely gone missing. The most basic change in the circumstances of those who came to Chapin Hall can be summed up thusly: They'd gone from being families in trouble to being troubled families.

Upon adoption of the progressive agenda, intake was not monitored as it had been before. No one distinguished between "worthy" and "unworthy" parents. At Chapin Hall, children began staying for years, something very rare in the nineteenth century. By the 1940s, welfare professionals were noting this as a fact for orphanages in general.[61]

Coupled with the increasing mismatch between child and program was the continued inability of the forces of managerial rationality to bring the private, service-providing agencies into line. The various orphanages scattered across the city stubbornly defied takeover, although the Depression gave the welfare managers a wedge that they would use very effectively after World War II. In the mid-1930s, however, Chapin Hall and other children's agencies deflected the efforts of the Council of Social Agencies and the newly created Community Fund to take over management of Chicago child welfare.

The coming of troubled families, the deference of social workers to parents, and the lengthening stay of children at Chapin Hall can all be related to the new concept of family and welfare developed in the early twentieth century. By the late 1940s, however, the trends were clear. Less than 30 percent of the children stayed under a year (as opposed to 74 percent in the 1870s). A full 50 percent spent over two years at Chapin Hall. During the nineteenth century only 14 percent of the children had a two-year stay. By the 1940s, it was not uncommon for children to spend six, seven, or eight years at Chapin Hall.[62]

The Depression staggered all of Chicago's social service agencies. For Chapin Hall, the old money sources—parental payment, endowment income, and yearly donations—were no longer enough. Public money came to Chapin Hall for the first time, as well as private federated charity through the Community Fund. The amounts were small, but had large effects. The Community Fund money was enough to challenge the managerial autonomy of the boards. When the outside money came, so too came outside pressure.

The expansion of welfare services during the Progressive Era undermined one of Chapin Hall's key sources of support, the downtown business community. The prosperity of the 1920s had allowed Chapin Hall to reconstitute its old financial base—the combination of endowment, donations, and parental board payments. Instead of downtown businessmen, fundraisers looked to traditional friends of Chapin Hall. Another modification of the 1920s was the increasing reliance on yearly donations, which made up almost 22 percent of costs, and parental board payments, which had crept up to 31 percent from 25 percent in 1914. Interest from the endowment covered only 34 percent of costs during the 1920s, as opposed to 53 percent before.[63]

By early 1931, the lack of money was the primary topic of conversation among the managers. For the next five years, financial problems never let the directors or managers alone. Several times they found themselves unable to pay the bills. In February 1931 the managers borrowed $3,000 from the endowment to cover expenses. Three months later they needed another $5,000. In April 1933 the managers asked the directors for $1,000 to spend "if it became necessary." It did. In October 1935, the directors made still another loan, this time for $4,000, so the managers could pay bills. None of these debts was ever repaid.[64]

Budget reductions of all kinds were resorted to again and again. Between April 1931 and August 1932, salaries were cut three times. In February 1932, sick leave benefits were drastically reduced. In August, paid vacations were eliminated. Some employees lost as much as 25 percent of their income in little over a year. When the social worker quit in March 1931, three months passed without any discussion of a replacement. Then the managers decided to do without a caseworker altogether. The same day, they also voted to close the nursery school and to dismiss the teacher.[65]

Closing the temporary emergency shelter for infants in

1931 was another service cut, occurring just a few months after Chapin Hall had worked out the arrangements with the Social Service Exchange of the Council of Social Service Agencies to be the city's primary caretaker for infants needing short-term emergency care.[66]

All cuts in services proved to be temporary. The managers turned to the State of Illinois and the local Community Fund to support the infant nursery. In November 1931, the managers hired a social worker who worked three days a week, at no salary but for room and board. A nursery school teacher was hired under the same arrangement. She got room and board for herself and her two-year-old, but no other income. House parents for the boys' and girls' cottages were hired in the same way.[67]

Central to the financial crisis was the asylum's deep dependence on income that had to be re-earned each year and which, once the Depression hit, began drying up. Yearly donations had come to account for 16.5 percent of the budget by the end of the 1920s, but that income dropped steadily during the 1930s.[68] The drop in money from parents did the most damage. While the number of children in the institution remained constant between 1928 and 1932, the amount of money that parents paid for their children's upkeep fell by 54.8 percent.[69] The managers, in keeping with a policy dating back to the 1860s, would not refuse children because their parents were indigent. In 1935, the worst year, on average ninety-one out of 134 children in the institution paid no board. Since, during the 1920s, Chapin Hall had come to rely on parental board for 30 percent of its yearly income, the loss was devastating.[70]

During the 1930s, the old system began a slow fade. In this, Chapin Hall was far from unique. By the early 1930s, literally hundreds of social service agencies in the Chicago area had similar financial problems. With so many agencies in chaos by 1931, the Community Fund saw its chance. A campaign in 1931 by the Community Fund raised $5.5 million, which was distributed to agencies that summer. Another campaign raised $10.5 million, distributed over four months.[71] Two other campaigns followed, and, in 1934, Chicago's Community Fund made the campaigns permanent.

As late as 1931, Chapin Hall's managers and directors clung to the stubborn faith that they could go it alone.[72] The managers (in consultation with the directors) in 1931 made major efforts at fundraising. The result, however, was that the 1931 donations equaled the 1930 donations. The added work did not increase income.[73] The board also turned to charity fundraising benefits.[74] Finally, the board tried to tighten up its collection of delinquent board payments, and, for the first time in years, charged parents when they took their children on vacation. (This policy was only applied to parents who had jobs.)[75]

In October 1932, the managers and directors agreed to accept Community Trust money to help keep open the infant nursery. By the end of 1934, the Community Fund had arranged monthly payments to Chapin Hall. Total support that year reached 4.2 percent of the orphanage's revenue. By 1936, Community Fund money accounted for 7.7 percent of Chapin Hall's budget, helping to fill the gap left by lost parental board payments.[76]

But there was a price for the money and Chapin Hall officials soon grew wary. By the late 1930s, both male and female boards were looking for ways to rid themselves of the Community Fund obligations. In 1941, they cut their ties with the Community Fund.[77] One reason that the orphanage could dismiss the Community Fund in the early 1940s was the steadily increasing amount of public money available. It first came as emergency aid in 1932 and 1933.[78] In 1935, Illinois revamped its welfare law, expanding the public presence in dozens of ways.[79] One change to affect Chapin Hall directly was that the Cook County Juvenile Court was now able to pay it to house wards of the court. By 1941, payments from Juvenile Court accounted for 8.8 percent of Chapin Hall's income. Other public money became available to Chapin Hall during World War II. By 1948, public funds accounted for 13.2 percent of the institution's operating expenses.[80]

The public money Chapin Hall received during the 1930s and 1940s was less than that received by similar institutions in Chicago and by most childcare institutions in the nation. Even as late as 1945, over 80 percent of Chapin Hall's income came from traditional sources—donations, the endowment, and parental payments.[81] A 1928 study of eight major cities (Chicago excluded) indicated that 25.5 percent of all money for care of dependent children came from the public treasury and that 36.1 percent came from the Community Fund. Even in 1937, according to the CSA study cited above, Protestant childcare institutions in Chicago still got only 21.9 percent of their income from public sources and only 15.8 percent from the Community Fund. Even after the increase in social spending due to the Depression, Chicago institutions relied more heavily on traditional sources of income (endowment, donations, and parental payments) than institutions in other cities did before the Depression.[82]

A Question of Authority Within

Changes at Chapin Hall led to movement on still another front—that of control within the institution. Slowly, the professional staff took on more responsibility while the managers did less. Part of this was the managers' own doing, part the result of a powerful push from the Council of Social Agencies.

It also became more difficult to find sufficient volunteers to adequately run the institution. The nineteenth-century managers of the Half-Orphan Asylum were committed urbanites. Even with the residential segregation that occurred in Chicago after the fire of 1871, managers like Helen Goudy or Elizabeth Chesbrough were never more than a mile or two away from the poorer neighborhood. These were women who saw themselves as attacking the problems of their own environment—in short, attacking their own problems as city dwellers. By the 1930s, the women managers increasingly saw themselves as maintaining family traditions. By the close of the 1930s, the Board of Managers was motivated by a honed sense of tradition combined with North Shore noblesse oblige.

If the movement away from the city contributed to the decline of the Board of Managers, so too did their own dependence upon expertise. Late into the 1920s, Julia Thompson had agonized over the new professionalism of the Half-Orphan Asylum.[83] But the next generation unabashedly praised the scientific spirit and readily looked to the Council of Social Agencies for guidance. Mrs. David McDougal and Mrs. Clarissa Haffner, two of the most engaged members of the managing board, lacked the sense of assurance that Helen Goudy had possessed in the late nineteenth century and which Julia Thompson mourned in the 1920s.

Despite the slow drift to staff control, the volunteer managers still made the major decisions into the 1940s. They still controlled the money. But the patterns of control were shifting. And to complicate the picture further, beginning in the 1930s, the coordinating agencies downtown, the Council of Social Agencies and the Community Fund, began to inject themselves into the management of Chapin Hall.

The impasse of the 1940s was eventually solved by a new generation of women managers, among the most important Clarissa Haffner and Kay Milliken. These women were the last generation of female volunteers to make really significant decisions about the institution. It is not too extreme to say that in the late 1940s their guidance saved Chapin Hall from closing.

What went on at Chapin Hall was happening at children's institutions all over the city. Postwar ideas about the importance of family life helped push welfare elites finally to destroy the nineteenth-century orphanage. "Normal" children should be in a home, the argument ran, and if the "natural" home was unavailable, a foster home should be provided. Orphanages, in turn, should be reconstituted as specialized institutions for emotionally disturbed children. Between 1945 and 1960, this thinking massively restructured child welfare throughout the city of Chicago.

At Chapin Hall, the restructuring began in earnest in 1947. In the next few years, the new generation of managers patiently instructed the male directors, soothed the egos of truculent staff, gently prodded the older and more skeptical female managers, and continually negotiated with downtown welfare professionals—all in an effort to remake Chapin Hall. By 1949, Chapin Hall would be in the middle of changes so extensive that the institution would no longer be an "orphanage" in any meaningful sense of the word.

After the war, the welfare professionals returned to Chapin Hall and the other children's institutions. By this time there were key managers more amenable to reform and who started to raise their voices. Kay Milliken, president of the Board of Managers by 1947, and Clarissa Haffner, who would serve as president later, began hunting around for ways that the institution could adapt to the new needs of child welfare in the mid-twentieth century, a search which led to an alliance with downtown professionals.

Behind the change in heart at Chapin Hall was the ongoing financial crisis during the 1940s. In 1947 and 1948, there was a $30,000 deficit, money taken from the general endowment. It was this financial problem that led Milliken, Haffner, and a few other key managers to begin to look for ways to reorient Chapin Hall. In 1948, after fundraising couldn't do enough to alleviate the problem, the managers decided to rejoin the Community Fund. This set in motion huge changes. As a condition of membership in the Community Fund, Chapin Hall had to undergo an intensive study. The report was done by Elizabeth Goddard, a Welfare Council staffer. Her suggestions were all in keeping with newly evolved notions of what a childcare institution should be. Psychiatric counseling, more extensive casework services, and more professionalization were recommended, along with a "richer and more creative" program for the children. All of this implied that emotionally disturbed children would be the norm. The whole drift of the report was to edge Chapin Hall toward becoming a residential group home.[84]

At the same time, Chapin Hall felt pressure from other

sources. In 1948, for the first time ever, the state's Department of Public Welfare gave a basically negative evaluation of Chapin Hall. Far more shocking to the managers and directors, in the fall of 1948, Chicago's Association of Commerce threatened to withhold accreditation from Chapin Hall. Since it was not a member of the Community Fund, about 15 percent of its yearly income came from donations from wealthy North Shore families. Without the Association's imprimatur such support would have been almost impossible. While the orphanage was endorsed in 1949, Clarissa Haffner warned the male directors that "they may come back at us again."[85]

Between the spring of 1949 and the middle of 1952, managers like Haffner and Milliken shepherded Chapin Hall through its greatest change. There were new written policies on intake and personnel. A consulting psychiatrist was hired. New caseworkers were brought in. Numerous house mothers were replaced. The responsibilities of the Board of Managers changed significantly. Even the physical plant was altered, as children were split into groups of ten to fifteen. All these changes, as well as others, revolved around creating a more "advanced" and "modern" program for the children.

The program change solved the institution's money woes, but it also subjected the agency to the de facto regulation of the downtown welfare agencies. After 1949, budgets had to be submitted each year to the Community Fund for approval. All fundraising, key hiring, and new building had to be approved in advance. Chapin Hall did not just join the Community Fund. It joined an urban welfare system managed by the fund, the Welfare Council of Metropolitan Chicago, Chicago's Association of Commerce, and key professors at the University of Chicago's School of Social Service Administration.

In the 1960s, federal law and the State of Illinois were critical catalysts for turning all of Chicago children's institutions, including Chapin Hall, in a far more intensely therapeutic direction. In terms of later developments, the

1950s Chapin Hall was a sort of way station between the orphanage of the earlier years and the more involved therapeutic environment of the 1960s through the 1980s.

Perhaps the most important move made by the managers in 1949 was to hire a new head administrator, Adrianna Bouterse, who had an M.A. in social work from the University of Chicago, and who threw herself into the remaking of Chapin Hall.[86]

After 1948, the number of dependent children living in institutions fell swiftly. As late as 1945, Chicago's ratio of children in institutions to children in foster homes was still about 1:1. There were still almost 5,000 children in orphanages and industrial schools. By 1960, however, 6,538 Chicago area children were in foster homes, with only 2,904 in institutions. By every yardstick, the fifteen years after World War II marked a huge change in attitudes about the institutionalization of dependent children.[87]

Bouterse's arrival signaled more than a change in attitude toward the children. It also marked a massive shift in the roles of staff and managers in Chapin Hall, and in the relationship among staff, managers, and the professional welfare community. In the 1950s, Chapin Hall's professional staff took control of the day-to-day running of the institution. Indirectly, downtown welfare professionals set the grand course of the institution. During the 1950s, the managers were marginalized. Ironically, in their effort to save Chapin Hall and to reset its course, Haffner and Milliken implemented policies that would make them the last volunteer managers to have a major say in how the institution was run.

By ending the managers' involvement with intake and finances, the professionals also effectively ended the managers' knowledge of the day-to-day workings of Chapin Hall. That Haffner and Milliken were themselves so captivated by professionalism augured ill for the future of any sort of active volunteerism. Then again, to resist, given what was happening in the late 1940s around the city, could very well have meant the death of Chapin Hall.

Between the middle of the 1960s and the end of the 1970s, Chapin Hall went on a roller coaster ride that raced from the heights of prosperity and promise to the depths of financial despair. At the outset, the institution, supported by new forms of government funding, dramatically modernized its program. New services were provided and more social workers hired. Increased psychiatric help allowed for the care of more problematic children. By the middle of the 1960s, Chapin Hall was referring to itself as a full-fledged "residential treatment center," a sign that it was in the vanguard of professional care for disturbed children.

Chapin Hall's history once again reflected much larger patterns. Behind the increased state funding available in the 1960s were changes in federal Social Security law (DCFS was primarily administering federal money). Similarly, in the 1960s, many Chicago children's institutions were, like Chapin Hall, turning themselves into residential treatment centers. This was, in fact, a nationwide trend.[88] And the problems Chapin Hall faced by the late 1970s were the byproduct of a new public policy affecting all of Chicago's homes for emotionally disturbed children. The policy once again reflected changed images about children, family life, and institutions. The "new" ideas, in fact, reflected a revival of those progressive anti-institutional notions set aside during the 1940s.

In the mid-1970s, the staff experimented with a variety of supplementary programs. In 1974, Chapin Hall joined a consortium of private agencies to plan with DCFS how services might be modified. With another group of private children's institutions, including Children's Memorial Hospital, the agency used a $1.6 million grant to develop a comprehensive child abuse program. In 1975, Chapin Hall opened a foster care program and an emergency care unit for abused and neglected children. In 1977, it accepted developmentally disabled children for the first time.[89]

Morale sank at Chapin Hall after 1979. Wages had to be frozen in 1982 and a post-1979 DCFS policy further reducing the number of institutionalized children also hurt. It was not only the staff that was damaged by sagging morale; the board suffered as well. The deficits of the late 1970s led to a revival of the boards. In 1979, Jay Buck, a downtown banker, became president of the board. He hoped to create a more active managing board that could steer Chapin Hall's residential program through tough times. Buck hoped that a reinvigorated board could manage the problems facing Chapin Hall. In September 1980, when he first took over as president, he was relatively confident that the operation would continue. Buck's strategy was to find ways to get a more active board, both to keep better watch over the institution and also to get a group of active fundraisers.[90]

Within a year, the board decided to embark on a major fundraising drive. It planned to go to United Way, get matching grant funds, and raise money to refurbish the endowment. This plan was derailed when United Way refused to support the idea. Trust officials simply did not believe that Chapin Hall would survive. The place was not at the cutting edge of child welfare. It did not take enough "problem" children to please DCFS and without state support there was no way the agency would last.[91]

Buck asked Bruce Newman of Community Trust to find someone from the outside who could evaluate the program. Newman suggested Harold Richman of the University of Chicago School of Social Service Administration. Richman thus became one of a long string of University of Chicago experts to give advice to Chapin Hall.

Richman's study, which was funded by Community Trust, suggested a series of options. Chapin Hall might reorient itself to take still more difficult children. It could diversify its program in a variety of ways. Another possibility was to merge with another agency. Finally, it could use its endowment to fund some sort of research or advocacy center. Whatever the option taken, Richman made clear, Chapin Hall could not go on as it had done. There was simply no longer the referral base for the agency to succeed in its present state.[92]

In the end, these frantic efforts were for naught. At a

special board meeting on 28 February 1984, the full board voted to close the residential treatment center. The decision was not unanimous. Some voted against; others were unhappy with the decision. One director, Julia McNulty, stood and resigned immediately after the vote. McNulty was the granddaughter of Julia Thompson, the manager who had put decades of work into Chapin Hall, capped by her 1929 fund drive to erect Chapin Hall's second cottage.

And so it was that the orphanage went down, not with a roar, but with a whimper. That institution that had arisen out of a sense of contributing to one's own community, of uplifting the worthy poor, could not a find a place in the late-twentieth-century system of child welfare. Just as the asylum's founders' beliefs were rooted in nineteenth-century ideas about society, the current Chapin Hall Center for Children in many ways was the logical next step. Chapin Hall has, in fact, transformed itself into one of the monitoring agencies that the orphanage sparred with over the years. Research at Chapin Hall often has immediate policy ramifications. At the same time, much of the new research recalls older issues of child welfare. In all this, the new Chapin Hall continues the postwar institution's commitment to troubled children, simply shifting its expression from the provision of services to research.

6 □ Fates of Orphans: Poor Children in Antebellum Charleston

John E. Murray[1]

A demographic regime of high adult mortality in early America resulted in many children losing one or both parents. Some of these children were cared for by the surviving parent and others by more distant kin. From the late eighteenth century onwards, many of them spent some of their childhood in orphanages. The fates of these unfortunates, and of those who were simply abandoned by their parents—both while they lived in orphanages and after they left them—can reveal a great deal about a society's attitudes towards its children. The history of the Charleston Orphan House and its residents can shed considerable light on such attitudes in the Old South. Upon discharge from the Orphan House, children followed a variety of different paths in life. Some were bound into apprenticeships and others returned to their families; still others ran away from or died in the institution. To understand the experiences of these orphaned children is the goal of this chapter. It focuses on post-orphanage outcomes of children who passed through the Charleston Orphan House, America's first public orphanage, from its founding in 1790 to the Civil War. As if in a mirror, the experiences of these children in and out of an institution can inform our understanding of family life among poor Southern whites of the time, as well as of extra-familial public welfare institutions.

The context of these findings can be located in two related but distinct literatures, the history of American children and the history of Southern families.[2] A stylized history of child-rearing practices in America usually begins with a picture of early New England children as miniature adults.[3] Parents of very young children imposed a harsh discipline with the intention of breaking their will, in order to rebuild it in a godly way. Evangelical parents, according to Philip Greven were not shy about using the rod when a child's conscience failed to induce proper behavior.[4] By the time they had reached ten or eleven years of age, many children were sent off to be raised in others' houses, which suggests little emotional investment by parents in their offspring. At the same time, other children in early America enjoyed the affection of their mothers and fathers. Parents in the eighteenth century Chesapeake region found great delight in their playful young ones.,[5] and even in New England some families believed that their offspring would benefit more from relatively gentle guidance than from physical punishment.[6] From an early time, then, American parents raised their children in a variety of ways, influenced by regional customs, religion, and family wealth.

From the time of the Revolution through the first quarter of the nineteenth century, the hypothesized formality of earlier marriages gave way to what has been called the companionate marriage, based on affection between spouses.[7] At the same time, falling fertility rates made it possible for parents to invest more love and emotion into each offspring. As parents specialized in market work for the father and house work for the mother, the so-called cult of domesticity showered praise on the diligent mother who attended to her children's needs, not the least of which was their education.[8] Indeed, by the mid-nineteenth century a powerful rationale for the education of girls was precisely that they needed to learn in order to teach their children. The use of corporal punishment waned, and according to foreign travelers' accounts, the consequent rise in visibility of spunky children reflected either American love of independence. or excessive permissiveness that boded poorly for the future.[9]

A study of early Southern families might recognize four different types, only one of which left behind much in the way of manuscript materials for later analysis. Perhaps the least well understood were families formed by free persons of color. Laboring under a variety of legal disabilities, they nevertheless married, raised children, and a few even prospered. Most of what we know is based on either a few exceptional families or relatively sparse legal records.[10] What is known of slave families is highly inferential in nature, heavily dependent upon slave censuses, oral tradition, and the occasional mention in masters' manuscript records. The history that emerges of efforts to raise children in the most straitened circumstances is truly heroic.[11] The best understood of all are families of the planter class.[12] If not as hyperliterate as the educated classes of New England, their letters, diaries, sermons, and prescriptive child-raising literature offer a wealth of insight into their daily lives. The familiar themes of patriarchy emerge, generally associated with slavery in the sense that planter desire for control over slaves more or less implied a desire to control wife and children as well. More recent analyses also emphasize differentiation of family responsibilities by gender, and they find mixed evidence of companionate marriage among the nineteenth century Southern elite. Whether such attitudes may have led to greater affection toward children is unclear. It does appear that siblings in such families formed close bonds,[13] which were of considerable importance after the death of one or both parents, even when the orphaned children were raised by extended family members, those of the famous "great, tangled cousinry."[14] Whether such attitudes as may be adduced from planter manuscripts were typical of the poorer classes of whites is not at all clear.

Narrative sources of the lives of poor whites in the South are virtually non-existent. Histories that either examine poor whites in particular or assay entire communities note the paucity of such manuscripts.[15] Local histories thus over-emphasize the middling and rich classes while poor whites have been "generally invisible" beyond the numerical data in census and tax records.[16] Available evidence suggests that the doctrine of the two spheres may not have described poor white households, who needed such wage earnings as the wife was able to gain, and that a fair amount of domestic violence may have interfered with the ideal of companionate marriage.[17]

How did poor white parents approach their obligations to their children? The families of the Charleston orphans offer some insight into family life among poor whites in the antebellum South, as they and Orphan House officials created a substantial body of both systematic data and manuscript narratives about their lives. While imperfect in many ways, due to limitations of geography and family status (much as in the case of the gentry, many of the Orphan House documents were written only in times of separation and crisis), they nonetheless offer insight into the workings of these families. In particular, as this chapter shows, we can examine systematically the attachments of parents to their offspring before, during, and after these children lived in the Orphan House.

Charleston and its Orphan House

The Orphan House was founded "for the purpose of supporting and educating poor orphan children, and those of poor, distressed and disabled parents who are unable to support and maintain them." Prior to the Revolution, responsibility for care of poor and orphaned children in Charleston lay with St. Philip's Parish, the mother church of the established Anglican faith. St. Philip's had the authority to levy poor rates and distribute them as its vestrymen saw fit to care for destitute adults and abandoned children. The Revolution brought disestablishment to the Anglican Church and devolution of its poor relief responsibilities to the city of Charleston, which enjoyed a slight subsidy from the state of South Carolina for relief efforts. After investigating Bethesda, the orphanage built by the great preacher George Whitefield in nearby Savannah, in 1790 City Council passed an ordinance that created the Charleston Orphan House as the first public orphanage in the country. The measure began by noting the "heavy expense" that attended the previous system of "supporting and educating poor children."[18] By the end of the year, 42 children had been legally bound into the Orphan House, and many more were to follow.

The Orphan House accepted nearly any white child between the ages of three and fourteen who could prove residence in Charleston and a dire family situation. Parents, guardians, and other adults brought children to the Orphan House following the death of a spouse, impoverishment, imprisonment, illness, unemployment, alcoholism, and combinations thereof. Many widows and widowers relinquished their children due to destitution or to a recalcitrant new wife or husband. Children who had lost a parent were by no means unusual in the early South. In seventeenth century Virginia, a third of children had lost one parent before they reached the age of nine, and an additional 10 percent had lost both.[19] In antebellum North Carolina, two-thirds of planter families lost a parent before the youngest child reached 21 years of age.[20] The Orphan House was an unusual, even unique, institution, but the children who came to it were not so unusual in their misfortune.

Once the Commissioners admitted a child to the Orphan House, all three parties (Orphan House, child, and adult sponsor) confirmed the arrangement by endorsing an indenture. This document stipulated that the adult relinquished all legal rights to the child, and that the child would remain in the Orphan House until its officials found a master for him. While in the institution, children received room, board, and schooling. Boys were expected to acquire a basic level of book learning; girls helped clothe themselves and the boys by spinning and weaving. When girls reached around age twelve and boys age fourteen they met their prospective masters, often in informal conversations on the Orphan House grounds. If Orphan House officials, master, parent or guardian, and the child approved, the master signed the very same indenture that had already bound the child to the Orphan House. He (and in a few cases, she) agreed to provide the child, now an apprentice, room, board, clothing, training in a craft, and some payment at the end of the term.[21] Many children in the early republic spent part of their youth bound as apprentices. In another Southern port city, Baltimore, about half of all teenaged boys had been apprenticed in the decade 1810 to 1820.[22] In rough terms, in a given year the Charleston Orphan House housed 8 to 12 percent of the poor white children of the city.[23]

Not all inmates left the institution to begin apprenticeships. Some returned to their homes after their families had overcome a temporary reversal of fortune and were able to support them. In many cases a widowed mother remarried a relatively prosperous man who was willing and able to act as a stepfather. Other children ran away from the institution or died there. Despite its stated policy, the Orphan House actually bound out children younger than twelve and older than fourteen, children from beyond the Ashley and Cooper Rivers and even north of Boundary Street in the Neck. In a few cases children or adults failed to sign or mark the indenture. But by and large this rough sketch accurately outlines the lives of most of children who passed through the antebellum Orphan House.

Other characteristics of the children and their families when they came to the Orphan House can be seen in Table 1. The left hand column shows mean values of variables for all the children and the right hand column for those for whom entrance and exit dates were known. There were approximately twice as many boys as girls. The average age for both at entrance was seven years. About 12 percent of the children were able to sign their names at entrance, while 64 percent could only make a mark, which usually resembled a capital X. That about a fourth of children failed to endorse the indenture may be a sign that, literally, not

Table 1. Mean values of available variables

variable	mean value in full sample	mean value in sample restricted to those with known entrance and exit dates
bound out	0.57	0.65
died in Orphan House	0.08	0.08
returned to family	0.27	0.25
ran away	0.08	0.02
boy	0.64	0.64
girl	0.36	0.36
under 6 years old at entrance	0.33	0.31
aged 6–9	0.34	0.35
aged 9–12	0.27	0.27
aged 12 and up	0.06	0.06
signed at entrance	0.12	0.14
marked at entrance	0.64	0.69
neither signed nor marked	0.24	0.17
resident of Charleston	0.86	0.86
from U.S. outside of Charleston	0.08	0.08
from overseas	0.04	0.04
bound in by public official	0.29	0.31
by kin other than parents	0.03	0.04
by mother	0.56	0.54
by father	0.11	0.11
share of mothers who signed	0.48	0.47
share of fathers who signed	0.83	0.83
n	2005	1718

all the *t*'s were crossed nor *i*'s dotted in the processing of the child. This laxness may indicate a certain informality which raised the probability that the child would eventually run away from the Orphan House.

The Orphan House's admissions and population levels rose, fell, and rose again over the seven decades covered by this study (see Figure 1). Estimated population levels are biased low because indentures without exit dates were omitted. Nearly every indenture was dated at the child's entrance, so the annual series of new children is likely very close to the real numbers. The population shows an arc beginning at about 100 children around 1800 that increased to 190 or so in the early 1820s and then declining back to 100 in the late 1840s. From 1850 both admissions and overall population rose sharply, probably due to increasing numbers of poor immigrants coming to Charleston.[24] This upward trend continued so that a few months after the firing on Fort Sumter the Orphan House held 356 children, a tripling of population in just a decade.[25]

The children came from a variety of previous family situations. Figure 2 indicates how these arrangements changed over time. Mothers delivered more than half of the children to the Orphan House. Given legal disabilities facing women in the realm of contract, these women must have been widowed or abandoned. Fathers signed for 11 percent of the children. Some of these men were still married to the children's mother, some had been widowed, and others remarried. In rare cases, two married, living parents brought children to the orphanage, but here one of the parents was typically ill and unable to work. Aunts, uncles, siblings, grandparents, or other family members accompanied about 3 percent of the children. Public officials or clergy were responsible for the remaining 29 percent, some of whom had been in the care of family friends, kind strangers, or the poor house, while others had been homeless, wandering and begging from door to door. The relatively small share of full orphans, who had lost both parents, was typical of later nineteenth century orphanages.

Life in the Orphan House was spartan to say the least, if marginally better than living conditions of other poor white children in the South. The Commissioners of the Orphan House, who acted as a combination trustee and general manager, made sure that the children in their charge received enough food, clothing, and education and not a bit more. A physician who observed in 1797 that the children looked sickly attributed their condition to an imbalance in their diet: too few vegetables relative to the amount of meat, he said. To bring the daily fare into balance the Commissioners cut the meat allotment.[26] Little had changed by the time of the Civil War, when Commissioners estimated that the Orphan House paid all of 5 ½ cents per day to feed each child.[27] The physical setting was no more comfortable. Privy vaults leaked into water wells, all dug on the Orphan House's sizable lot. At times the sky could be seen on the top floor through holes in the roof. The rainwater that leaked in as a result was "particularly dreadful during the prevalence among them of whooping cough," according to a Commissioner in his response to complaints by women monitors (the "Superintending Ladies"). Bedding left in the courtyard to air out became covered with chicken droppings.[28] Education was probably quite a bit better than what was available on the outside. It centered on teaching girls the needle trades and giving boys the rudiments of reading, writing, and arithmetic, and appears to have had the desired effect on the inmates.[29]

What happened to these children after a few years of this life? This study considers four outcomes that cover nearly all cases: indenturing, returning to families, running away, and death in the Orphan House. Most of the children were bound out to new masters, but the share of apprentices declined over time (Figure 3). Of the entering cohort of 1800 to 1809, four-fifths were eventually indentured as apprentices, and then as time went by this proportion gradually declined. The next largest group consisted of children who were returned to their families, and this proportion rose over time. Figure 3 shows that the decline in bindings-out was matched in nearly every decade by a corresponding increase in the share of children returned to their families, from a low of 10 percent among the 1800s' entering cohort to 40 percent in the 1850s' cohort. By the end of the period more children were restored to their families than were bound out. The share of runaways and of children who died in the Orphan House remained roughly constant at about 10 percent. While there were other children not appearing in this accounting–those who were lost to the record keepers, sent into naval service, or granted further education in Charleston or Columbia—approximately 94 percent of all children who came to the Orphan House fell into one of these four categories.

The process of matching apprentice to master prized consensus from all parties: master, child, parent, and officials.[30] The Orphan House circulated a list of those children eligible for binding and occasionally advertised in the local papers that children were available for service. In other cases merchants and artisans visited the Orphan House and interviewed children before applying for particular youngsters. A prospective master like W.L. Graham who wanted to impress the Commissioners might carefully describe how he had "conversed with one of your boys (James Williams) who has expressed his willingness to live with me." That willingness was necessary for a master to gain in order for any indenture to be approved. The Orphan House denied many applications on the grounds that the child simply did not want to be bound to that master. As examples, Commissioners approved an application by a prospective master from out of town in part because it was "the choice of the girl," while another girl named Mary Mitchell, "having changed her mind, and expressed her dis-inclination to go to Mrs. Belin, the Board agreed not to force her inclinations." Mrs. Belin received another girl and Mary Mitchell was immediately bound to another mistress of whom she approved.[31]

The process became a family affair if the child had a surviving parent. Graham, who operated a dry goods store in

Mississippi, assured the Commissioners that he had "also seen [James Williams'] mother who has consented for him to go" along with him back to the West. In some cases the mother implied approval of a particular master or mistress when she asked him or her to take in her child. Margaret Moles, one of Charleston's intrepid women entrepreneurs, applied for Sarah Fields after "being solicited by her mother Mrs. Clipper to make application for her daughter." Consent of the surviving parent or guardian was not automatically granted. One mother rejected a master's application because she thought house painting was an "unworthy trade" for her son. This boy was bound to a house carpenter four months later. If master, child, and family were amenable to the apprenticeship, the Commissioners then checked the child's age to make sure he was old enough to be bound. Often they tested him to see if he had received an education that would enable him to perform his duties—or *her* duties, as even girls to be bound to learn housewifery were examined as well. Not all children passed. "Upon examination," they noted in one girl's case, "the commissioners did not think her sufficiently advanced in her education to be bound out." Several prospective apothecaries had to remain in the Orphan House to continue their learning.[32]

Surviving parents often retrieved children before they could be bound to a master. Children formally bound to a family member who signed the indenture are treated here as apprentices, in part because the records do not consistently note if the master was or was not related by blood or marriage to the child. The description "returned to family" applies to those children whose parent or other relative retrieved them from the Orphan House without going through the formal binding process. J. R. Cook, for one, applied to have his three sons restored to him because he had "returned to the city under favorable circumstances and being convinced that I will be able to provide for and maintain my children in a proper manner I now make application to withdraw them from the institution." Following the custom of consensus, this letter was also endorsed with the signature of his wife Martha, who had bound them into the Orphan House a year previously. The boys returned to their parents' custody two days later.[33]

In other cases a widowed mother who had attained a measure of prosperity after remarriage returned with her new husband to regain custody of the child. The Orphan House rarely turned down such applications from parents. When it happened the rejected family member was often a stepfather who had applied for his new wife's children.[34] It was much more typical for the parent to take the child home. Out of town kin such as uncles or grandparents were required to have officials in their locality send a letter to Charleston vouching for their character.[35]

Far fewer children ran away from the Orphan House or died there than left as apprentices or returned to families. Commissioners felt bound by their position to act *in loco parentis*, and they aimed to retrieve those children who absconded from the institution. Some of the escapees they admonished and allowed to remain, but the obvious troublemakers were immediately bound out, typically as an unskilled seaman on a cargo ship. The intent was to keep malcontents away from the other children. It may have been common for children who had been bound out to run away from their master. Hamilton (1995, 556) suggests that in Canada, "relatively few desertions occurred," but that American evidence is "inconclusive."[36] Lack of any systematic data on the Charleston orphans after binding prevents further exploration of this interesting topic.[37]

A few truly unfortunate orphans died in the institution. Statistics that would allow comparison of the Orphan House death rate with mortality of other contemporary children are scarce, but suggest that the Charleston orphans were not at significantly higher risk than others. About 2,000 children appear in the present dataset and each stayed an average of 5.5 years in the Orphan House, yielding some 10,500 child-years at risk of death. Of all children in the sample. (including those with missing dates of entrance or exit and who were omitted from further analysis), 164 died in residence, so that the Orphan House mortality rate was 15.6 per 1000 child-years at risk. Mortality data from the 1850 census, usually discounted by historians due to uneven coverage, supply a comparison, even if one to be regarded warily. According to the census, in the city of Charleston mortality among one to 20 year olds was 9.8 per 1000.[38] National estimates of child mortality suggest 28 per 1000 among five to nine year olds and 19 per 1000 among 10 to 14 year olds.[39]

In a world lacking any understanding of the germ theory of disease, and in a high-mortality environment, the young and epidemiologically vulnerable residents of the Orphan House probably received medical attention as efficacious as that given to any other child of the day. Physicians such as George Logan, Jr., who had earned his medical degree at the University of Pennsylvania, visited sick children and examined others regularly.[40] According to Logan's records over his forty years of service, children who died in the Orphan House had suffered from a variety of ailments. Infectious diseases such as measles or yellow fever had disastrous effects, especially when the Orphan House was unusually crowded. Frequent cases of worms or worm fever indicates a problem with intestinal parasites, perhaps related to continual difficulties in the disposing of waste–a problem common to much of low-lying Charleston.[41]

Long-term Influences of Family on Orphanage Outcomes

Charleston Orphan House residents came from a variety of prior family situations, spent varying lengths of time in the institution, and followed several different paths upon leaving. A child's earlier experiences might well have influenced what happened to him or her later in youth. For example, children brought to the Orphan House by their mother were much more likely to return to some configuration of their natal family than were those bound in by public officials. Table 2 outlines what ultimately happened to children brought by particular family members or other adults. The identity of the responsible adult seems to have had substantial influ-

Table 2. Proportions of children by identity of responsible adult and post-orphan house destination

	Bound out apprentice	Restored to family	Died in Orphan House	Ran away	Total
Mother	52.7%	35.4%	8.0%	3.9%	100%
Father	64.7	21.3	9.5	4.5	100
Other kin	70.3	17.6	8.1	4.1	100
Public official or unrelated guardian	72.7	14.2	7.7	5.4	100

Note: Percentages show share of children bound in by that adult who continued on to particular outcome; thus, 52.7% of those bound in by mothers were bound out apprentice. Includes children with missing entrance and/or exit dates.

ence upon how the child's stay in the Orphan House ended. The greater the familial distance from the child, the more likely that child was to be bound out to a master. Just over half of children bound in by their mothers became apprentices. This proportion rose to nearly two-thirds among those bound by their fathers, rose again among those bound by more distant kin, and was highest among those bound in by public officials. Similarly, the closer the blood relationship the more likely it was that the child would be returned to a family member.

Occasionally an unrelated person such as a church warden brought an abandoned child to the Orphan House, and then a family member retrieved the child. For example, in 1814 poor wardens bound in nine-year-old Sarah Adams, who was restored to her brother-in-law five years later. Altogether, a seventh of those bound in by unrelated strangers eventually were returned to family members, and among those bound in by their mothers this share was one-third. The role of prior family structure in the orphan's disposition is worthy of a closer look.[42]

The child's length of stay in the institution offers another perspective into the ongoing role of the family. Time spent in the Orphan House varied considerably from child to child and reflected different life histories for the inmates. A child who returned to his or her family after six months and one who returned after six years had quite different experiences at the Orphan House. Fortunately, reasonably precise dates of both entrance and exit are available for 86 percent of the Charleston children, which allows for estimated influences on children's time spent in the Orphan House. While virtually every indenture recorded the date on which the child entered the institution, unfortunately the missing dates were not distributed proportionally across all four outcomes. For nearly every child who was bound out to apprentice the date he or she left the Orphan House was recorded on the bottom part of the indenture. The share of missing dates among the children who died was the same as among all the children. However, missing exit dates were more likely to be found in records of children who were returned to their family and much more likely among those who ran away. When the Steward, who managed the Orphan House on a daily basis, and the Commissioners determined that a child had in fact absconded, digging out that child's records to note the date was probably a low priority for the harried officials.

Simple estimates of length of stay in the Charleston Orphan House can be compared to those found in other nineteenth century orphanages. Table 3 describes the distributions of length of stay at the Charleston Orphan House for boys and girls. The central tendencies obscure the wide range of spell lengths. Eleven percent of the children spent less than two years in the Orphan House, while 26 percent lived there for eight or more years. Hacsi offered round estimates of one to four years as typical lengths of stay, but most of these examples refer to later in the century. Early in the century girls at the Boston Female Asylum stayed two to three years; after a policy change in the 1840s that kept girls in-house longer before binding them out, they stayed over six years.[43] The children at the Orphan House

Table 3. Length of stay in months by sex and outcome

measure	bound out	returned to family	died in Orphan House	ran away	total
boys					
n	717	244	93	37	1091
mean	75.9	41.7	32.1	55.2	63.8
standard deviation	38.3	33.7	29.9	36.5	40.4
median	72.0	34.5	23.0	50.0	58.0
girls					
n	405	178	43	1	627
mean	64.2	46.5	34.6	26	57.1
standard deviation	36.6	33.5	32.9	0	36.6
median	61.0	39.5	23.0	26.0	50.0

may have stayed slightly longer in their institution than other contemporary children did in theirs, although there is too little data on antebellum orphanages to make such comparisons confidently.

Table 3 also shows length of stay measured in months. Both boys and girls who ultimately returned to their families or who died in the Orphan House lived about equally long there, three and a half years in the former case and just under three years in the latter. Differences between means and medians among these children indicate a skewing of distributions in which a few children with rather long length of stays before being returned or dying increased the mean without affecting the median. A sizable difference between the sexes can be seen among those children who were bound out, among whom the boys stayed about a full year longer than did the girls (76 months versus 64 months).

This difference probably reflects the policy of aiming to bind boys out at age 14 and girls at age 12.

The availability of length of stay data for the majority of children allows the estimation of more sophisticated models that address the fate of these children with more precision. In the orphanage history literature some effort has been expended to examine the length of stay in the institution, but less work has been done on differentiating among the outcomes based on those time periods.[44] To extract such information requires individual level data on children, which is scarce historically and in present day studies. In the child welfare literature the duration in question often begins when the child enters the foster care system, but the outcome remains unknown when the study ends, because the child is yet to be adopted.[45] This type of observation is called right-censored, since the beginning of the period (visually, the left hand end of a graph describing the spell) is known but the end of the period (the right hand end of the spell) is unknown. Spells that are censored after just a year or two of observation omit potentially important information that could be obtained by following the children through a longer period of time, which of course results in a more expensive study. Historical data, which trace subjects through sufficiently long spells of interest, offers some advantages in this way over present-day data, although this advantage is offset to some extent by the deterioration and loss of historical records through time. Even those only interested in present-day issues of child welfare may find that historical studies offer useful examples of data with relatively few censored spells.

Influences on length of stay that ended in one of several possible outcomes can be estimated with competing risk models. These are a class of regression models which estimate hazard functions (in the present case, proportional hazards), which report the conditional probability of an event in a given time period, given that the event has not occurred in any previous time period. It is possible that the event of interest will fail to occur because of another event that preempts it—say, in the present case, a mother retrieving her son from the Orphan House, which would thereby eliminate any chance that he would be bound out. In this case, we say that the observation was censored at the time of the child's return to his family, because he was no longer at risk of binding. One proportional hazard model was estimated for each of the four outcomes: binding, restoration, death, and running away. In each of these a censored observation was defined as having ended in any of the other three outcomes; the time of censoring was set at the date of the intervening outcome. These models can easily be fitted to the kinds of duration data that child welfare organizations generate.[46]

How the broken and suffering families of antebellum Charleston viewed their children can be inferred from the results in Table 4. As noted above, the natal family structure strongly influenced the child's future, mothers in particular being key determinants. Children bound into the Orphan House by their fathers or a family member other than a parent faced hazards of various outcomes that were identical to those bound in by public officials such as poor house commissioners and church wardens. That is to say, the child's fate depended not on orphan status *per se*, but on whether his or her mother was alive. Children with surviving fathers, siblings, aunts, uncles, and grandparents looked forward to futures little different from those faced by full orphans. Children bound in by mothers were much more likely—78 percent more—to return to their natal families, which often meant the mother and a new stepfather. (The effect of a coefficient on the hazard is given by exponentiating it.)

The ability of parents and children to sign their names had several consequences, some economic and others related to deeper kinds of well-being. A literate child was sure to be more useful to a master than one unable to sign his or her name. Results in Table 4 indicate that children who were already literate at entrance were significantly more likely to be bound out soon (i.e., in that time period given that they remained in the Orphan House up to that time) than children who could only mark their name, holding all other characteristics constant. In part, such children could pass the Commissioners' own examinations more easily, and in part they might impress the prospective master with their skills. Masters could and did observe child literacy and took that into account in deciding to indent the child. A merchant from Lancaster, S.C., explained his interest in a particular boy: "The boy Wm. R. Bull, whom I have seen & conversed with & whose writing, ciphering &c I have also seen, I am pleased with him." The more literate children may also have been more attractive to the extent that their higher level of education spared their masters the contractual burden of promising additional schooling.[47]

A child's ability to sign also reflected accumulated interactions with the parents, particularly the mother, that led to literacy acquisition. Previous research has indicated the importance of the mother's literacy in enabling the child to acquire it.[48] When a mother engaged her child in reading and writing lessons, she not only taught a skill but helped form a bond that grew through repeated interactions and emerged in the path that the child followed. The results in Table 4 suggest the durability of the parent-child bond. The power of the maternal relationship is manifest in the determination of mothers to regain custody of their offspring. For children of literate mothers, the hazard of binding out was significantly reduced by 26 percent and corresponding prospects for the child's return to her were significantly raised by 54 percent, holding constant the child's literacy as well as age and other influences. Earlier research has questioned exactly what kinds of behavioral changes are induced by literacy.[49] The present results suggest that literate parents held a greater desire and ability to keep their family together than did illiterate parents.

As the previous paragraph suggests, acquisition of literacy reflected more than just a learning process. It was the result of parental investment in the child early in life, as such had life-and-death consequences for the child, ac-

Table 4. Competing risk model results

variable	hazard of being bound out	hazard of return to family	hazard of death	hazard of running away
child characteristics				
girl	0.27***	0.34***	-0.23	-3.22***
	(0.07)	(0.10)	(0.19)	(1.02)
aged 3-6	0.94***	0.49*	-0.80***	0.99
	(0.17)	(0.29)	(0.27)	(1.10)
aged 6-9	1.87***	0.71**	-1.17***	1.96*
	(0.17)	(0.29)	(0.28)	(1.08)
aged 9-12	3.26***	1.19***	-1.53***	3.29***
	(0.18)	(0.30)	(0.35)	(1.10)
aged 12 and up	4.38***	1.04***	-2.31**	3.84***
	(0.21)	(0.40)	(1.03)	(1.31)
signed at entrance	0.49***	-0.99***	-1.99***	-0.78
	(0.10)	(0.29)	(0.76)	(0.70)
did not sign or mark indenture	-0.59***	0.80***	0.46	1.33***
	(0.15)	(0.22)	(0.40)	(0.50)
from S.C. low country not Chas.	-0.04	0.23	-0.09	1.06*
	(0.20)	(0.24)	(0.47)	(0.64)
from S.C. up country	0.36	0.60	-0.03	-15.84
	(0.30)	(0.51)	(1.01)	(5721)
from else-where in America	0.04	0.23	-0.99	1.16*
	(0.14)	(0.24)	(0.71)	(0.64)
from overseas	0.40**	1.05***	-0.27	-0.45
	(0.18)	(0.19)	(0.59)	(1.03)
family characteristics				
bound in by kin other than parents	-0.05	-0.04	0.15	-0.86
	(0.16)	(0.34)	(0.48)	(1.03)
mother	-0.08	0.61***	0.17	-1.39***
	(0.08)	(0.15)	(0.23)	(0.47)
father	-0.09	-0.26	0.53	-0.56
	(0.15)	(0.37)	(0.47)	(0.81)

variable	hazard of being bound out	hazard of return to family	hazard of death	hazard of running away
mother * literate	-0.30*** (0.09)	0.43*** (0.12)	-0.43 (0.50)	0.89* (0.53)
father * literate	-0.16 (0.16)	0.56 (0.38)	-0.26 (0.24)	-0.17 (0.84)
decade of admission				
1800s	-0.16 (0.11)	-0.51* (0.30)	0.001 (0.39)	-15.38 (1043)
1810s	0.01 (0.11)	0.71*** (0.22)	0.27 (0.36)	-15.41 (1163)
1820s	-0.06 (0.11)	1.01*** (0.22)	0.29 (0.36)	0.94 (0.69)
1830s	-0.29** (0.12)	0.62*** (0.24)	0.50 (0.37)	0.78 (0.74)
1840s	-0.58 (0.13)***	0.95*** (0.26)	0.04 (0.45)	0.94 (0.71)
1850s	-1.10*** (0.14)	0.37 (0.28)	0.16 (0.50)	-0.10 (0.77)

Notes: *=significant at 0.10 level; ** at 0.05 level; and *** at 0.01 level. Omitted categories: boy, aged 3 or less at entrance, did not sign or mark indenture at entrance, resident of Charleston, bound in by public official, bound in during 1790s.

cording to Table 4. A child who was literate enjoyed a substantial and significant reduction in mortality hazard of about 86 percent. Literacy did not cause longevity, but both followed from the same investment by the parents in the child, in what economists call human capital. Gary Becker defined investment in human capital as "activities that influence future monetary and psychic income by increasing the resources in people," which subsumes both health and education.[50] Most likely, the literacy that some children who entered the Orphan House had acquired from their parents came to them as part of a bundle of many different interactions.[51] These parents taught them how to write, fed them a decent diet, and provided sufficient shelter and rest that enabled them to withstand the rigors of the Orphan House. That is to say, these parents loved their children.

The control variables of sex, age, residence of the child, and the decade of entry influenced the child's path as well. In hazard function terms, girls were at significantly increased risk of both being bound out soon (31 percent more likely than boys) and being returned to their family soon (40 percent more likely than boys); this is not unexpected given the findings in Table 3 and the policy of binding girls at a younger age than boys. They were, though, much (96 percent) less likely to runaway soon than were boys, which was consistent with the multinomial logit model estimates. Mark Courtney and Yin-Ling Irene Wong (1996) reported similar results for present day foster care, which suggests that running away from temporary care then and now has been largely a boys' gambit.[52] At the same time it is worth noting that running away was the category most affected by the loss of observations that lacked exit dates, which could have introduced a bias into the parameter estimates.

Few regional differences were apparent. Non-South Carolinians were at greater risk to run away. Children from overseas were more likely than Charleston residents to return to their families and to be bound out. These latter children were primarily of two groups. In the 1790s the Orphan House accepted with little of the usual investigations children of white refugees from the St. Dominigue (Haitian) rebellion, nearly all of whom were reclaimed by their parents. Much later, toward the end of the period, children native to Ireland and Germany predominated among immigrants.

The age of the child at entrance strongly influenced each hazard. It hardly seems necessary to note the critical role of age in any kind of systematic study of children, but precisely because age matters so much it illustrates how powerful regression analysis is in this regard. Use of inferential statistics does not fetishize the method. Rather, the ability to hold key developmental variables such as age constant while examining other influences sharply reduces the likelihood of incorrectly imputing causal power to a variable of interest rather than a more powerful characteristic such as the child's age. For each age category (under three years of age, three to six years of age, six to nine years, nine to twelve years, and over twelve years), the older the child at entrance the greater the hazard of being bound out, which is intuitively reasonable, and the magnitude of the increase was substantial: in very rough terms children in each age group were more than twice as likely to be bound out soon as the children in the next youngest age group.

The return-to-family hazard was also influenced significantly by the age of the child at entry. Three to six year olds were 63 percent more likely to return soon than were toddlers, and six to nine year olds about twice as likely to return compared to toddlers. All children above nine years of age had similar and elevated reunion hazards. The effect of age on the death hazard was especially telling. Although older children were at reduced mortality risk, the increase with age was not great. Clearly, the children at greatest risk of immediate death were those aged three and younger, which may have been a result of their particular vulnerability to diarrheal diseases contracted through contaminated food and water. Finally, and again consistent with present day findings, the hazard of running away was lowest for all children under six years of age, and was especially elevated for those aged nine and up.

Changes in hazards over time were restricted to the apprenticeship and reunification hazards. The chances of a quick transfer into apprenticeship declined markedly in the last three decades. The hazard of returning to family initially declined by 40 percent in the first decade of the nineteenth century before rising to elevated levels from 1810 to 1850. As shown in Figure 3, entry into apprenticeship eventually declined in importance and the return to family began to predominate. The hazard of death remained constant over time. Whatever changes might have been made in the nutrition or disease environment of the Orphan House, or in the level of medical attention paid to the children, they seem to have had little effect on the inmate's ability to survive in the institution.

Conclusions

The record of entry to, residence in, and departure from the Charleston Orphan House provides a detailed view of the lives of poor white families in the urban, antebellum South. In addition to contributing new estimates of length of stay for an earlier period than historians have already studied, this chapter addresses previously unanswered questions of how those lengths of stay ended. The analysis suggests that relationships between parents and children in poor Southern families had powerful effects, and, in the process, it affords a better understanding of a group largely lost to history.

The beneficial consequences of maternal bonds formed when mothers taught, or helped to teach, their children to write are clear in this study. The mothers of the literate children at the Orphan House committed themselves to bringing them home even after facing the direst of hardships. The quantitative study of human capital transmission from generation to generation points to deeper and more humane relationships between mothers and very young children than the present analysis can fully express. But the relationships between these destitute Southern mothers and their literate children in the nineteenth century appear to have been as close as any reported in historical studies of wealthier, Northern families or any considered to be exemplary from a more modern perspective. Did these destitute mothers love their children in such a way that we might recognize? The answer is *yes*.

The record of the Charleston Orphan House invites assessment of its effectiveness. While its purpose, to care for children of deceased, ill, and impoverished whites, did not change over the period in question, the ways it arranged for such care did. The large majority of children who were bound out to apprentice from the Orphan House suggests that in its early days the Orphan House was something of a hiring hall for artisans and housewives who wanted to employ young children at fairly low rates. Deeper into the antebellum period, the Orphan House returned more and more children to their natal families, until that was the most typical outcome by the eve of the Civil War. The manuscript records in both periods indicate ongoing relationships between children and parents, and after binding out, among apprentices, their parents, and the masters and mistresses. The Charleston Orphan House did prepare young children for adulthood, in large measure because it could rely on resources and clear communications from all members of its community.

7 □ The Transformation of Catholic Orphanages: Cleveland, 1851–1996

Marian J. Morton

In 1886, the formidable three-storied brick structure of St. Vincent's Orphanage in Cleveland—already more than three decades old—housed about 200 boys, the children of impoverished Catholics. Many were German or Irish, and, almost without exception, they were white. The orphanage was staffed by thirty Sisters of Charity of St. Augustine and funded by diocesan collections and orphans' fairs. A century later, St. Vincent's had merged with other Catholic orphanages and evolved into Parmadale System of Family Services. Very few children with serious emotional and behavioral problems lived on-site; its professional staff provided a wide range of off-site psychiatric and social services. Funding was almost completely public and the clients were children and families of all creeds and races. Responding to national developments, the needs of the local community, and their own institutional imperatives, Cleveland's Catholic orphanages had transformed themselves and Catholic social services in general.

Catholic orphanages were possibly the most used and are certainly the least studied of American childcare institutions. Although most sectarian orphanages experienced similar changes in services, staff, and clientele from the mid-nineteenth to the late twentieth centuries, the Catholic experience has been differentiated and—to some extent—

shaped by the presence of the National Conference of Catholic Charities (NCCC), founded in 1910. The NCCC's challenging mission was to modernize Catholic charities—to bring them into the American social welfare mainstream—and at the same time to maintain their Catholic identity. The annual proceedings of the NCCC and its journals, *Catholic Charities Review* and its successor, *Charities USA*, provide the national context within which the changes in Catholic orphanages, "the hallmark of Catholic social provision," can be understood and assessed.[1]

Preserving the Faith: 1851–1900

Orphanages were a creation of the nineteenth century, when Americans believed that institutions could solve many social problems, including crime, mental and physical illness, and dependence. In an age of minimal government, the vast majority of social welfare institutions was sponsored by religious organizations and was fervently sectarian, intended by their Protestant, Jewish, and Catholic founders to shelter the bodies and preserve the faith of their coreligionists.

Catholic dioceses founded scores of care-taking institutions, including schools and hospitals, as well as homes for the aged, infants and unwed mothers, and working women. This prolific institution-building was prompted not only by the common belief in the value of institutions, but also by the pressing spiritual and material needs of impoverished Catholics; by the well-founded fear that they would fall victim to Protestant proselytizing, and by rivalries between dioceses.

Perhaps most importantly, dioceses built institutions because there were men and especially women religious to staff them. European orders such as the Ursuline Sisters and the Sisters of the Good Shepherd were joined by indigenous orders such as the Sisters of Charity of Emmitsburg. By 1900, more than 40,000 nuns, most of them American-born, served Catholic schools, hospitals, and charitable institutions. Because women religious received less compensation than men, these institutions became efficient, relatively inexpensive ways of providing charity.[2]

During the nineteenth century, orphanages became the most characteristic venue for Catholic charity. According to the secretary of the NCCC, Monsignor John O'Grady, "the care of children away from their own homes . . . occupied a larger place in Catholic welfare in the United States than any other type of work."[3] Catholics led the way in founding orphanages, establishing sixteen institutions for dependent and neglected children before 1840 and 175 by 1890. These orphanages maintained the ethnic traditions of German, Irish, Polish, Bohemian, and Italian immigrants. Most significantly, they sustained the children's religious faith, acting as a "preventive against [the] Protestantism" of the dominant culture.[4]

Because the care of dependent children was recognized as a public responsibility, Catholic orphanages in many states received public subsidies. In New York, Illinois, Pennsylvania, Maryland, California, Michigan, Wisconsin, and Iowa, the counties subsidized private institutions. Other states, like Ohio, maintained their own county children's homes.

There were no county homes in Cleveland, however, and dependent children were housed in the city poorhouse, the Cleveland Infirmary. The poorhouse sheltered those impoverished by unemployment, accident, and illness who had absolutely nowhere else to go. The sick were housed with the insane, the criminal, and the indigent of all ages. The Infirmary was a stark, uninviting place; inmates were not supposed to linger at taxpayers' expense. Although public, the Infirmary was also distinctly Protestant—overseen by Protestants and visited by Protestant missionaries.

Cleveland attracted a rapidly growing, ethnically diverse population, especially from Ireland and Germany. Many were Catholic. In 1836, there was one Catholic church with a membership of 200. The diocese of Cleveland was established in 1849, and by 1860, nine Catholic churches claimed 20,000 members (about 30 percent of Cleveland's population).[5] Catholic immigrants were probably the poorest group in Cleveland at mid-century. In 1856, of the 159 persons admitted to the Infirmary, forty-two were born in Ireland and fifty-nine in Germany; sixty-two were children.[6] The problem was urgent: Catholics "could not let their children go to the poorhouse because it would be an eternal disgrace; they could not permit them to become beneficiaries of Protestant philanthropy because they would be lost to the faith."[7] Accordingly, one of the first tasks of Cleveland's first bishop, Amadeus Rappe, was to persuade three Ladies of the Sacred Heart, a wealthy order from Paris, to emigrate and found St. Mary's Asylum for girls in 1851. Members of the order, who were called "Miss" rather than "Sister" and who did not wear religious habits, also taught in several parish schools in Cleveland. In 1863, the order opened a second orphanage, St. Joseph's, for younger girls, on five acres on the city's far east side. In 1894, these two institutions merged as St. Joseph's Orphanage.[8] In 1853, the Sisters of Charity of St. Augustine, led by Sister Mary Ursula, opened St. Vincent's Orphan Asylum for boys. This order also had its roots in France but was organized by Bishop Rappe. The sisters' primary mission was nursing, and they administered five hospitals in Ohio, including Cleveland's first permanent general hospital, St. Vincent Charity Hospital, in 1865. In 1873, the sisters opened a home for unwed mothers, and the children born there sometimes were placed at St. Vincent's.[9]

Other denominations also founded orphanages. The Cleveland Protestant Orphan Asylum was organized by members of the First Presbyterian (Old Stone) Church in 1852. Methodists sustained the Children's Aid Society (1854) and the Berea Children's Home (1864). In 1869, the Independent Order of B'nai Brith opened the Jewish Orphan Asylum for the children of Jewish veterans of the Civil War from the Midwest.

Regardless of denomination, orphans were children of the poor. Although dramatic events like cholera epidemics occasionally robbed children of both parents, most "orphans" had at least one parent, unable to care for his or her child because of unemployment, physical or mental disability, or the death or desertion of a spouse. These parents asked that orphanages, or orphan asylums, care for their children. Timothy A. Hacsi has described orphanages as "often the final desperate step in a series of attempts [by a parent] to deal with poverty brought on by some family calamity."[10] Children might also be placed in orphanages by clergy or public officials who judged parents negligent and incapable of caring for their offspring.

In 1853, a child entered St. Vincent's whose mother had died and whose father was "sick and poor"; another child had been abandoned by his parents, who had left his sister at St. Mary's. In 1861, St. Vincent's admitted seven boys from the Infirmary. In one month in 1895, St. Joseph's admitted a child whose father was dead and whose mother had run off; a child whose father had left his family, including his sick wife; a child whose father was alive but whose mother was missing; and a child whose mother was alive but whose father was a "drinker."[11]

Parents were supposed to pay for their children's board. Although few did, their payments were a way of retaining connections to their offspring. Sometimes children were "placed out" or "given to" a family that would raise them, presumably in return for work around the house or farm; girls were occasionally placed "in situations"—that is, in domestic service.[12] Most children, however, eventually returned to parents or other family members. Some children stayed only a few days or weeks; most stayed much longer, sometimes for years until the family could care for them again or until they could support themselves. Martin Styles, "the son of a respectable widow," stayed at St. Vincent's ten years; when he left, he became an accountant, "the support of his mother and an exemplary member of the church."[13] Orphanages, in short, "served as early welfare agencies by caring for the children of impoverished families" that did not want to give up their offspring permanently.

Orphanages provided children with food, shelter, clothing, and some education, especially in job skills so that children could escape their parents' poverty. Sometimes these skills were acquired in classes, more often by working around the institution. The girls at St. Mary's were taught to sew; their handiwork was sold to "benevolent ladies" to raise funds for the institution. The children were meant to live a rigorous, disciplined life, symbolized by their uniforms, originally "satinette trousers and coats with good-sized brass buttons" for the boys at St. Vincent's.[14]

Religious services were mandatory and daily. In St. Vincent's early years, the boys rose at 5:30 a.m., had morning prayer at 6 and mass at 6:30, said the rosary at 1:30 p.m., had catechism and Bible history at 6:30 p.m., and said "night prayers" at 7:30. The registers of the orphanages routinely noted when the child made his or her First Communion.[15]

The presence of the nuns was crucial. Although the institutions were nominally under the control of the bishop, the sisters staffed them, acting as surrogate parents, teachers, nurses, housekeepers, cooks, disciplinarians, and religious role models. In their spare time, nuns also raised funds.

All Catholic childcare institutions in Cleveland were entirely privately funded. Catholic and sometimes Protestant philanthropists made gifts to the orphanages. The diocese held special collections at Sunday Masses and sponsored annual orphans' fairs. In 1894, the boys from St. Vincent's performed "drills, speeches, music, songs, etc" in a fundraiser before 4,000 people in Music Hall.[16] Yet there was seldom enough money. In 1881, for instance, the Cleveland Orphans' Fair collected $8,248 to support the almost 400 children at St. Vincent's, St. Mary's, and St. Joseph's. The nuns had to beg for the deficit.[17]

At the turn of the century, St. Joseph's and St. Vincent's had become large congregate facilities. St. Joseph's had sold one of its five acres; the neighborhood had become Jewish (the Jewish Orphan Asylum was down the street) and commercial. A tall iron fence surrounded the institution, which housed more than 200 girls. St. Vincent's overlooked the city's industrial valley; 225 boys crowded into its buildings.[18]

Across the country, the number of orphanages rose from

624 in 1880 to 1,067 in 1910. Although the median number of children sheltered in 1910 was sixty, 109 orphanages cared for more than 200 children each, and twenty-four institutions cared for 400 or more. The largest childcare institution, the New York Catholic Protectory, housed 2,500 children.[19] These large orphanages, almost always sectarian and often committed to lengthy stays for their inmates, were viewed with increasing dismay by the emerging social work profession.

Preserving the Home: 1900-1929

Rejecting the nineteenth-century belief that institutions could save and reform inmates, child welfare workers now argued that dependent children should be raised in their own homes or foster homes, not in orphanages. Although conceding that homes were best for children, the leaders of the newly-formed National Conference of Catholic Charities generally continued to endorse orphanages while attempting to move them in new directions.

At the 1898 meeting of the National Conference of Charities and Corrections, critics argued that orphanages stifled children's individuality and initiative: "The home develops reliance, the institution, dependence. . . . Children [in orphanages] are often taught too much about heaven and too little about earth."[20] The National Conference of Charities and Corrections had been established in 1874 in an effort to rationalize and professionalize the nation's rapidly multiplying social welfare agencies. Renamed the National Conference on Social Work in 1917 and the National Conference on Social Welfare in 1956, the organization formed the vanguard of the new profession of social work by the turn of the century.

Following suit, Catholic clergy and lay leaders of the St. Vincent DePaul Society founded the NCCC to play a similar role: to impose order and social work standards on the hundreds of Catholic social welfare agencies and institutions, maintained by scores of dioceses and dozens of religious orders for children of various ethnic backgrounds.[21] The NCCC leadership placed itself at the forefront of "the Catholic philosophy of social work" and generally endorsed the principle articulated at the 1909 White House Conference on Dependent Children that became—and still is—social work dogma: "Home life . . . is 'the highest and finest product of civilization.'" Children should not be removed from their own homes "unless unusual conditions exist."[22] Some speakers offered cautious endorsements of foster homes over institutions and cautious criticism of the regimentation of orphanage life.[23] In 1923, the *Catholic Charities Review (CCR)* urged "child-caring homes" (the organization did not use the term "orphanage") to "keep up with advancing standards of health, education, recreation, and social life [and to] be in the vanguard of all genuine improvements." First and foremost, caretakers of children should remember that "our [child-caring] homes are at best only substitutes for good families which are to be preserved or rehabilitated if possible."[24]

Other members of the NCCC, however, were more traditional. They (probably correctly) interpreted anti-orphanage sentiment expressed at the National Conference of Charities and Corrections and elsewhere as anti-Catholic, especially targeted at public aid to Catholic institutions. Although no one claimed that an orphanage was preferable to a good home, defenders of orphanages argued that it was difficult to find good foster homes for children, especially Catholic homes; institutions, they insisted, could provide greater spiritual direction than foster homes. A priest and director of the Catholic Charities of Baltimore raised these practical questions: if childcare institutions disappeared, "it would mean the loss of several million dollars in property." More important, "thousands of our religious will have found themselves without the occupation for which they have been especially trained."[25]

In the wake of the 1909 White House Conference, thirty-nine states (including Ohio in 1913) enacted mothers' pensions. These provided subsidies to mothers so that they could raise their children at home rather than place them in orphanages. But the stipends were very small and selectively awarded. The numbers of orphanages continued to rise, responding to the huge waves of European immigration and the poverty and family dislocation of urban life. Fifty-one new Catholic institutions were founded between 1900 and 1915. In 1923, Catholics maintained 558 institutions that cared for 81,000 children and only eighteen child-placing agencies, responsible for 10,500 children in foster homes.[26]

Catholic childcare in Cleveland was also torn between the old traditions and the new directions. On the one hand, four new non-diocesan orphanages had been established. The Home of the Holy Family, founded in 1895, sheltered forty-four boys and girls. Three very small Catholic ethnic orphanages, each housing about a dozen children, had also opened: Holy Ghost Greek Catholic Orphanage, Holy Ghost Roman Catholic Orphanage, and St. Basil's Orphanage for Ukrainian Catholic children. Children. Hungarian Lutherans and Orthodox Jews had also opened orphanages.[27] In addition, the diocese established two small institutions for older dependent children with special needs: for girls, Catherine Horstman Training Home in 1909, and for boys, St. Anthony's Home in 1908.

On the other hand, the diocese also moved to modernize its charitable activities, as did other urban dioceses.[28] In 1910, Bishop John Farrelly established the Catholic Charities Bureau to oversee and coordinate diocesan child welfare activities, especially fundraising. In 1901, Bishop Ignatius Horstman had written to the Superior at St. Joseph's: "Repeated complaints have reached me that on pay days various sisterhoods in this city have had representatives at the same hour and place, for the purpose of soliciting alms from persons then receiving their pay . . . especially at the City Hall."[29]

This competitive begging was a public relations disaster in a Protestant city; worse, it did not raise sufficient funds. Neither did the orphans' fairs. St. Vincent's and St. Joseph's were perpetually in debt.[30] The diocesan bureau replaced the fairs and the begging nuns with systematic assessments of each parish that yielded more satisfactory returns.

The first director of the bureau, the Reverend C. Hubert LeBlond, was an early member of the NCCC and a frequent speaker at its annual meetings. Probably at his urging, the diocesan orphanages joined the Cleveland Federation for Charity and Philanthropy, founded in 1913 and renamed the Cleveland Welfare Federation in 1917. Although sensitive —by necessity—to the sectarian missions of its members, the federation nevertheless hoped to modernize the city's private charities. The federation raised and distributed community fund monies to its member agencies; in return, agencies were to implement modern social work principles. Because they housed large numbers of children, St. Joseph's and especially St. Vincent's got substantial operating funds from the federation.[31]

In 1921, a survey of Cleveland's overcrowded orphanages revealed that 91 percent of their 2,065 inmates from 1915 to 1919 had at least one parent, and 66 percent returned to their families. The survey also criticized the orphanages' haphazard record-keeping, their "inadequate investigation of family situations, their unhealthy, crowded, unsanitary conditions, insufficient board payments by parents and relatives" and the children's lengthy stays.[32] As a result, the Welfare Federation funded the Cleveland Children's Bureau. Many of the bureau's staff were professionally trained caseworkers, who screened all applicants for admission to orphanages. Admissions decisions by this nonsectarian agency represented a loss of autonomy for the orphanages, even though the Catholic Charities Bureau still made the final recommendations.

The Children's Bureau's investigations also revealed the persistent immiserization of Cleveland's Catholic population. From 1922 to 1925, 844 of the 1,416 applicant families— almost 60 percent—were Catholic. As in the nineteenth century, the children's parents were deserted, divorced, widowed, dead, physically or mentally disabled, or unemployed; more than half were foreign-born.[33]

Farrelly also established the Catholic Charities Corporation in 1919 to raise funds to rebuild Catholic institutions in "deplorable financial and physical condition . . . especially the child-caring institutions."[34] The Corporation's greatest success was a brand new orphanage for the boys from St. Vincent's and an orphanage in Louisville, Ohio. Although the facility on 180 acres in rural Parma would house more than 300 children, they would live in a dozen Tudor-style cottages, intended to be as much like private homes as possible. In 1922, *CCR* predicted, "Cleveland will have one of the finest, largest, and most modern child-caring institutions, not only among Catholic, but among all those of the nation."[35]

In 1925, when the institution opened, it was renamed Parmadale Children's Village. Although its new name was nonsectarian, Parmadale remained distinctly Catholic, and the Sisters of Charity of St. Augustine, led by Sister M. Carmelita Riley, staffed and administered the institution. Life at Parmadale reflected the new thinking that orphanages should be more flexible, more humane, and more like home. The orphanage stressed vigorous outdoor activity and provided football, baseball, basketball, volleyball, and track and field, and boasted of its marching band. The boys attended local Catholic schools. The institution did not "retain its children for very long periods," claimed *CCR*. "Its ideal is to provide short intensive training and then return the children to their own homes or have them placed in foster homes."[36]

Although Catholic orphanages across the country were slow to adopt the cottage system—probably because of its cost—two other sectarian Cleveland orphanages switched to the cottage system during the 1920s. The Protestant Orphan Asylum moved to Orange Township, becoming Beech Brook; the Jewish Orphan Asylum moved to University Heights and was renamed Bellefaire. The Home of the Holy Family and St. Joseph's remained in the city.

In 1931, John M. Cooper, the author of a massive study of childcare institutions commissioned by the NCCC, maintained that because of mothers' pensions, "poverty alone . . . is not sufficient ground . . . for breaking up a home."[37] The Great Depression, however, had already made his advice irrelevant.

Two Emergencies: 1929–1947

The childcare emergencies created by the Great Depression and World War II prolonged the traditional role of orphanages as caretakers of dependent children. Local and federal governments, however, increasingly shouldered this responsibility.

In December 1933, 102,000 dependent and neglected children in the United States were in foster homes, and more than 140,000, a record number, were in orphanages.[38] In 1931, orphanage administrators noted at the NCCC annual meeting that families requesting placement for their children were of a "higher type" than usual and that relatives were less able to help out and parents less able to pay board. In 1933, *CCR* warned, "The depression has increased the demand made on child-caring agencies and diminished their resources. Many child-caring agencies have long waiting lists. Relief agencies are asking children's agencies to accept children without any compensation." Catholic orphanages across the country felt the pinch, especially where state or local subsidies were cut.[39]

Cleveland orphanages were already full in the late 1920s, as the city's heavy industries began to lay off workers; Parmadale had a long waiting list.[40] As the Depression deepened, the first public childcare agency, the Cuyahoga County Child Welfare Bureau (CCCWB), was established. The orphanages and private child-placing agencies like the Children's Bureau continued to take responsibility for children needing short-term care or children whose parents could pay some board. The CCCWB assumed financial responsibility for children needing long-term care. The agency's staff of professional social workers preferred foster homes to institutions even though the CCCWB was not obligated to pay the board of county wards in orphanages that received community fund monies.

The orphanages struggled to survive. Full to the brim, they had to feed, shelter, and clothe more children with less money than ever before. Children stayed longer, and their parents, unemployed, working part-time, and bearing other crushing financial obligations, paid less and less. Only eighteen of the ninety-seven families with girls at St. Joseph's had any employment; their average compensation was $8.66 a week; only forty-five of the families of the Parmadale children had work; seventeen of those earned from $1 to $5 a week. Board payments dried up.[41] In 1927, Parmadale received $14,742 in board monies; in 1933, $3,322. Both the Welfare Federation and Catholic Charities slashed their subsidies. Parmadale cut per capita expenditures from $1.15 a child in 1930 to $.92 a child in 1933. The boys' meals cost seven cents each. Parmadale had $26,000 in unpaid bills in September, 1933.[42] St. Joseph's ended 1931 with $12.23 on hand and 1932 with $10.43. When the Welfare Federation and Catholic Charities bailed out the institution, its Superior rejoiced: "Divine Providence steered our over-freighted barque safely over the first half of 1935."[43].

In the midst of the financial crisis, the children's lives probably remained substantially unchanged. The boys at Parmadale rose at 6:15 a.m. and attended Mass before breakfast. They tidied their own rooms, scrubbed the bathrooms, locker rooms, and basements, cleaned the dining halls, classrooms, yards, and playgrounds, washed the dishes, and set the tables for meals. They spent most of their day in school and their free time in band or choir practice and went to bed at 9:30 in the evening.[44] Life for the girls at St. Joseph's remained regimented and limited. This last large congregate facility in the city was still on Woodland Avenue, now an African-American neighborhood. Two brick structures housed between 170 to 140 girls, ages five to fifteen, who slept in dormitories in the school building, the smallest children in its basement. The girls "marched" or were "conducted to" their daily activities. For recreation, they roller-skated in the gym or rode bicycles or walked around the grounds for an hour. The girls did a substantial amount of the institution's housekeeping. Even the oldest were in bed by 9 p.m.[45]

In 1941, when the United States entered World War II, the Depression was over, but the dislocations created by family members entering the armed services or moving around the country in search of jobs once more created a pressing need for childcare institutions. By March 1943, Catholic childcare institutions were "taxed to capacity," reported the *CCR*, and hard put to cope with the loss of staff to war-related jobs, food rationing, and continued "demands of placement."[46]

In Cleveland, prosperity returned, but children again fell victim to family disarray. Foster homes for dependent children were in short supply, and the orphanages were soon almost as full as they had been during the darkest days of the Depression. The county Detention Home was crowded with dependent and delinquent children waiting for permanent placement.[47]

To fill the crying need for shelter, the diocese opened St. Theresa's, a temporary facility for preschool children, in 1943; in 1946, this facility was replaced by St. Edward's, across the street from Parmadale. Probably in response to criticism by the Welfare Federation, St. Joseph's began "extensive remodeling to make it more homelike and cheerful," and the girls were allowed to attend the nearby parochial school. The remodeling was not completed, however, and in 1942 the institution and the children were moved to a diocesan property on the Lake Erie shore, a former hospital. The sisters found the facility inadequate for their increased population of 141 girls.[48] In 1947, although the small ethnic orphanages had not survived, Cleveland's Catholic institutions sheltered far more children than did the Protestant and Jewish childcare institutions combined.[49]

Yet the public agency, the CCCWB, had emerged as the primary caretaker of Cleveland's dependent children. Moreover, the old age and unemployment insurances and especially the provision of Aid to Dependent Children of the Social Security Act of 1935 were intended to eliminate the economic insecurity that had earlier forced parents to place their children in orphanages.

At the NCCC annual meetings, orphanages still had vigorous defenders, who affirmed the institutions' historic mission to preserve the Catholic faith and feared that the public childcare agencies such as the CCCWB would not safeguard Catholic children's religion. But other NCCC speakers warned that because of public programs, "The place of the institution is changing." Its new clientele must be children whose emotional difficulties made placement in their own or foster homes inappropriate.[50]

Redefining Orphans: 1947–1971

During the next decades, psychological or emotional problems became the rationale endorsed by social workers for institutionalizing healthy children. Catholic orphanages began the slow, difficult transition from institutions for children orphaned by poverty and dependency to institutions for "emotional" orphans.

This transition was complicated by the difficulty of reconciling the institutions' historic staff of women religious with the secular professional staff and services required by these new orphans. The issue of professionalizing orphanage staff had been raised at NCCC meetings during the second and third decades of the century, since foster home placement presumably required a professional caseworker. The issue resurfaced during the 1930s when public relief agencies, often staffed by professionals, assumed responsibility for the placement of Catholic children. The NCCC held several sessions on social work to encourage Catholics to enter public agencies to protect the children's faith. In 1941, *CCR* urged "Catholic training for social work" and listed the seven Catholic schools of social work.[51] In the postwar years, this issue of new clientele and staff dominated discussions about childcare institutions at the NCCC annual meetings and in *CCR*. In 1955, a caseworker advised *CCR* readers that "the 'normal child-caring institution' . . . no longer exists" because the children entering institutions had serious "behavior and personality problems" that must be addressed by trained psychiatric social workers. He also noted "hesitation and doubt" about this "new approach . . . [that] calls for an occasional readjustment or modification of practices which have been carried on for many years."[52]

The NCCC leadership had early recognized that "The Sisterhoods and Brotherhoods [were] the most conservative elements in Catholic Charity."[53] Yet nuns, not social workers, had been absolutely essential not only in founding and running the orphanages but also in identifying them as Catholic. Nuns had become the "universally recognized symbol of Catholic charity." Beginning in 1920, nuns had met separately at the NCCC annual meetings as the Conference of Religious, which remained more interested in and more supportive of orphanages than the general meetings of the NCCC. After decades of service in institutions, "sisters found arguments that the institutional approach to charity was now outmoded very hard to accept."[54] In 1951, *CCR* published an article "in praise of institutions" by a member of the Daughters of Charity of St. Vincent DePaul: "[T]hese religious [will] preserve, without financial aid or State standing the Church's standard of charity; they will still be bringing the charity of Christ to the poor and needy because they see Christ in them."[55] As late as the mid-1960s, *CCR* articles noted the reluctance of the religious orders to provide in-service or other training for the sisters as well as tension between sisters and caseworkers.[56]

Despite pressures from the NCCC, as well as from the Cleveland Welfare Federation, Parmadale in 1951 had on staff only one trained social worker, Sister Mary Beatrice, and no psychiatrist or psychologist; children with emotional problems were sent elsewhere for counseling.[57] Parmadale remained an institution for dependent Catholic children, serving its historic clientele of children deprived of family

by "death, illness, desertion, or family breakdown."[58] For although many of Cleveland's Catholics participated in the
wartime and postwar prosperity, many others did not. In
1950, almost 40 percent of the dependent children under
care of the Child Welfare Division of the Cuyahoga County
Welfare Department (formerly the CCCWB) were Catholic;
in 1954, more than a third were. These were children who
presumably needed shelter that could be provided by nuns,
not psychiatric care from medical personnel.[59]

Parmadale increased its enrollment by absorbing other
Catholic institutions. In 1947, St. Joseph's closed its doors,
and its 100 girls were moved to Parmadale, boosting its
numbers to 431 children.[60] In 1952, the boys and girls of the
Home of the Holy Family and, in 1953, the small children
from St. Edward's, joined them.

Parmadale had struggled to make ends meet even with
substantial financial support from the Welfare Federation,
Catholic Charities, and local foundations. The merger with
St. Joseph's had necessitated building new cottages for the
girls and had incurred substantial debt to Catholic Charities. By 1958, the institution's costs had continued to rise,
although the numbers of children in residence had begun
to decline.[61] Parmadale's financial difficulties were exacerbated by the fact that the county child welfare agency was
not required to compensate Parmadale for the care of its
wards. In 1961, for example, Parmadale sheltered in an average month eighty-one county wards for whom it received
no county subsidy, although the institution did receive subsidies from the Welfare Federation.[62]

In 1962, Parmadale took its first significant steps toward changing its clientele and function. In order to receive
public subsidies, Parmadale agreed to provide specialized
services for emotionally disturbed children. (Bellefaire had
done so since 1954, and Beech Brook also would soon receive
county funds.) Since the mid-1950s, a nun social worker had
headed the Social Service Department, often with only one
other nun to assist her. Now, however, Parmadale hired

four full-time caseworkers and several part-time caseworkers, all lay people. Although Parmadale was still described as a "general care" facility," its staff now also included a part-time psychologist and a part-time psychiatrist.[63]

By 1966, eighty of Parmadale's 180 children in residence were county wards, and the institution received $84,000 in county monies, almost 15 percent of its total budget. Yet all of the children at Parmadale in 1968 were Catholic, as were all of its staff and advisory board.[64]

In the late 1960s, however, the numbers of women religious in the United States began a slow but steady decline that had a dramatic effect on Catholic social welfare institutions.[65] In 1967, *CCR* lamented the closing of an institution of the Sisters of the Good Shepherd due to an "acute shortage of religious personnel. . . . Most of our Catholic institutions are feeling this same pinch as vocations decline. . . . This decline in vocations also gives rise to the philosophical question as to whether there will be a change in the role of the religious functioning in the institutions."[66]

The number of nuns at Parmadale also declined. In 1968, there were fifty-four Sisters of Charity of St. Augustine at Parmadale; in 1970, there were only thirty-two. Sisters continued to staff the cottages, but lay teachers joined the sisters on the staff of Parmadale's school. The loss of the sisters exacerbated the institution's financial problems. In 1969, Parmadale's Advisory Board estimated that the nuns had contributed $181,000 in services to the institution; now "additional lay personnel" would have to be hired—and paid.[67] In 1972, an article in *CCR* announced a "crisis in child-caring institutions." Its author noted a "fairly extensive deterioration in the field of child-care institutions . . . characterized by the closing of many institutions throughout the country because of high cost, low population, lack of staff, [and] insufficiently trained staff." He warned that the orphanages must soon address "critical questions of survival."[68]

Redefining Catholic Charity: 1971–1996

Catholic orphanages were about to face their most serious challenges. They would respond by redefining their historic services and purpose.

Beginning in the 1970s, powerful political and financial pressures to deinstitutionalize all populations challenged the long Catholic tradition of childcare institutions. The numbers of dependent and neglected children in childcare institutions had fallen throughout the 1960s, even as those institutions became more and more dependent on public funds. In 1973, the federal government provided a quarter of all income for Catholic agencies.[69] The desire to save taxpayers' dollars spurred the movement toward deinstitutionalization. Alternative off-site services such as community mental health programs appeared just as effective in treating troubled children and were much less expensive.

Parmadale fell upon desperate times. Its population had dipped perilously low—from 288 in 1961 to 149 in 1971, partly because social workers renewed their criticism of institutionalizing children and partly because Parmadale experienced difficulties adapting to its new clientele. By 1973, only twenty nuns remained on the Parmadale staff.[70]

In late 1973, the Reverend John H. Leahy became director of the institution, stabilized its enrollment, and initiated significant changes. Parmadale absorbed adolescent girls from Carmelita Hall in 1974 and in 1975 adolescent boys from St. Anthony's Home. In 1977, Parmadale's enrollment had risen to 234 children.[71]

These were different children. In 1960 the "average child" at Parmadale was a nine-year-old placed because of family difficulties; in 1974, the "average child" was a thirteen-year-old placed "for behavior problems in the home or in the community." In 1974, only 10 percent of Parmadale's children had been referred by Catholic Charities; the rest had come from the county child welfare agency or from juvenile court, as adjudicated juveniles.[72] In 1983, Leahy described Parmadale's 221 residents as "multi-problemed";

those problems included chemical dependency, truancy, unacceptable school behavior, and delinquency: "[A] vast majority . . . are at least mildly emotionally disturbed." Leahy developed new on- and off-site programs eligible for public funding, including classes for mentally retarded children, a day care center, chemical dependency services, and family therapy.[73]

In the early 1980s, when local agencies felt the impact of the Reagan administration's budget cuts, the county and the juvenile court cut back their placements at Parmadale. In response, the new Executive Director, Thomas W. Woll, developed a range of specialized residential services such as a victim protection program for adolescent sex offenders, and more off-site services such as a foster care program. By the 1990s, the institution had created a network of integrated services—renamed Parmadale System of Family Services—aimed at "family survival." Those services included day care, in-home counseling, placement of children in foster care, an outpatient treatment program, family therapy services, a group home for young adults, and training and consultation for social workers. (Bellefaire, now Bellefaire Jewish Children's Bureau, and Beech Brook also developed a wide variety of on- and off-site services.)

As had Catholic charities around the country, the institution had become increasingly dependent on public funds—from Cuyahoga County, from the state, and from the federal government, including Medicaid payments. In 1985, these sources provided almost 80 percent of Parmadale's budget, and in 1993, almost 88 percent.[74]

More and more of Parmadale's children were black: 18 percent of its children in 1971, 28 percent in 1981, and more than 50 percent in 1985. Increasingly, the beneficiaries of Parmadale programs were non-Catholic children and their families. In 1971, 75 percent of the children at Parmadale were Catholic; in 1981, only half were. In 1987, only seventy-seven of the 389 children receiving institutional care were identified as Catholic; only 62 of the children in classes for the mentally retarded were; only forty-seven of the 132 children in the drug treatment program were.[75] In 1990, the last Sister of Charity of St. Augustine left, although other religious staff remained.

Parmadale's changed population reflected significant new trends in Catholic charities. As American Catholics increasingly entered the middle class, Catholic charitable organizations across the country became more sensitive to the needs of the non-Catholic poor. Inspired by the War on Poverty and the "social concerns of the Vatican Council," they broadened their focus.[76] In 1986, a national conference on Catholic Residential Care for Children contemplated "an emerging new identity" for their institutions. Deinstitutionalization had forced some to close; others survived by developing innovative programs. Catholic institutions were also forced to answer the question of "whether or not our call is to serve the child and the family of another faith." Responding both to the spirit of ecumenism that followed Vatican Council II and to practical necessity, the conference answered yes: The inclusion of non-Catholic children in residential care institutions illustrated the Catholic Church's mission to "reach out to absolutely every person and every need. . . . [I]t is in this apostolic identification with all people that we witness our Christianity."[77] In 1988, the mission statement of Catholic residential childcare providers reiterated this broadened definition of clientele as "the youngest and most vulnerable members of society" and affirmed these goals: "the creation of an environment which fosters the spiritual, physical and moral development of each child. . . . The integration of the human and spiritual dimensions of service which promote each child's self-actualization and meaningful participation in life."[78]

Like other Catholic residential care providers, Parmadale adapted its religious life and redefined its religious mission. In 1985, the agency offered "a cultural hour as an alternative to mass" and "a variety of services, both religious and civic."[79] In spring 1991, Parmadale celebrated Easter and held a Seder for its staff; the pastor of a leading black Baptist church, also a Parmadale advisory board member, led a prayer service.[80] Current brochures boast: "We provide services to young people in need regardless of race or religion. . . . No attempt is made to dictate or influence a client or staff member's religious preferences."[81]

According to Executive Director Woll, in 1996, only about 20 to 30 percent of Parmadale's clients were Catholic. Yet, he maintained, the agency remained "Catholic" in its sustained mission to provide spiritual leadership for children; it served as "the social action arm" of the Church and "proof of [its] compassion." Moreover, Parmadale served more children and families than it ever had. He estimated that in one year, the agency served 360 children in treatment, 250 in foster care, and fifty in group or transitional housing.[82]

Revisiting Orphanages

Catholic orphanages have been not only the signature institutions of Catholic charity but also, in public memory, representative of all orphanages. When the debate over the future of welfare took shape in the late 1980s and 1990s, policymakers who suggested that the orphanage be used again as a shelter for dependent children probably imagined an orphanage like Parmadale's Children's Village in 1925—home-like cottages in the country where well-behaved children stayed temporarily until they rejoined their families. This suggestion ignited opposition from those who probably imagined an orphanage like St. Joseph's in the 1930s—a bleak, cheerless congregate facility with an iron fence and an asphalt playground. But St. Joseph's is gone, as are St. Vincent's, St. Mary's, the Home of the Holy Family, St. Theresa's, St. Edward's, St. Anthony's, and the three small ethnic orphanages. Parmadale, the most significant beneficiary of Catholic and nonsectarian funds, has survived, but in a form that would scarcely be recognizable to its founders. As they consider the future of orphanages, it is imperative that policymakers revisit their past. That past illustrates the "complex encounter between modernity and tradition" that, according to Elizabeth McKeown, has characterized the development of Catholic charities from the mid-nineteenth century to the present.[83]

The Catholic tradition of childcare developed in an age when government was weak, sectarian identities were strong, and Catholics were poor. Accordingly, Cleveland's Catholic orphanages were founded by the diocese to save the bodies and souls of indigent coreligionists, often immigrants. This mission was reinforced by Catholic monies and the presence of Catholic nuns. Today government takes primary responsibility for dependence, sectarian identities are less narrow, and most Catholics have achieved the middle class. Parmadale Family Services, although still under the auspices of the diocese and Catholic Charities, is funded by public monies, staffed by medical and social work professionals, and serves primarily non-Catholic children. Adapting to dramatically different circumstances, Cleveland's most significant childcare institution has reinvented itself and redefined Catholic charity. Modernity has triumphed.

But this case study reveals that the victory was hard-fought and astonishingly recent, for Cleveland's Catholic orphanages long resisted the modernization endorsed by the NCCC leadership. By the time Bishop Farrelly and Father LeBlond began their efforts to bring Catholic charities into the twentieth century, St. Vincent's and St. Joseph's were well established (although not well funded). For six decades, two orders of nuns had sheltered indigent Catholic children whose families counted on the orphanages to get them through hard times. And the hard times kept on coming, perpetuated by new waves of Catholic immigration and exacerbated by the Great Depression. World War II disrupted families and did not bring prosperity to all Catholics. Their sectarian identity firmly rooted in service to the community that provided financial and moral support, Cleveland orphanages often discounted advice and suggestions from national Catholic leaders. The needs of the community and of the institutions themselves were more compelling. Even the most "modern" orphanage, Parmadale, remained committed to its original constituency of dependent Catholic children and its historic staff of women religious until the 1960s, long after the NCCC urged professionalization and specialized services for emotionally disturbed children. Only when the Sisters of Charity of St. Augustine, founders and sustainers of the institution's traditions, began to leave did rapid change occur—in large part because their leaving created the dramatic need for greater public funding. During the ensuing crises of the 1970s and 1980s, when the alternative to change seemed to be the institution's extinction, Parmadale's new directors did follow the lead of the NCCC, innovating and developing off-site services, broadening the institution's clientele and its Catholic mission. Any consideration of the future of orphanages by national policymakers, therefore, must take into account the practical difficulties, the soul-searching, and the healthy dose of institutional self-interest that accompany the encounter between tradition and modernity revealed at the local level.

Catholic Child Care Institutions in Cleveland 1851–1996

Name and Date opened	Renamed or merged
St. Mary's Female Asylum (1851)	Merged with St. Joseph's (1894)
St. Joseph's Orphanage (1853)	Merged with Parmadale (1947)
St. Vincent's Orphan Asylum (1852)	Renamed Parmadale Children's Village (1925) Parmadale System of Family Services (1996)
Home of the Holy Family (1895)	Merged with Parmadale (1952)
St. Theresa's (1943)\St. Edwards (1946)	Merged with Parmadale (1953)
St. Anthony's Home (1908)	Merged with Parmadale (1975)
Carmelita Hall (1969)	Merged with Parmadale (1974)
Catherine Horstman Home (1909)	
Holy Ghost Greek Catholic Orphanage (1918)*	
Holy Ghost Roman Catholic Orphanage (1919)*	
St. Basil's Orphanage (1920)*	

* These tiny institutions, listed in *Children Under Institutional Care 1923* (Washington, D.C.: 1927), Table 22, 107, were not diocesan institutions and were located in and/or closely affiliated with ethnic churches or sisters' convents. Because they are not clearly identified in city directories, it is impossible to know exactly when they closed.

8 □ Baltimore's Nineteenth-Century Orphanages

Nurith Zmora

Recent debate in the United States concerning orphanages has spurred new consideration of the viability of this child-care solution. Even those critics convinced that institutions can create a family-like atmosphere, preparing children for life outside their sheltering walls, remain skeptical about the possibility of building and maintaining such institutions. Good orphanages, the argument goes, require a very large initial investment in buildings, programs, and staff, as well as continuing financial support to maintain them.

Yet in the nineteenth century, communities around the United States far less endowed than ours today organized, built, and financed childcare institutions for their children. This fact raises a host of questions. Why did they take the initiative? What did they hope to achieve? How did they manage and finance the orphanages? Who were the children sheltered in the orphanages? How were they treated, and what happened to them after they left the orphanages? What lessons can we draw from their experience?

This essay will address these questions by focusing on three childcare institutions built by ethnic and religious communities in Baltimore, Maryland, during the nineteenth century.

In contrast to many cities in the United States in the nineteenth century that had both public and private orphanages, Baltimore had only private ones. Its population in the late nineteenth century was a mixture of ethnic and religious groups, with well-established citizens, newcomers from Maryland's rural areas, and new immigrants from Europe. Baltimore was a large urban center, a seaport where immigrants arrived, and an industrial and commercial city with a rural hinterland. It had the same social problems that plagued other cities in the United States.

Late-nineteenth-century Baltimore's social reformers were mainly concerned with child welfare and public health. Their achievements in child welfare brought to Baltimore a compulsory education law (1901), a new child labor law that raised the employment age to fourteen (1902), a juvenile court (1902), and a playground movement (1898). Those interested in the different classes of dependent children—such as the orphaned, the neglected and abused, the insane, and the feeble-minded[1]—spearheaded the establishment of orphanages,[2] but this was not an innovation of post-Civil War reform. In Baltimore, twelve orphanages had been founded between 1778 and 1856, all belonging to religious and ethnic groups (seven were Protestant, and six were Catholic).[3] Almost twice as many were established between 1860 and 1910. By 1910, Baltimore had twenty-eight orphanages: twelve Catholic, two Jewish, seven declared Protestant, and seven labeled as private corporations but organized and run by Protestant philanthropists. Racial and ethnic identity further divided them: six were for blacks, three for Germans, two for the Irish, and one for Russian Jews. The rest served either the old American community or were parish or congregation orphanages and had a mixture of children from various ethnic groups.[4] Thus, Baltimore seems to have had a history of continuous care and interest in the welfare of dependent children by religious and ethnic groups.

Baltimore orphanages were always founded through private initiatives, a collective volunteer effort that required a long-term time commitment and dedication. The orphanages in this study were similarly structured but differed according to financial status and the respective needs of the communities they served. All began with a private donation of a lot, a building, an endowment, or a combination of these. All three were managed by the social and economic elite of the religious and ethnic community. Administrators had to deal with a variety of people including parents, children, educators, and the community to which the orphanage belonged, as well as with a variety of responsibilities related to finances, public relations, education, legal issues, welfare management, and building maintenance.

The Hebrew Orphan Asylum

The Hebrew Orphan Asylum was established in 1872 after several attempts by B'nai B'rith to build an orphanage had failed. After the Hebrew Benevolent Society, the charity organization of German Jews, adopted the idea of an orphanage, the resources for such an enterprise quickly appeared when Dr. Benjamin Szold, William S. Rayner, and Alfred Y. Ulman became involved.[5] Dr. Szold, the Conservative rabbi of Oheb Shalom congregation, promoted the idea, and William S. Rayner, a businessman and a Reformed Jew, donated the land and the old almshouse building situated on it. The orphanage was located on the outskirts of the city in Calverton Heights, then a small village. Alfred Y. Ulman, another wealthy German Jew, gave the money needed for remodeling the building and preparing it for children.[6]

At the end of the first year, during which the Hebrew Orphan Asylum (HOA) sheltered and educated about thirty children, a fire destroyed the building. The children who were not hurt spent the first few nights in the directors' homes, and then were transferred to a rented apartment in downtown Baltimore. Meanwhile, the directors collected the insurance money, hired architects, and mobilized the Jewish community to contribute to the new building, a beautiful and spacious structure an HOA graduate recalled as "an arresting building in its beauty."[7] Some of those graduates who did not know its history thought it was built as a mansion for one of Maryland's gentry.[8] The building was well-equipped with the most modern inventions, starting with the heating system, indoor toilets, and the well-drained grounds. In years to come, this policy of installing the newest modern appliances for the orphans' convenience was repeated.[9]

What was the aim of the founders? At the opening ceremony of the new building, William Rayner told a large crowd from the Jewish community, and city dignitaries, that the community could have sheltered orphans in the German Asylum, but "children of our faith we intend to raise in our own way to become good American citizens as well as true Israelites."[10] The aspirations of the founders were high. Rayner did not speak merely of maintaining the new institution, but of enlarging its scope and operation. "I think you all will agree with me," he said,

> that it ought to be our joyful duty and sacred pride not only to maintain the same, but to make it one of the model institutions of this country. I hope the day is not far distant when the endowments and donations will be ample to make it also a first-class institution of learning, where the intelligent youth can not only be instructed in the rudiments but also in those higher branches of education necessary for professional life, and when it will be considered an honor and a high testimonial to have been a graduate of the school of the Hebrew Orphan Asylum of Baltimore.[11]

Rayner, however, did not have any illusions about the ability of an orphanage to give children parental love and affection. Still, he expected the children to be achievers and to overcome the disadvantages that were often the poor orphans' lot, advising them to be obedient to their guardians, to be truthful, and above all to have self-confidence. Rayner suggested that the Jewish community regard donations as an investment that one day would bear fruit; some of the children in the future would contribute to the welfare of the community, and the rest would serve as the contributors' advocates in heaven.

Rayner's speech was compatible with Jewish laws regarding orphans, but it also carried the American ideology of its day. It reminded the Jewish community that taking care of and educating its orphans was a religious obligation that carried remuneration in the next world; it also voiced the sentiments of an American Jew who viewed poor children's education as a great benefit for the Jewish community in particular and for American society as a whole.[12] In Leroy Ashby's words, children in post-Civil War America became increasingly "indispensable in the battle for the nation's destiny."[13] Save the children in order to create a better society in the future—that was the reformers' belief.

The Asylum's Board of Directors was made up entirely of prominent members of the German Jewish community. In the 1870s, they were immigrants who had made their way to the United States in their youth and become wealthy. Some had started working at an early age and did not have much formal education. Others had a Jewish or professional education. What they shared was not only German Jewish culture and wealth, but also social bonds. They belonged to the same German Jewish elite, frequented the same social clubs, and were involved in organizing and financing the community's Jewish institutions. In some cases the ties binding them were made even stronger when children from these families married each other.[14]

This generation of directors was marked by its dedication to the HOA. They were rising businessmen with many social and philanthropic obligations, but they spent long years on the Board when such service, far from being merely an honorary position, required real work. The directors supervised the administration of the orphanage, decided the general educational program of the institution and each child's particular education, and raised the funds for the whole venture. Some of its founding members remained on the Board into the 1900s, alongside new members. A large number of the latter were the sons or other relatives of the first-generation members. Thus, the Hutzlers, the Hamburgers, the Gutmans, the Friedenwalds, the Rayners, and the Adlers continued to be represented in the 1900s, along with new directors who were also prominent members of the Baltimore German Jewish community.[15] The second generation of directors was more educated, and represented the professions more than the business community.

Medicine and law were the most represented professions among the new directors. Doctors had a special place on the Board. No fewer than four famous doctors in the Jewish Community served on the Board during various periods, and they closely supervised the orphans' diet and medical care. Besides serving as directors on various committees, the doctors also screened applicants for the HOA and children were admitted upon their recommendation. Lawyers on the board provided the legal advice needed for financial matters and other questions regarding the children.

The second generation of directors was educated either in the private or public schools of Baltimore City and went on to colleges and universities. Most graduated from Johns Hopkins University and continued their studies in their professions.[16] The high level of formal education of the second-generation directors affected their attitudes towards the orphans' education. There is a correlation between the standards of education for orphans in the 1870s and 1900s and the educational backgrounds of the Board of Directors.[17] Although these views reflect changing standards of education in the Jewish community and in the United States in general, they also demonstrate that the directors did not see poor orphans as inferior or doomed to minor positions in society. It seems that Rayner's belief in education as a vehicle for social mobility was shared by the directors. Moreover, the success of the directors and their relatively rapid ascent to wealth and high social position probably served as an example for the children.

The records show that the directors ran the HOA such that all decisions regarding the children's welfare were subject to their approval. The superintendent, chosen or approved by them annually, had little liberty in operating the institution and frequently had to consult committees. The superintendent was not the only one who frequently talked to the various directors. Parents approached the directors when they wanted to admit or release their children.[18] The directors chose and confirmed all of the HOA's employees. Their most important appointment was the superintendent, who had to seek reappointment every year.

The first three superintendents served only for short periods, but in 1886 the directors hired Samuel Freudenthal, a rabbi and a Doctor of Philosophy from Germany, where he had taught and directed Hebrew schools. In 1865, Freudenthal emigrated to the United States and served as a rabbi for nineteen years in congregations in Pennsylvania before becoming the superintendent of the HOA. He remained a superintendent for almost twenty-five years and was responsible for shaping the development of the HOA.[19]

Part of the human touch in the orphanage came from the role played by Dr. Freudenthal's wife. Although the wife of a superintendent was not paid separately, his hiring included hers as well. He was responsible for the whole operation; she ministered to the needs of the girls. His daughter also worked in the HOA (although she was not paid separately, either). His eldest daughter, Dora, and later her sister, Ray, were in charge of the preschool children. This enabled the superintendent to concentrate on the children's education.[20]

The time Freudenthal served as superintendent was marked by vigorous debates in the United States about childcare institutions and the methods by which children should be raised. During this time, the number of children in the HOA also rose due to the flow of Russian immigrants to the United States. Freudenthal was well aware of changes in the theory and practice of childcare during this era, and he suggested improvements both in physical and educational conditions to the directors. These suggestions included requests for an improved playground and to shorten the period of institutionalization of girls. His requests for improvements show that he was familiar with changes in other Jewish communities in regard to childcare institutions and he urged the Board to adopt similar changes. But Freudenthal was also a good administrator and knew the limits of his budget. He did not press for expensive programs and changes all at once and seemed to give more emphasis to educational programs than to improvement in physical conditions.[21]

After his death and a short interim period, the directors appointed Dr. Milton Reizenstein. Reizenstein was also a doctor in philosophy from Johns Hopkins University, which was considered at that time a center for reform and professionalism. Dr. Reizenstein, a Reform Jew but not a devoted one, did not have the Jewish education of his predecessor, but it seemed less important in the 1910s than it had in the 1880s. The fact that he was a reformer, a professional social worker, and was trained in economics seemed the right qualifications for the office.[22] He immediately suggested changes in both the educational programs and facilities in order to modernize the HOA.

The extensive repairs and changes, which included reassigning rooms and installing new toilets, baths, and appliances, strained the HOA's budget.[23] The wish of the superintendent and the directors to adapt the institution to recent innovations was not matched by contributions. By that time, many projects were claiming community attention, such as the Jewish Educational Alliance (a settlement house), consumption cottages, Girls' Home (a house for working girls), Friendly Inn (a temporary shelter for immigrants), and another orphanage, the Betsy Levy Home. Besides the competition for funds, there was a large increase in the number of children in the HOA, from seventy children in the Freudenthal era to 120 in early 1910. When World War I broke out, competition over funds became even greater, although by that time the HOA no longer solicited contributions directly, as it was part of an organization that supported all charity causes run by the German Jewish community in Baltimore.[24]

In 1918, Reizenstein left the superintendency. There were rumors among social workers at that time that he was forced to leave because he was not handling the HOA's budget to the Board's satisfaction.[25] His reforms both in educational programs and physical layout were indeed expensive, as were those of the next superintendent. Michael Sharlitt, another dedicated reformer, argued powerfully for replacing the congregate living arrangements with a cottage system, a change that Reizenstein had recommended and one that required huge sums of money. Sharlitt, himself a teacher, a social worker, and a graduate of a New York Jewish Orphanage, left within only two years to run Cleveland's large cottage-system Jewish Orphanage.[26] The irony was that Sharlitt's cottage-system plans materialized only after he had been replaced, and by that time, the Jewish community had hired Jacob Kepecs, a social worker, to close the orphanage and to establish a foster care system.[27]

The Samuel Ready School

Samuel Ready, a sailmaker and later an owner of a lumber business, died in 1871 at the age of eighty-two, leaving most of his property to establish an orphanage for girls. There was no indication in Ready's business career that he would be such a generous philanthropist. He was a modest and frugal bachelor who lived with his sister's family until his death. In 1864, the retired Samuel Ready asked David M. Perine, the register of wills of Baltimore city, to prepare a charter for a girls' orphanage. He chose the trustees who would carry out the plan after his death and obtained a charter for the future institution from the Maryland General Assembly, which exempted the institution from inheritance taxes. He bequeathed the bulk of his money, $370,999, to the future institution, with the addition of the property left to his nieces that was given to them only for life. In the sixteen years between Samuel Ready's death and the opening of the orphanage, the trustees settled the problems arising from his estate. The property was composed of many lots that were leased. Wise management during those years brought the fund's holdings to $554,110 in 1882. At that point, the trustees started carefully planning for the opening of the new institution. After inspecting the lot designated by Samuel Ready for the orphanage, they concluded that it was not suitable. Bounded by Washington and North Avenue, which by then were paved and graded, the lot did not have enough ground in front and was not high enough to avoid drainage problems in the fall and winter, because Baltimore lacked a sewage system in the 1880s.

The trustees found and purchased another lot in the same area on North Avenue and Harford Street, which included sixteen acres of well-drained ground.[28] Then they turned to Col. William Allan, principal of the McDonogh School, for advice on how the orphanage should be built and operated. Col. Allan used his own school as a model. Built outside the city of Baltimore by the trustees of John McDonogh's will, the McDonogh School was also a gift from a philanthropist for poor children's education, and although it was not solely committed to the education of orphans, about 90 percent of the boys on its premises were orphans and half-orphans.[29] Col. Allan's twenty-three page recommendation is an interesting document, in that it reveals an ideology shared and endorsed by the trustees.

By giving so few specifications about the kind of institution he wanted (except that it would serve orphan girls), Ready gave the trustees a free hand in molding it. Pointing out that the city already had satisfactory institutions that provided plain education for destitute girls, Col. Allan advised selectivity; he supported an orphanage for healthy orphan girls, with fair ability, from good, industrious families.

The school should give such girls a good vocational education, besides a general education, that would enable them to be self-supporting once they graduated. Allan advised the trustees not to invest in new buildings, but rather to remodel the existing ones, which were large enough to lodge about thirty girls and staff. The most important decision, he stressed, was choosing the right superintendent and teachers to run the institution.[30]

The trustees proceeded according to Allan's guidelines. They hired Miss Helen J. Rowe, then a principal of the

Female High School in Frederick County, an experienced teacher in her early forties with a strong personality. She was hired in 1886, a year before the orphanage opened, so she could study other childcare institutions and form the best program for the Ready School. While the buildings were remodeled, Rowe visited schools and orphanages in Philadelphia, New York, Boston, Cleveland, Xenia, Cincinnati, and Coldwater (Michigan). Her reports reveal the issues that preoccupied the trustees and the superintendent: the curriculum, the nature of vocational education, and living accommodations for the girls. From Rowe's reports it is clear that the trustees' intentions were to combine the best programs and accommodations and to develop a model institution.

The correspondence regarding the final moves and decisions with regards to the institution show that by that time, the trustees respected Rowe's opinions and accepted her judgment. She recommended a female colleague from Frederick High School as a teacher (this was accepted by the trustees) and vehemently objected to the suggestion that a man should help her in running the institution. She preferred a housekeeper rather than a matron for fear that the latter would challenge her authority. In all educational matters that came to be debated in the first year, her opinion seems to have prevailed. Her correspondence with the trustees was always very respectful and her tone was confident as she suggested rather than asserted her view—which clearly mattered most.[31] Rowe remained the principal decision-maker of the Samuel Ready School for the next thirty-three years.

The trustees of the Samuel Ready Orphanage were respectable gentlemen of the old Baltimore upper class. They belonged to the same commercial and social circles, and some of them were neighbors. Like the directors of the Hebrew Orphan Asylum, these people viewed their involvement in philanthropic work as part of their obligation to society. Also like the HOA's directors, their philanthropic work passed like a tradition through their families, and they served on the board of trustees of the "Samuel Ready" for decades or until their deaths.

Like the HOA, the Samuel Ready also had representatives of the professions on its board: Charles H. Latrobe, a well-known civil engineer in the city who also designed the orphanage's site, and Dr. Daniel C. Gilman, the first president of Johns Hopkins University.[32]

The Board of the Samuel Ready, not as large as the HOA's, had between five and seven members at a time. Although they had great influence in shaping the policy of the institution, they left day-to-day decisions to Rowe, and once the institution was stabilized in terms of staff and recruitment, the trustees took a back seat. They convened formally twice a year to hear reports from Rowe, to give annual reports to the governor, and to decide upon new candidates and reappointments of children for the following academic year.[33] Decisions that had to be made during the year were referred to the secretary, who contacted the trustees. While the trustees left many of the decisions regarding the children to Rowe, they controlled the finances, investing the money Samuel Ready left and overseeing expenditures. Every decision involving an expenditure not previously approved had to pass through the Board.[34]

The Dolan Children's Aid Society

In 1847, three ships carrying Irish immigrants fleeing the Potato Famine docked in Baltimore Harbor. The immigrants on board were starving and plagued with sea fever. Some died during the trip, some upon arrival, leaving behind about forty orphans. Among the members of the Hibernian Society (an Irish aid society founded in the early nineteenth century) who came to the newcomers' aid was a Catholic priest, James Dolan, from St. Patrick's church. Father Dolan borrowed money from an Irish Protestant, the President of the Hibernian Society, Hugh Jenkins, and established an orphanage for these children.[35] Twenty-three years later, when Father Dolan died, he bequeathed two-thirds of his money and property to the orphanages he had founded. One was for boys from St. Patrick's parish and one was a new orphanage for Irish boys and girls from all denominations in the city of Baltimore and its counties. Father Dolan was a devout Catholic, but also a very proud Irish-American. His will, in which he also left money to disperse among the poor in his native parish in Ireland, testifies to his strong ethnic ties.[36]

The parish orphanage was given to St. Patrick's church to organize and manage, but the Irish orphanage would, by his will, be established and run by the Young Catholic's Friend Society. This was a group of prominent members of all Catholic parishes in Baltimore and its counties who devoted their time to poor children's education, organizing free schools and supplying young children with clothes and shoes, so they would be able to go to school during the winter.[37]

Father Dolan asked the Young Catholic's Friend Society to use his own house on Gough Street for the new orphanage, which he designated as a home for children between the ages of six and twelve of both sexes, so siblings would not be separated.[38] The organization was called the Dolan Children's Aid Society and aimed to shelter and educate about thirty children. The Young Catholic's Friend Society invited the Holy Cross Sisters to run the new orphanage. The Sisters of the Holy Cross were also employed in the St. Patrick's orphanage and in the school for girls and boys next to St. Patrick's church. The Sisters of the Order also ran an academy and a normal school for young ladies. Thus, the Order took charge of both caring for the children and educating them, since the children of the Dolan Children's Aid Society went to the parish school.[39]

The orphanage opened in 1874. Although day-to-day care was left in the hands of two Sisters and a helper, the trustees of the Dolan Home oversaw all other aspects of running the orphanage. The list of roles which these trustees filled without pay and in their free time was similar to those filled by the directors of the Hebrew Orphan Asylum, with the exception that the superintendent of the Dolan Home had fewer administrative responsibilities, devoting more time to the actual care of the children. No doubt the fact that all the children in the Dolan Home were young, coupled with the shortage of help in providing for their needs, forced the superintendent to concentrate on the basic necessities. The Sisters' poor record-keeping illustrates the problem caused by the lack of a secretary to handle correspondence, registration, and the children's record book.[40]

Like the Hebrew Orphan Asylum's directors, the Dolan's trustees heard requests for admission and release. The trustees also had to place the children in homes or schools whenever relatives or parents did not take charge of the children. Unlike the HOA's children, who were not sent to work or study before the age of fourteen, the children of the Dolan Home had to leave the orphanage at the age of twelve at the latest. Some were committed through the Court and could not return to their parents, a situation that forced the trustees to find homes for them, sometimes at an earlier age, in order to make the adjustment necessary for such young children. The result was a need either to employ an investigator who would look for homes and supervise the welfare of the children or to devote their own time to correspondence and visits to homes for the children. The fact that they looked for such homes in the counties, among Catholic farmers, complicated their task. The admission and release procedure in the small orphanage of about thirty children, therefore, included correspondence with the court, parents, other orphan asylums in the city, and farmers and priests who could help verify information as well as letters recommending children, parents, and foster parents.[41]

The secretary of the Dolan Home, who was in charge of this correspondence, was the only paid member of the board of trustees (although the small payments suggest that he was merely compensated for expenses related to traveling and correspondence). Unlike the Samuel Ready or the HOA, the Dolan Children's Aid Society did not have enough money to have an office for the secretary and treasurer. The secretary's work was apparently done at his own home. The endowment left by Father Dolan was mainly investment in city land. The scattered lots were leased to different people, and the trustees were required to keep them leased. To keep track of the property, the treasurer had to hire a rent collector and also to solicit contributions, as the money from the fund was insufficient for the maintenance of the orphanage.

Even the oversight of the superintendent and the Sisters was more complicated than at the other two orphanages, because regular relations between employer and employees did not exist. The Mother Superior of the Order of the Holy Cross, not the board of trustees, was the final authority for the Sisters. She sent them to their mission and could ask them to leave. When the Mother Superior did not approve of certain conditions in the orphanage, she openly threatened to withdraw her nuns from the service. The trustees found themselves more than once in conflict with the Sisters on questions regarding both the children's welfare and the administration of the institution.[42]

The trustees of the Dolan Home who were representatives of the Young Catholic's Friend Society from all Catholic churches in Baltimore met every three months to hear the superintendent's report and to approve the budget, but they had an executive committee that worked constantly during the three-month period to solve problems that required the trustees' attention. The trustees were, as one might expect, prominent Catholic laymen.

The composition of the board of trustees of the Dolan Children's Aid Society resembled that of the board of trustees of the Samuel Ready and the HOA. It had representatives from the professions, such as physicians, attorneys, and engineers, as well as those from the business and financial community. These board members were all very involved in their communities, contributing time and money to charities, and were devout members of their religious congregations. Although many of them were born in Maryland, they tended to preserve their ethnic ties in addition to their religious affiliation. The trustees were part of an elite group that lived in comfort and had servants at home; they sent their children to colleges and universities at a time when only a few could afford such an education. They belonged to the most prominent social clubs and appeared in the society column in the press.[43]

On the surface, it seems that these elites lived in different circles, each according to its religious and ethnic affiliation, in a divided city. Yet orphanage trustees belonging to different ethnic and religious groups knew and helped each other at the turn of the century, when the city was still an intimate town. Some were very active in other reform movements in Baltimore.[44] Some were partners in businesses and financial institutions. This elite group not only met for business, but also shared city-sponsored relief institutions' directorships, as well as service on several boards of charities and institutions of their own denominations. They did not serve on all of them at the same time, but the fact that the same people were chosen for the same kind of service shows that they regarded the service as their civic and religious obligation, whatever the additional claims of their particular groups might be. The involvement of their families—second and third generations as well as wives— in charitable causes further indicates that they viewed the work as important, valuable, and transcending ethnic and religious lines.[45]

Long-term commitment was a source of stability, provided continuity of care, served as a model of civic responsibility to the community, and underscored the importance of philanthropic work. These gentlemen and ladies were also able to establish strong ties with contributors, volunteers, and the business community, connections that helped the orphans find jobs and scholarships for further studies when they left the orphanage. There was, however, the danger of preserving existing conditions without adopting necessary reforms. It was the role of the superintendent to push for changes whenever he or she felt they were needed. Continued adaptation of the orphanages to the latest innovations in childcare shows that the superintendents and the trustees (directors) were sympathetic to change whenever finances allowed.

The trustees of the three orphanages were preoccupied with finances. Whether the institution had an endowment or depended on contributions, the trustees had to plan the budget, invest the money, and control expenses. It was not accidental that the majority of the trustees in all three institutions were businessmen.

Financial Management of the Orphanages

The Samuel Ready was the wealthiest and most secure of the institutions because it had a large endowment. Wise investments made by the trustees during the years between the death of Samuel Ready, the donor, and the opening of the institution, yielded significant profit and changed the nature of the endowment, which was initially mainly invested in land. In 1910, the financial report showed that income from investments of the original capital came from two almost equal sources: the rent of grounds and houses, and bank interest. The grounds and houses were long-term investments because some of them were mortgaged and required payments of loans, mortgages, taxes and improvements. When examining the expenses on land and houses and the income from them, the balance appears negative. There was more cost in maintaining the property than profit made by it. But the overall value of the assets of the Samuel Ready endowment increased during the years 1886 to 1910 by more than 50 percent as a result of the investment in land and houses: from about $550,000 in 1883 to about $845,000 in 1910.[46] The 1910 report also showed that the interest paid on money invested in banks covered the expenses of the orphanage and the negative balance from investments on land and houses, leaving a cash balance of about $4000. In other words, the diversification of the investments that the trustees pursued was calculated to achieve two goals: to cover all expenses, and to increase capital at the same time.

The actual cost of educating a girl in the orphanage was $220 annually. This sum was reasonable in comparison with other childcare institutions.[47] But comparing the direct cost of the orphanage in 1910 with the direct cost in 1888, the first year the school operated, shows that in 1888 the expenses per girl were about $250. The reason for this difference was that the garden and repairs on the house cost proportionally more in 1888 since the institution was just starting out. Yet, the girls in 1910 enjoyed far better conditions than the girls who stayed at the Ready School in 1888.[48]

The difference in the standard of living was primarily due to the increased contributions from the trustees to the school. Contributions included new buildings, special rooms for vocational education, a new dormitory, and a new library. Such improvements did not come from the endowment and allowed the trustees to dedicate money otherwise spent for improvements and repairs to expanding educational programs and raising standards of living, without increasing the annual cost of the orphanage.[49]

The Dolan Home also was financed by an endowment, but as the introduction to the Minute Book reveals, the revenue derived from it amounted to "very little more than seven hundred dollars per annum."[50] By that year, 1874, there were only thirteen children in the orphanage. The situation did not improve much in the years to come. The report from 5 October 1890 gives the finances of the Dolan Home for the previous six months. The income was $1,164 and the expenditure for six months was $647.61. Of that sum, the treasurer gave the Sisters $471. The rest was made up of $159 paid by parents whose children were boarders and $14 given in donations. The Sisters also solicited contributions of food in the Lexington Market, worth $70 for that period.

The Sisters' salaries, administration, school expenditures, and medical care were not included in the budget.

These items were covered by other institutions and organizations that provided the services. For example, the parochial school that the children attended was financed by the Parish of St. Patrick, and the yard in which the children played also belonged to the church, which most likely paid for its maintenance. There were no doctors' fees in the budget and no administrative expenses except $20 every three months, paid to the treasurer, for stamps, telephone bills, and other office expenses.[51] Even then, the orphanage's expenditures were very low. By comparison, the cost for the items of clothing and fuel in the Samuel Ready School for the same year (forty children in 1890) was equivalent to the Dolan Home's whole budget, without taking food bills into account. Even if we take into consideration that the Dolan Home sheltered only young children, who most probably consumed less food than teenagers, and who wore uniforms, the sum per child remains very low.[52]

The Hebrew Orphan Asylum did not have an endowment. The building and the lot had been donated and were free from debt, but operation of the orphanage depended on contributions from people of all walks of life in the Jewish community and arrived through different channels. There were people who left legacies, or donated a considerable amount of money in memory of a family member. This money was invested, and the HOA received some of the benefits of an endowment, since the investments yielded a steady income. Another source of income came from members of the HOA association or from subscribers. Many were from the wealthy German Jewish community, but there were also less affluent Jews and former alumni who paid annual fees. Some of the alumni asked not to be mentioned by name, and the records only identify them as ex-inmates.[53]

The Purim Association also helped raise funds. Traditionally, during the Purim holiday, food was sent as a present to the poor. The Jewish community of Baltimore used the holiday to solicit money for its two main charitable projects: the Hebrew hospital and the Hebrew Orphan Asylum. Money raised by the big ball at Purim was given alternately one year to the hospital and one year to the HOA. Although the Purim Association was a separate organization, many of its members were also members, directors, and former directors of the HOA.

Another organization that helped cover the HOA's expenses was the Hebrew Orphan Asylum Ladies Aid Society. This was a women's organization that included women of the German Jewish elite in the city, many of whom were the wives and other female members of the directors' families. They took it upon themselves to supply the orphanage with clothes and linen by collecting membership fees with which they bought the materials and by donating their time to sew the clothes. They provided entertainment for holidays and special occasions and were responsible for providing sewing lessons at the HOA. Once a girl graduated and needed vocational education and a home, these ladies provided for her and looked after her needs until she no longer required their help.[54]

The HOA received other contributions of services and supplies on a regular basis. Every month, the superintendent's reports recorded the contributions received, which included meals and toys, clothes and sports outfits, and books for the library or money specifically given for that purpose. Presents given on Hanukkah and prizes on commencement were also part of the donations received.

Volunteering was another form of contribution to the HOA's finances. The teacher who taught vocal music and organized the choir donated his time, as did the tutor who helped some of the children prepare for high school. The stenography and typewriting teachers, as well as those who taught the musical instruments, were all volunteers. Jewish newspapers gave the HOA free subscriptions and the directors gave the children rides in their automobiles whenever they were entertained outside the orphanage. These donations represented the Jewish community at large. Although many of the monthly contributions came from the directors and their families, there were alumni contributions as well as those from members of the HOA association. Some of these contributors supported the HOA for decades. Similar to those who gave to the Samuel Ready School, Bernard Cahn donated an addition to the HOA that was organized as a gymnasium; William S. Rayner gave an additional lot to the orphanage to enlarge its playground; and Bertha Rayner Frank, his daughter, built a manual training school in the asylum in her husband's memory.[55]

The Hebrew Orphan Asylum was a community project dependent entirely on community support. The Dolan Home relied on some community support (St. Patrick's Church) and on a small and insufficient endowment, and supplemented its income by taking in boarders—children whose parents needed the orphanage as a temporary shelter and were able to pay some money towards their keep. The Samuel Ready School had a big endowment and enjoyed large contributions from its trustees and their friends. Differences in endowments and patterns of giving make it difficult to compare conditions in the three orphanages only on the basis of per capita expenditures. The annual budget included different items in each orphanage; there was no way to calculate volunteer work or donations—nor do expenses indicate the quality of services and provisions provided.

In other words, comparing conditions in childcare institutions based on annual reports does not necessarily yield accurate results and does not reflect the reality of the children's lives there. Having an endowment could sometimes isolate an institution from the community and deprive it of broad-based support. An institution dependent on donations and contributions from a community was not necessarily poorer than an institution with a large endowment.

Children's Lives in the Institutions and After Leaving Them

The populations in the three orphanages had much in common. A sample of 129 children who entered the three institutions between 1887 and 1890 shows that the majority of children had only one surviving parent, typically a widowed or abandoned mother. Many had siblings in the orphan-ages. The majority of the children entered the orphanages between the ages of six and twelve. A few children younger than six were admitted to the Dolan Home and to the HOA. A small number of children older than twelve were also ad-mitted to the three orphanages.

Children in the Dolan Home and the HOA stayed in the orphanages until their families were able to take them home. For the families in the Samuel Ready School, the in-stitution served only as a boarding school. At the turn of the twentieth century, single parents, mainly poor women, used orphanages as temporary shelter or as boarding schools.[56]

The Dickensian image of nineteenth-century orphanages as jail-like institutions where children dressed in rags, suf-fered from malnutrition, were often sick, and died of com-mon diseases, does not fit with the reality of children's lives in these three orphanages. Although the orphanages differed in their levels of expenditure on children's food, clothes, and medical care, all three provided the children with far better living conditions than their peers had in the neighborhoods from which they came. In an era in which many poor families relied on one potato dish per day, there were three to four meals served daily in all three orphan-ages. While graduates of the HOA and the Samuel Ready School had different memories of the quality, quantity, and taste of the food, their food would have been considered rich people's meals by their peers outside of the institutions. Standards of care continued to improve during that period, and the diets of the children in the orphanages changed accordingly.[57]

Clothes in the Samuel Ready School were made partly by the students, following their choices of color and style. In the HOA, they were made by the wives of the directors, and in the Dolan Home, the children wore uniforms. Children in the orphanages were raised with middle-class values and their appearance, apparel, and personal hygiene were care-fully monitored. The children in the HOA were not different in appearance from their counterparts in the public Baltimore high school they attended. Decades later, one of the graduates of the high school was surprised to discover that one of his friends actually came to school every morning from the orphanage.[58]

Physicians had the most influence on standards of care in the three institutions, and their main concern was the health of the children. Children in the orphanages had medical and dental care, in addition to access to hospitals. As a result, few children died of disease in the three institutions. Physicians placed a great emphasis on the environment to prevent the spread of contagious diseases. In the three orphanages, cleanliness, personal hygiene, fresh air, and isolation of the sick were used to keep the children healthy.[59]

All three orphanages had connections with their immediate neighborhoods. The HOA used the public school nearby; the Samuel Ready girls frequented the churches in their neighborhood; the Dolan Home's children went to school at the nearby St. Patrick's Catholic school and church. The superintendents and boards of trustees encouraged relationships between the children and their families and attempted to preserve family ties during the years of separation. The presence of siblings, the company of friends, and the understanding and caring of superintendents and staff in most cases diminished the pain of orphanhood and enabled children to have as "normal" a childhood as possible under the circumstances. Testimony from children in the HOA and Samuel Ready School and letters and visits by alumni of the two institutions testify to the close relationships formed with the superintendents, matrons, teachers, and staff. The superintendents served long terms, thereby remaining, for many graduates, the close friend and parent figure they consulted during their adult lives.[60]

The three orphanages strove to provide an academically sound education as well as ethical and religious instruction and an appreciation of culture. Their success is evident from comparisons of the achievements of children in their care with those of their peers who did not live in institutions. In the 1890s, school was not mandatory and although Americans had access to free education, parents who were economically stressed often removed their children from school. Children in the three orphanages received a better education and richer range of activities than they could have expected in their homes. The orphanages monitored their progress in school and encouraged them to improve and excel. The orphanages also attended to their moral, ethical, and cultural well-being by providing them with extensive extracurricular enrichment. Children in the HOA and the Samuel Ready School formed literary clubs, played instrumental music, participated in choirs, played sports, and visited cultural sites in the city. They had religious instruction, and frequented the church or synagogue regularly.[61]

Although only forty-five children from two of the orphanages (the Samuel Ready School and the HOA) were traced in the years after they left the institutions, generalizations about their success in life can be made. The orphanages sent home teenagers capable of working and helping their families. They challenged and aided achievers among the orphans to pursue further studies and to excel. The number of students who not only graduated from high school but also continued their studies afterwards is impressive, considering the educational norms of the era. Most graduates, as can be judged from the sources, integrated into society, found employment, and formed families of their own.[62]

Graduates viewed the orphanage as their home and were grateful for their education, but they suffered from the stigma attached to childcare institutions and as a result sometimes concealed their association with the orphanage. The three institutions had much in common: They were founded as a result of private initiative, and were administrated by prominent community leaders who viewed their work as part of their civic and religious obligation to their community and to the country. They all had common goals of returning children to the community as self-sufficient and educated citizens. They all considered these children *their* children and therefore their responsibility.

Some historians view nineteenth-century orphanages as financially strained institutions for poor children, claiming that these institutions isolated children from the community either to protect them from the vices of the city or to protect the community from them.[63] Historians also have questioned the effectiveness of the volunteering social elites who operated private childcare institutions in the nineteenth and early twentieth centuries.[64] Some historians view these elites as conservative and slow to move towards reform.[65] They credited the emerging social work professional class as the messengers of change.

My research suggests that no two orphanages in the nineteenth-century were the same. Communities built childcare institutions to fit their needs. Private orphanages were flexible, practical, and adaptable to community needs,[66] and community leaders and professional managers were not necessarily in discord.[67] Some orphanages were quick to adopt the latest innovations in child welfare, while others moved more slowly, mainly because of financial constraints. Yet the volunteering trustees and professional managers of the nineteenth-century orphanage were deeply engaged in caring for the welfare and education of the children entrusted to them. They brought stability and continuity of care to their institutions, and fostered bonds between the children and the community, which served to benefit both.

During the twentieth century, childcare institutions were brought gradually under the control of the government, through financial contributions, regulation, and laws. Orphanages for dependent healthy children largely disappeared, and instead children entered the foster care system. These children became wards of the state, and, to protect their privacy, also invisible to the public. While there was some public oversight of the decisions made by the professional social workers in regard to dependent children, the ties between communities and children were largely severed.

From time to time, when problems in the foster care system surface and become part of a public debate, the possibility of resurrecting the nineteenth-century orphanage is raised. Orphanages or boarding schools for healthy but neglected and abandoned children can be a good alternative for teenagers who are not likely to be adopted, and who often end up bouncing from one foster home to another. Good boarding schools, however, like the nineteenth-century Samuel Ready School and the McDonough School in Baltimore, require a great investment of funds, which neither the government nor the private sector seems ready to provide. Unless communities start claiming these children, and press the government for such a solution, boarding schools for healthy dependent children will remain a relic of the past.

9 □ The Orphan Trains as an Alternative to Orphanages

Marilyn Irvin Holt

They put us all on a big platform in some big building while people came from all around the countryside to pick out those of us they wished to take home. I was four years old, and my sister was only two. . . . It was a nice train ride, and we were fed mustard and bread during the trip.[1]

This is Margaret Braden's account of her trip and arrival in a small South Dakota town in 1914, via the home placement practice known today as the "orphan trains." By the time of this girl's experience, the transportation of dependent children out of eastern metropolitan areas had been accepted as a form of child welfare for sixty-one years, and the orphan trains would continue for another sixteen years, until 1930.

The story of the orphan trains, like that of orphanages, is tied to the history of childcare in nineteenth-century America. Although the two forms of care are linked through the common problems they sought to address, they represent parallel stories. The orphan train practice, in fact, was hailed by its supporters as a viable alternative to and more favorable option than the institutionalization of children. The man credited with creating the blueprint for child relocation, Charles Loring Brace, strenuously argued throughout his lifetime that placement in private homes was preferable to life in an orphanage.

Brace hoped to replace orphanage care, much as orphanages were touted in the early 1800s as positive alternatives to the almshouses, poor farms, and pauper jails that routinely housed children with an adult population that might include their parents but also included the mentally ill, physically disabled, and sometimes criminal elements. Orphanages, supporters argued, not only provided a safer environment for children, but they also offered basic education and trade skills. In the 1830s orphanages were a rarity, but by the mid-1800s, there were over fifty east of the Mississippi River. They could be found in places as geographically diverse as Chicago and Mobile, and a number served specific populations, based on religious, ethnic, or racial background.

Orphanages also began to appear on America's west coast as travelers of the Overland Trail and gold seekers arrived in California and Oregon. In 1851, for example, San Francisco opened its first orphan asylum as a direct response to its newly arrived and newly orphaned.[2] The public perception of an orphanage—often called an orphan asylum—was that of an institution that took in parentless children. In practice, however, orphanages were never populated by just the truly orphaned. Families used orphanages as a solution to personal crises, usually paying a stipend to the institution that housed their children. Often this was a stopgap measure. When the family situation improved, parents reclaimed their children. Nineteenth-century terminology gave the word "orphan" many meanings that were, nevertheless, understood in the national discussion of dependent children. Observed one writer in the 1870s: "Soon, the word *orphan* became expanded in its significations to include the half-orphan [one-parent child] and later, to embrace destitute children having both parents, living, many of whom were in a condition yet more unfortunate than orphanages."[3]

An increase in the number of orphanages demonstrated American society's acceptance of these institutions. At the same time, the number signaled the ongoing struggle faced by charities and civil authorities as they attempted to deal

with the less-than-desirable results of mid-century urbanization, industrialization, immigration, and western settlement. An influx of a rural population seeking work in cities, as well as foreign immigration, swelled the ranks of the
poverty-stricken and marginally employed in urban centers.
Children lost parental or extended-family protection when
adults were disabled or killed through industrial accidents,
died of illness, or succumbed during periodic epidemics of
disease such as cholera. The numbers needing aid, even to
overcome short-term family problems, often overwhelmed
public officials and existing programs for the poor. City and
county governments largely relied on private charities to
provide needed aid, while government entities were more
likely to punish the poor with incarceration, work laws, or
inadequately funded and maintained poorhouses and inef-
ficient orphanages. Cities such as Boston and New York
found it near impossible to deal with dependent children,
whose numbers only seemed to grow. In 1848 and 1849,
New York officials estimated that 10,000 vagrant children
roamed the city. How many were actually homeless was unknown, but it was believed that at least 3,000 made a liveli-
hood by stealing. In 1850, Boston officials put the number
of jailed boys (under the age of nineteen) at 500; most were
incarcerated for such offenses as vagrancy, selling newspapers without a license, and petty theft.[4]

Child Relocation

Among those individuals determined to effect change was
Charles Loring Brace, who attended Yale Divinity School
and the Union Theological Seminary before becoming a city
missionary. He worked first at New York City's Five Points
Mission and then at Blackwell's Island, with its workhouse
and penitentiary, but his efforts to reform adults left him
disillusioned. Deciding that adults were beyond redemp-
tion, Brace turned to child-saving projects. He was instrumental in establishing the New York Children's Aid Society
(CAS) in 1853. The organization developed and supported a

number of in-city programs for children, including lodging houses for newspaper boys, but CAS's best-known practice became its transportation of dependent children to rural locations.

The idea of placing children in homes was not new. Since colonial times, youngsters had been placed out through indenture, and in the mid-1850s, there was an increase in foster care. Yet the concept of transporting children in large numbers across state and territorial boundaries was new in America. The plan was largely borrowed from the European system of "transportation." During the 1700s, magistrates in Paris ordered compulsory immigration to French colonies in North America for some of the city's imprisoned poor, including children.[5] At the same time, Britain shipped its poor and undesirables to North America, South Africa, and Australia. By the mid-1800s, both the British government and private charities were sending women and children to Canada and Australia as supplemental labor for the Empire. Brace, having traveled in Europe, was familiar with the concept of transportation, and he shared his enthusiasm for the plan in America with Robert M. Hartley, of the New York Association for Improving the Condition of the Poor, and with John Earl Williams, of the Boston-based Children's Mission to the Children of the Destitute. In fact, the Children's Mission initiated a modest in-state placement program in 1850, moving children out of Boston to homes in rural areas of Massachusetts.[6]

A grander, larger-scale plan than the Children's Mission program was envisioned by Brace. Soon after CAS was established, Brace began "communicating with farmers, manufacturers, or families who may have need of [child] employment," and in 1853 CAS began to send adolescents and teenagers to "manufacturers" in Connecticut, New Jersey, and Massachusetts.[7] Places were found in the trades, such as millwork or printing. Far more employment opportunities were located on farms. Encouraged by these early successes, the society's first annual report in 1854 announced: "We have thus far sent off to homes in the country, or to places where they could earn an honest living, 164 boys and 43 girls, of whom some 20 were taken from prison, where they had been placed for being homeless on the streets."[8] These placements seemed to be a continuation of the practice, going back to the colonial period, when local authorities claimed the right to act as guardians for the poor and orphaned, and then transferred them into the homes of farmers and businessmen where they were usually indentured servants or apprentices.[9] Brace's plan, however, did not condone indenture, and it exceeded the bounds of placements beyond a few local communities. CAS's out-of-state placements quickly expanded to include all of New England, and in 1854 the organization sent its first group to a Midwestern state. In March of that year, the town of Dowagiac, Michigan, on the Michigan Central Railroad, received the first of several groups of orphan train children. Within two years, Ohio, Indiana, and Illinois were added to the list of "western" states receiving children.[10]

Fundamentally, transportation was based on the concept of child-saving. Not only physical survival but also spiritual well-being was at risk. It was imperative that children be removed from the worst of urban life. The CAS program began with gathering youngsters into "companies" of traveling groups. The number per group generally ranged from five to thirty youngsters for the simple reason that more would have severely taxed the abilities of the lone CAS agent escorting the group. For the general readership of *Harper's*, a popular magazine, Brace described the process: "On a given day in New York the ragged and dirty little ones are gathered to a central office . . . [they] are cleaned and dressed, and sent away, under the charge of an experienced agent."[11] There was a planned destination to specific towns, where CAS worked to build local support for the children's reception. Before their arrival, stories began to appear in town and county newspapers explaining the purpose of CAS's child-saving efforts, and the organization made it clear that its charges were good potential farm labor. Typically, newspaper stories followed the line of that found in one 1860

Illinois paper: "If any of our readers . . . desire to get boys who will render them a valuable service on their farms, they now have the opportunity."[12] Less advertised, but no less sought after, were girls, for domestic work. To Brace's way of thinking, people would be more likely to take young strangers into their homes if there was the promise that these children had something to contribute. Their labor would benefit the family. The placed out would gain as well. In the wholesome environment of country life, the urban poor would learn moral temperance, the value of work, and the importance of civic responsibility. Brace argued that everyone benefited. Children had an opportunity to better their circumstances; they would, he said, learn that "industry and self help [were] better than alms."[13] At the same time, both established and developing regions of the country gained an additional labor force. As an expanding network of railroads opened new areas for settlement, Brace discovered an "endless demand for children's labor in the Western country."[14]

The Placed Out

The children and teenagers relocated via the orphan trains came from a variety of circumstances. Some vagrant children were gathered off the streets, as noted by a CAS agent describing one of his charges: "Samuel (Picelle) Thompson was named after the street in New York on which he was picked up."[15] Other children were turned over to CAS by parents. In some cases, both parents were living, but more commonly the children came from single-parent households that for any number of reasons could not, or would not, care for the children. For women, the loss of a spouse meant the lack of a breadwinner and support for her children; for men, the loss of a wife meant children left alone while he worked or sought employment. In one instance, an agent told the story of three siblings whose mother, on her deathbed, begged CAS to place the children "where they will grow up church people."[16] Both poverty and the stigma of having an illegitimate child also prompted unwed women to give up their children. CAS found some candidates for relocation among the newspaper boys that frequented the agency's lodging houses, but institutions were a prime source.

CAS had a working relationship with a number of orphanages and juvenile asylums that seemed more than willing to deplete their populations through relocation. A review of CAS reports and the personal histories of those placed out confirm that the majority of children had at least one parent living and were removed from institutions. A 1912 newspaper story from Kansas, for instance, stated that most of the children coming to that state were "from the best orphanages" in and about New York City.[17] It was a point often repeated, as in a 1914 announcement of CAS placements in South Dakota: "The children are well disciplined, having come from various orphanages."[18] Among those cooperative charities were the New York Infant Asylum, Five Points House of Industry, the New York Home for the Friendless, Salvation Army Brooklyn Nursery and Infants Hospital, and New York's Sheltering Arms Nursery. Also counted among CAS's allies was the Orphan Asylum Society of New York which, in 1875, noted an already long association through which "a large number of our boys [go] West . . . under the watchful eye of the Children's Aid Society."[19] Children also came from institutions outside the New York City area. Howard Dowell and his two siblings, for instance, were true orphans, living at the United Helpers Orphanage in St. Lawrence County, New York, when they were turned over the CAS for home placements in Kansas.[20] On other occasions, children were taken from county poorhouses and orphanages in upper New York State, and from at least one orphanage in New Jersey.

CAS had no written guidelines for determining who made good candidates for placement. It was understood that youngsters with apparent physical or emotional problems were unacceptable, but CAS's statements concerning who its charges were and their backgrounds were hardly specific. Broad generalizations portrayed the children as "mostly American born, [with] no fault but poor parent-age and limited education."[21] Nevertheless, Brace's personal writings and CAS reports suggest a preference for American-born and immigrant children of Western European background. Between 1860 and 1890, CAS records indicate that approximately 94 percent of its placements were either Caucasians born in the United States or immigrant children from Germany, England, and Ireland. African-American and Native American children were ignored by the system.[22] Less than 1 percent of CAS placements were Italian or Jewish, although the first group sent to Michigan included "a little German Jew, who . . . found his way into the [CAS] Newsboys Lodging-house," and Brace noted another boy, an Italian, who was removed from New York's Home for the Friendless and placed in a "superior home" in Kansas.[23] For the most part, CAS placements reflected a bias for children of Western European extraction. It was not an uncommon attitude for nineteenth-century America, and CAS, cognizant of public attitudes and prejudices, found it easier to place urban children when they blended, and easily assimilated, into the Caucasian rural communities chosen as destination sites.

Upon their arrival in rural towns, the youngsters were taken to that "big building" recalled by Margaret Braden in her reminiscence. This might be an opera house, church, school, or county courthouse. There, the selection process took place. Before an audience that might include as many as 200 people, the agent reiterated the goals of CAS and introduced the youngsters. Many accounts from those placed out, as well as from local observers, noted that people interested in taking a child might check youngsters' teeth and muscles. Interested parties then applied to the agent or to the local arrangements committee (usually consisting of prominent businessmen and clergy) which, presumably, knew which homes would best serve the children. Those taking children were expected to provide religious training, a common school education, and fair treatment. The receiving families' responsibilities were printed on a card handed out by the agent. CAS did not approve of indenture. As for legal adoption, CAS did not have a formal statement regarding this form of guardianship until the late 1800s when agents began to state, verbally and in writing, that children under the age of fifteen, "if not adopted must be retained as members of the family until they are 18 years of age, and they must be sent to school regularly."[24] Legal adoption was not, in fact, an option in some states and territories. While one state had adoption statutes, another did not. In 1851, Massachusetts was the first to expand the English code of guardianship to recognize adoption as a legal relationship between a minor and an adult. Other states, including Illinois and Kansas, enacted adoption laws in the 1860s, but some states, including Minnesota, did not recognize the legal mechanics of adoption until the early 1900s.[25]

On the face of it, CAS was rather blasé on the point of defining the children's place in their new households. Brace, however, believed that more families would be willing to take children if they were not tied to legalities or the expectation that they accept a specific form of guardianship. For this reason, the refusal to demand indenture or adoption created a child-adult relationship much more in line with foster care than with other forms of home placement. No matter the arrangement, placing agents were responsible for monitoring the homes and noting any changes in a child's status within a household. Typically, agents were pleased when children were legally adopted, although there was one recorded Nebraska incident when an agent went to court demanding that an adoption be voided and CAS be reinstated as legal guardian. In an opinion that pleased no one, the judge reestablished CAS guardianship but refused to remove the teenage girl at the center of the feud from the family that tried to adopt her.[26]

An Expanded Program

Those who shared Brace's dislike of orphanages considered child relocation a good alternative to the institution, and as CAS began to demonstrate transportation's workability, other organizations initiated their own programs in the 1850s. Among the first to launch a relocation plan were the Children's Mission to the Children of the Destitute and the New York Juvenile Asylum. The former had initiated a limited in-state placement program in 1850, but in 1857, the mission's directors decided to replicate the CAS model. The Children's Mission focused on placements within New England, but until the end of the nineteenth century, it sent one or two groups each year to Midwestern states.[27] The Children's Mission did not operate an orphanage or other type of institution for congregate care, but the New York Juvenile Asylum was a self-described "reformatory and disciplinary institution." Incorporated in 1851 under the direction of the New York Association for Improving the Condition of the Poor, the asylum's inmates were labeled as vagrants, delinquents, and "vicious children." Both boys and girls were housed in the facility, but males had priority in out-of-state relocation. And, unlike other orphan train organizations, the asylum demanded indenture. Binding agreements were signed and filed at the county courthouse. An early account, from 1856, noted the practice when it was reported that adolescents, all males, had gone to Illinois where they were indentured to "become agriculturists or engage in other useful employments."[28]

The Civil War and its aftermath dramatically affected families and domestic life. The absence of a provider and the loss of men in battle produced a population of destitute women and children. Although the impact was most visible in large cities, rural areas also saw an upturn in the numbers of dependent children. One response was institution building, with as many orphanages founded in the 1860s as the combined total of the previous two decades.[29] The number and size of orphanages increased during the remainder of the nineteenth century. Some were private institutions established by religious organizations and fraternal societies. Others were county- or state-supported homes. By 1876, twenty institutions existed for the sole purpose of housing the children of war veterans, and more were built before the end of the century.[30] There was a flurry of orphanage building for the tribal groups of Cherokee, Chickasaw, Choctaw, and Creek, which were devastated by the Civil War in present-day Oklahoma.[31] A number of orphanages addressed the needs of African-American children, either displaced by the Civil War and Reconstruction or ignored by charities whose missions did not include people of color. Among this group were the Carrie Steele Orphan Home in Atlanta, the Home for Destitute Colored Children in Philadelphia, the Colored Orphan Asylum in Indianapolis, and the Kansas City Colored Children's Home.

Child relocation might be expected to have slowed or even to have stopped during the turmoil of the Civil War, but the practice continued. Men going off to war produced a severe labor shortage on farms and in small towns in northern and Midwestern states. CAS found that the drain on adult labor created an additional demand for child workers. "In spite of the calamities inflicted by the war," Brace later wrote, "and the absence of heads of families, the West had never contributed [financially to CAS] so liberally, or called for so many children." In 1863, CAS placed 884 youngsters; in 1864, the number rose to 1,034. The figures surpassed those for yearly prewar placements.[32]

To these numbers were added those of new organizations interested in child relocation. Among them was a charity established by a former CAS agent. Reverend W. C. Van Meter stopped escorting CAS "companies" to found the Howard Mission and Home for Little Wanderers in 1861. Located in New York's notorious Five Points district, the mission handed out food and fuel to those in need, established a day nursery for working mothers, and opened an employment agency. It also arranged home placements, although the scope was limited to New York State, and the numbers of children affected were miniscule compared to CAS numbers.[33] In a cross-pollination of ideas and people, Howard Mission contributed to another organization's practice when one of the mission's workers, Reverend Russell G.

Toles, was asked to transfer his experience and expertise to Boston as the first superintendent of the New England Home for Little Wanderers. Originally known as Baldwin Place Home for Little Wanderers, this charity was established in 1865 in response to the Boston's rising number of Civil War orphans and other dependent children. By war's end, the city's estimate of vagrant children stood at 6,000, and one of every four boys incarcerated in Boston jails were the children of soldiers, either dead or unable to support their offspring. The city was overwhelmed by the depth of need among its younger population.[34]

The Home for Little Wanderers was established to aid the orphaned and dependent by providing temporary institutional care in the home's orphanage. Some children received short-term housing and schooling while parents recovered from illness or found work. Other children lived at the home while waiting for home placement. Little Wanderers never planned to be an orphanage providing long-term residence. Rather, it intended either to return children to their families or to serve as a place for children to make the transition from whatever their lives had been to new private homes. During its first year of operation, the home had 200 residents. Of that number, 100 were placed out to homes in New England and Midwestern states. Within five years, the total number of placed out reached 2,500. The manner of placement did not differ dramatically from the blueprint established by CAS. There was a selection process when groups of children reached their destination, but Little Wanderers did not advertise its charges as a potential source of labor. Would-be families were urged to legally adopt the children. At the very least, there was the expectation that children would be treated as members of the family, receive religious instruction, and have a classroom education.[35]

The majority of child-transportation organizations were Protestant-based, but they made little attempt to differentiate between Protestant, Catholic, or Jewish children when making placements, despite claims to the contrary.

Leaders in the Catholic community were suspicious, accusing Protestant charities of intentionally converting children through home placement. To counter the Protestants' hold, the New York Foundling Hospital expanded its in-city, in-state foster care program to include placement through transportation. Established in 1869 by the Sisters of Charity of St. Vincent de Paul, the foundling hospital was both an orphanage and a home placement organization. According to its charter, the foundling hospital was "to receive and keep under its care, charge, custody and management children of the age of two years and under, found in the city of New York, abandoned and deserted or left with [the hospital] and to keep such children during their infancy."[36] Besides infants, the institution also took in children up to four or five years of age. Although the foundling hospital continued to maintain its foster care programs in and near New York City, its transportation system came to rival CAS in geographical scope and in number of children placed.

The foundling hospital inaugurated its transportation program in the 1870s by contacting priests and asking if their parishioners would be willing to provide homes to children. If the answer came in the affirmative, placements began, and like other orphan train organizations, the foundling hospital visited some locations numerous times over a period of years. One difference of the CAS model was the absence of a selection process after children reached their destination. Youngsters were matched to a receiving family before the children left New York, and, as with private adoptions, would-be parents sometimes requested a child with a certain color of hair or eyes. Children did not leave the foundling hospital without the assurance that someone would be waiting for them at the end of their journeys. One account of a placement in a Kansas community illustrated the point: "The children were attended by nurses and must have ranged from 2 to 4 or 5 years of age. The people were lined up all around the station and the nurses brought the little ones out. All of them had tags on their clothes with the name of the person who was to adopt them and the nurses passed them out to the people who called for them."[37] A placing agent, sisters, and nurses traveled with each group, and the numbers in each party generally exceeded those of other organizations' traveling companies. A 1910 newspaper story, for instance, told of "a whole carload of babies not one of whom was over three years old." All were destined for Texas. Probably the largest single transport occurred in 1909 when one train, bound for Louisiana, carried three hundred babies and toddlers. It was little wonder that some called the foundling hospital placements "baby trains."[38]

By the end of the nineteenth century, child relocation was used by a number of organizations to remove children from desperate circumstances, as well as to keep them out of orphanages. Children from New York and Boston continued to arrive in Ohio, Indiana, and Illinois, but institutions and aid societies in those states added another layer to the program. These states were no longer the "western" regions they had been when the orphan train program began in the 1850s. The social ills that came with urbanization and immigration, as well as the number of families left in chaos and poverty when husbands and brothers did not return from the battles of the Civil War, meant increasing problems of dependent and orphaned children. Private and public charities multiplied. Most of these organizations never considered child relocation a solution. A small charity in central Illinois, for example, made it a point to proclaim that it did not "ship children . . . out of state."[39] Nevertheless, a few institutions in Ohio, Indiana, and Illinois transported their own poor and orphaned to states farther west. By the 1890s, there were at least eleven childcare institutions in Cleveland, Ohio. Two transported children out of state. So did the Children's Home of Cincinnati, Ohio. Meanwhile, the Children's Aid Society of Indiana and the Children's Home Society of Chicago also sent groups out of state. The number of children relocated by Midwestern institutions was miniscule, in the hundreds, when compared to those of CAS or other eastern organizations, which numbered collectively at about 200,000, but that they occurred at all offers a commentary on the program's acceptance as an alternative to institutionalization.[40]

Controversy and Criticisms

During the early years of child transportation, there were isolated criticisms. Most came from "employers" when their little laborers did not perform as expected or when they ran away. One agent, writing of his experiences, noted that "a frequent complaint and cause for removal of a child was that he or she did not like to work."[41] By the mid-1870s, however, the orphan trains were increasingly questioned. A growing chorus from within the ranks of reformers and social welfare practitioners took a critical look and found the system wanting. Representatives from Wisconsin, Michigan, Illinois, and Indiana spoke out at prison reform conferences, accusing CAS in particular of saddling unsuspecting communities with "criminal juveniles . . . vagabonds, and gutter snipes."[42] In ridding eastern cities of their poor, these critics said, transportation agencies were really draining away its worst problems. Other commentators accused placing agencies of wrenching children from the arms of their parents, and, in a pique of anti-Catholic feeling, some accused the foundling home of selling its charges for profit. Questions mounted, with a rising voice of reformers concerned with the adequacy of home investigations and follow-up visits.[43] There was little doubt that placing agencies did not usually investigate homes before placement, and certainly there were instances when agents failed to check on children after placement or to make a serious effort to find youngsters, particularly older boys, that picked up and moved on.

To quiet at least some of its critics, CAS launched internal investigations in 1881 and 1883 to disprove claims of "dumping" undesirables. In 1881, a CAS agent took a list of forty-five names, chosen at random, and set out to find the placed out who, by that time, were older teenagers or adults. After a search of six weeks, the agent had located thirty-four on his list. They were ordinary people going about their business; only one had ended up in trouble with the law. Agents reported much the same in the 1883 investigation of placements in Wisconsin, Minnesota, and Kansas. Opponents of transportation were not persuaded by these in-house studies, however. Hoping to bring some clarity, Hastings Hornell Hart, later director of the Department of Child Help for the Russell Sage Foundation, conducted an outside, impartial investigation in 1884. Hart chose Minnesota for the study, and his conclusions were generally favorable to CAS. He found no evidence of rampant crime or incarceration among the placed out. His report also concluded that while CAS did not investigate all homes on a regular basis, it did act responsibly when there were reports of child abuse; Hart discovered that many charges of abuse stemmed from local gossip, not fact. If there was a failing in home placement, said Hart, it was the public distribution of children through the selection process. The investigator was appalled by the rather cavalier attitude of the local committees responsible for approving homes, by the agency's failure to investigate homes, and by the rather hurried attitude of agents. Despite these misgivings, Hart's report generally came down in favor of CAS's program, and in 1899, partly because of this investigation, the Conference of Charities and Correction gave its official approval to the practice. This seal of approval did not, of course, silence all critics, but it played a role in allowing the orphan trains to continue into the twentieth century.[44]

Opposition to child transportation continued, and complaints became more persistent. Despite evidence to the contrary, some continued to accuse agencies of transporting undesirables. An agent for the New York Foundling Hospital hotly responded in one instance, saying, "We do not dump our children but see that they get good homes . . . [and] look after them until they are twenty one."[45] CAS also fought back with more reports and studies that supported its contention that the transported and their new communities benefited from their experience. CAS agent

Anna Laura Hill, for example, provided a report in 1924 on the outcome for all children placed in and near McPherson, Kansas, since 1911. She found that the majority were attending school or employed and making homes of their own; only one, "a bright boy but of a very peculiar disposition," was considered a failure because he returned to New York on his own.[46] The placed out identified in Hill's investigation had become just what CAS expected from transportation—ordinary men and women with jobs and families.

This was the gauge for success, but when possible, CAS pointed to those who had risen much higher in life than their humble beginnings would have allowed. Counted in this small group were John Brady and Andrew Burke. Both were residents of the Nursery Department of the House of Refuge on Randall's Island when they were removed by CAS and sent in the same group to Indiana in 1859. Through very different paths of education and careers, both became governors; Burke served as governor of North Dakota from 1870 to 1873, and Brady, who became a missionary, was named territorial governor of Alaska in 1897. These men's successes were attributed to the life-changing experience of the orphan trains.[47] Nevertheless, it is impossible to state with any authority that children taken out of orphanages and other institutions fared better in their new homes than those who had not been institutionalized at some point in their young lives. It is also difficult to know if time spent in an institution influenced the children as adults, leading them to seek out institutional life, either as inmates or as concerned workers, administrators, or teachers.

Age at the time of placement, length of time spent in an institution, separation from parents or siblings, and the circumstances within the children's new homes affected outcomes. Burke and Brady were very visible success stories, but there were more failures than CAS or other agencies wished to acknowledge. CAS agent Reverend H. D. Clarke, for instance, recorded a number of unhappy outcomes, and was particularly dismayed by what became of most of a

Five Points House of Industry group placed in Iowa. "We had an interesting company [of children]," he wrote, "but later events brought very discouraging results." Among the disappointments in the Five Points group was a girl, "bold and defiant, but very nice in many ways," who was placed with twelve different families in three short years. She was finally sent back to New York City and committed to reform school until she reached the age of eighteen.[48]

Supporters of transportation might argue that there were more successes than failures among those placed out, but state officials, in conjunction with an increasing number of professional social workers and reformers, argued that states were responsible for their own dependent children and should not be forced to contend with out-of-state children that might become wards of state institutions or private orphanages. State governments took matters into their own hands, passing laws that regulated "the importation of dependent children." In 1895, Michigan required institutions to post a bond with county probate judges for each child resettled; four years later, Indiana, Illinois, and Minnesota established more stringent standards for placement homes. Missouri passed a similar statue in 1901. In the same year, Kansas law demanded that out-of-state agencies provide a "certificate of good character" for each child brought into the state, and out-of-state agencies were required to post a $5,000 guaranty bond. Three years later, Kansas stiffened its statute by prohibiting adoption of out-of-state children unless placing agencies could meet all the requirements stipulated in the state's adoption code. Kansas governor William Stanley announced: "We can not afford to have the state made a dumping ground for the dependent children of other states, especially New York." By 1924, twenty-eight states had laws regulating the transportation of children across state lines, and the U.S. Children's Bureau investigated the practice to identify and study state requirements.[49]

Options and Methodologies

Professionals in the developing field of social work worried about the strain these dependent children might place on state agencies and institutions, but fundamentally they questioned the correctness of transportation. Both orphan train supporters and proponents of new methodologies in social welfare agreed that home care was preferable, but they diverged on the point of what made the best home environment. Brace argued that it was essential for children to break all ties to any family left behind. Placements were intended to be permanent, without interference from, or future appearance of, biological parents or extended family. The Progressive movement of the early twentieth century, however, put more emphasis on children remaining with, or near, their families. Progressives stressed that, whenever possible, programs such as aid-to-mothers should enable children to stay at home. When that was not an option, foster care and short-term placement in orphanages would allow youngsters to remain in fairly close proximity to the family home and/or neighborhood. Charities and state agencies began to address the needs of the whole family, not just those of children. Social workers saw themselves as "making the family an asset and not a liability to society, economically and socially."[50]

Although the orphan trains and orphanages offered divergent forms of childcare, neither was immune from criticisms that arose in the Progressive period. Among those to reconsider orphanages and their place in social welfare was Dr. Rex Rudolph Reeder, superintendent of the Orphan Asylum Society of New York. In 1900, Reeder began to reorganize the society's traditional orphanage environment to reflect the more popular progressive model of cottage living. Convinced that an orphan asylum was "not a real childhood home," Reeder argued that only children with physical and mental disabilities needed institutional care. Most children, he said, did better in home-like situations, and he argued for the scientific approach in considering the place of orphanages in childcare. In 1925, he wrote: "That they [orphan asylums] are now drawn within the scope of social investigation as to methods, results, [and reason for being] is entirely due to an awakening of social consciousness and the application of scientific procedure of all ways and means employed in child welfare work."[51]

The walled, regimented orphanage of the nineteenth century received its share of criticism in the early 1900s. Nevertheless, acceptance of institutionalized congregate care did not dwindle as it did for child transportation. Rather, while transportation became a past chapter in the history of child welfare, more institutions were established through the 1920s. In part this was a result of social reform laws, including those that specifically defined parents' responsibilities in childrearing and those that addressed juvenile delinquency. When families seemed to be failing, outside agencies and welfare workers had the right, even the "sacred obligation," to intervene.[52] Progressives argued that when it was necessary to remove children from their home environments, foster care and cottage-care programs were the best solutions. Failing the availability of the more modern cottage model of institutionalization, however, congregate care in large buildings remained an acceptable and widespread practice in the care of dependent and orphaned children.

Conclusions

Orphanages continued to function, while the orphan trains slowly met their demise. Many factors brought the practice to an end, but the influence of the Progressives cannot be ignored or underestimated. The new, scientific approach to social welfare affected strategies and changed the thinking among some organizations still engaged in transportation. The New York Foundling Home, for instance, moved away from child transportation and expanded its efforts to establish more foster care opportunities in New York neighborhoods. Meanwhile, the New England Home for Little Wanderers and the Children's Mission to the Children of the Destitute (by the 1920s, it was simply known as the Children's Mission to Children) added an increasing number of professional social workers to their staffs, and both eliminated transportation from their childcare programs. The Children's Mission focused its resources on foster care in the city of Boston, and it developed a rural cottage program. The Home for Little Wanderers began to concentrate exclusively on those children with emotional problems and learning disabilities.[53] When transportation ended in 1930, only CAS was still engaged in the practice, although its placements had drastically dwindled from the robust numbers found at the beginning of the century. By the late 1920s, it was transporting fewer children, and the organization was redirecting more time and money to in-state foster care, urban fresh-air programs, and construction of in-city neighborhood playgrounds.

By the early twentieth century, reformers and childcare advocates agreed that home was preferable to institutionalization, but orphanages, they believed, still had a place in social welfare. Families still used the institution to house their children when personal crises, death, or unemployment left them unable to deal with urgent problems. Professionals in the field of social work began to agree that not every child was "a proper subject for adoption" or foster care.[54] In all probability, some children as well as their biological parents were better served by orphanages than by home placement.

The same could not be said for child transportation. The orphan trains and agencies' placement programs were not legislated out of operation, although state laws made the practice more difficult. Nor was child transportation ended out of public outrage. The era of the orphan trains eventually came to a close because professionals trained in methodologies based on serving specific populations thought about home care and child welfare in ways that were not grounded in the nineteenth-century rhetoric of child-saving. The religious connotations of child-saving were replaced with a scientific approach that demanded more than the basic belief that Christian charity was all that was required to provide a child with a good home. Advertising children as prospective laborers was considered antiquated and hardly acceptable when one considered the question of what best served children. Nevertheless, criticisms surrounding the orphan trains, as well as the practice's inherent weaknesses, proved to be instructive tools for reformers. Thanks to the scenes of public distribution of children during the selection process, and agents' failure consistently to investigate homes after placement, reformers developed methods and ideologies that elaborated on the criteria for homes and the legalities of guardianship. Unintentionally, child transportation played a role in shaping twentieth-century public policy, state laws, and society's attitudes toward home versus institutional care.

10 □ Orphanages as a National Institution: History and Its Lessons

Timothy A. Hacsi

Between the 1830s and 1850s, orphanages swept across the nation, founded in dozens of cities as America urbanized and passed through the early stages of industrialization. They became not only a place for children without stable homes but also a symbol of community pride. Founded by private citizens and associations, and by churches of all kinds, they became an expected part of the developing urban landscape during the second half of the nineteenth century in America. Despite facing harsh criticism beginning in the 1890s and escalating in the 1910s and 1920s, more than a thousand orphanages were still functioning in the early 1930s. By the 1940s, however, the orphanage as a widespread community institution was clearly in decline, overtaken by government provisions for the poor and by different ideas about the kind of settings proper for children. But they have never left the popular imagination, and have continued on in a variety of incarnations, most notably as residential institutions for emotionally or psychologically troubled children, and as group homes within foster care settings. In an era when welfare has been curtailed, the number of homeless Americans (including women and children) is on the rise, and foster care systems regularly come under heavy criticism, the history of orphanages holds some lessons about the options available to a society that is seeking solutions for disadvantaged children who lack stable homes.

Founding Asylums

There is a tendency to think of the era before the New Deal as a period when private charity cared for the poor, with little or no government involvement. In fact, government was already far more active in providing for the poor in the colonial era and in the first few decades of the nation's existence than is generally recognized. Dependent families and individuals were often given "outdoor relief" in the form of firewood, coal, food, and other non-monetary aid. "Indoor relief" was also provided in the form of almshouses, also known as poorhouses, which were catch-all institutions that cared for many different kinds of people in need: the elderly, the physically ill, the mentally ill, broken families without means, the blind or deaf, and children. Indoor and outdoor relief were provided by local town governments, or by county governments. Across the nineteenth century, a number of state governments became increasingly active in the care of the needy, but public welfare, like private charity, remained largely a local affair. In fact, assuming there was a clear-cut distinction between public and private aid would be a mistake. Governments often provided aid by contracting with private agencies or individuals, rather than by providing aid directly to recipients.[1]

The boundaries that we see now between "public" government and "private" charity were extremely fluid, to the extent that they existed at all in people's minds or in practice. In part, this was probably due to the much smaller nature of government, and the much smaller national population; individuals simply had much greater access to their town's government in the early republic than they do to city (much less state or federal) government now.

This does not mean that welfare and/or charity were either generous or easily available. Despite government involvement and the development of numerous private charities, there was never enough help available to care for everyone in need, especially during the economic downturns that became regular occurrences as the economy industrialized. Indoor and outdoor relief were provided by local governments in small quantities, both in the amount given to individual families and in the number of people helped. That should hardly be surprising, since local, state, and federal government were all quite limited institutions in the first half of the nineteenth century. The budgets for each kind of relief were small and targeted towards a few specific goals. Attempts to raise taxes or to introduce new taxes were viewed with suspicion. For example, the creation of common school systems across the Midwest in the middle of the century took decades because of strong opposition to the increased taxes schools would require. In the South, where opposition to taxes was even fiercer than in the Midwest, and where support for widespread schooling was much weaker, public school systems were an even later development.[2]

Given that government actually was involved in addressing poverty long before the twentieth century, it is not immediately clear why many private citizens saw the problem of orphans as something they themselves, and not their government, ought to address. Most basically, when people thought about how to solve a social problem in nineteenth-century America, they did not *automatically* think in terms of government as being an obvious or appropriate source of a solution. Like most social issues, children without homes were something to be solved by citizens. The government-provided solution that did exist for homeless children (whether actually orphaned or not) in many communities before the Civil War—the almshouse—was a last resort. Those who became concerned about children living on the street and decided to help might seek to do so individually, or in small or not-so-small associations. They might do so through existing organizations, most notably churches, or they might create a new association to address the perceived problem. They did not, however, always assume that government should play *no* role; orphanage founders often turned to local or even state government for certain kinds of help. That private citizens took the lead in developing and trying to implement solutions, in this case usually in the form of institutional care for orphans and other dependent children, did not necessarily rule out seeking government involvement.

When one traces the origin of an individual orphanage, one often comes to one or two people who were the motivating force; in other cases, one finds a small handful of people, usually bound together by an organization of some sort—often a church or religious order. The Chicago Nursery and Half-Orphan Asylum soon developed from a day nursery founded by either one or three women in 1859 and 1860. Two German Catholic parishes in Philadelphia joined forces to establish St. Vincent's Orphan Asylum in the 1850s. A Jewish voluntary organization dominated by German Jews, the B'nai B'rith, took the lead in founding the Cleveland Jewish Orphan Asylum in 1868. Sometimes the small handful of people who began an orphanage were public officials, as with the Charleston Orphan House, which opened in 1792 and was the creation of the Charleston city council, apparently led by one member, John Robertson.[3] (This kind of government-based origin was rare prior to the 1860s, but shows the way that citizens used government in various ways to achieve their goals.)

Why did so many people, individually and in associations, decide to build orphanages? One reason is that they knew such institutions existed elsewhere, in Europe and in other parts of the United States. More immediately, however, it was the combination of this knowledge and the sight of needy children in their own communities that spurred people to action. Just as homeless people are now visible in more than a few places in most American cities, in the nineteenth century street children were a part of everyday life in urban America. These children became needy—and visible—in a variety of ways. Their parents might have died, and if there were no relatives or friends both able and willing to take them in, they would have had to take to the streets. In other cases, their parents might be ill and unable to provide any support, forcing the children to seek whatever work they could; newsboys were perhaps the most commonly visible children in this category. Adults became used to the sight of children living and working on the streets, but not all adults accepted its inevitability. Some decided to act. Sometimes the problem that motivated people to build an orphanage was the actual sight of a few orphaned and/or homeless children on the street. In other instances, it was an awareness that large numbers of children were without homes. Sometimes specific disastrous events, such as a cholera epidemic, created the need; so did the most devastating event of the nineteenth century, the Civil War.

Growing cities saw the founding of multiple asylums for children within a decade or two. Chicago is a case in point. The Chicago Nursery and Half-Orphan Asylum, mentioned above and later known as Chapin Hall, was just one of many orphan asylums that opened in Illinois in the middle of the century; the details surrounding the founding of these orphanages varied, though the broader goal of each was to provide a home for desperate children. Chicago's first orphanage, the Chicago Orphan Asylum, opened in 1848 as a response to a cholera epidemic that swept the city and the nation. The next year Chicago's Roman Catholic Orphan Asylum opened due both to cholera and to the Catholic community's desire to keep Catholic children in need out of the COA, which was a Protestant institution. The Illinois Soldiers' Orphans' Home, founded in 1865, was created to care for the children of soldiers who had died or been disabled in the Civil War, though it soon expanded to take in children of Civil War veterans more generally when they needed care.[4]

By the middle of the nineteenth century, orphanages were a widely recognized response to the problem of children without homes. In the early years of the century orphanage founders had known about orphanages elsewhere; by the 1850s, and probably earlier, *everyone* knew about orphanages, whether or not they had any personal involvement with them. Dozens of orphanages had opened within a few years of the cholera epidemic that swept the nation in 1832 and 1833, and even more were founded immediately after the epidemic of 1849. While not all orphanages that opened in those years were responses to that epidemic—some opened in cities that had not really been hit by cholera—most were founded to care for children from immigrant communities that had been devastated by the disease. By the 1850s people throughout the nation not only knew about orphanages, but also saw them as an appropriate response to children in need, and even as a desirable community institution that showed the community's financial health and social responsibility to care for its own. They had become prevalent enough and prominent enough that opening one seemed an obvious thing to do when confronted with dozens of families suddenly left destitute and damaged due to illness or death. It was not just individuals and churches that saw orphanages as the answer to needy children in the second half of the nineteenth century. As with Illinois, a number of state governments built their own orphanages after the Civil War, to help care for the children of soldiers who died.

By the 1870s orphanages were opening in ever-increasing numbers at *all* times, not just in response to disasters. Ongoing urban growth, industrialization, and immigration combined to create concentrated poverty and large, highly vulnerable urban populations. Epidemics and depressions could lead to large numbers of children in need of homes at the same time, but even when times were good there was a steady flow of children whose families were suddenly unable to care for them. The supply of new orphans and other needy children, in other words, ebbed and flowed but never stopped. Several states, most notably Ohio, built their own publicly-funded and -managed orphanages, usually on a county-by-county basis. Private orphanages also appeared everywhere, run by different Catholic orders, by various Protestant churches, or by avowedly nonsectarian (usually Protestant) groups. As Jewish immigration increased, Jewish orphanages appeared in a number of cities. Orphanages for African-American, Native American, Japanese, and Mexican children also opened in the second half of the nineteenth century, sometimes managed by those communities for their own children, sometimes by whites who became especially concerned about the needy children in these communities.[5]

While the people who founded orphanages in the nineteenth century were usually individuals or small groups acting as private citizens, or as church members, it would be a mistake to see the spread of orphanages as something that was driven and supported completely by private donations. Town and state governments played a crucial role in helping many orphanages get started or expand, perhaps most often by granting them land on which to build. Several states went much farther either by establishing public asylums themselves or by paying private asylums a certain amount for each child under care. By 1910, nearly one-quarter of the money in orphanage budgets nationwide came from government appropriations. This amount was not simply a sign that most publicly-managed asylums were almost completely funded through public monies; Catholic asylums as a group received 22 percent of their funds from public sources, and Jewish asylums as a group received 11 percent of their funding the same way.[6] In practice, of course, this meant that some Catholic and Jewish orphanages received little or no public money, while for others it made up a considerable part of their annual budgets.

The Variety of Asylums

When discussing orphanages, as with other things so extraordinarily varied and complex, we simplify the historical reality to find useful generalizations. Lumping all asylums for children into one category is just such a simplification; it provides a powerful and useful symbol of a certain kind of institution, but misses the reality of most of the actual institutions that existed. It is important to recognize that orphan asylums varied on many fronts. What type of children did they admit and care for? Some took only full orphans who had lost both parents, but most also accepted half-orphans with one living parent. Well before 1900, most orphanages were already admitting children with two living parents, so long as they were destitute and in need of aid. How did asylum managers view the children they admitted, and the parents and relations of those children? More than a few viewed poor parents with disdain, while others saw them as people in need and worthy of help; some managers started with the former view, but shifted to the latter after years of interaction with parents who clearly loved their children. Some asylums would only accept children over whom they were given complete legal control (to limit parental interference), while others took children in with the expectation that the children would be returned to relatives as soon as possible. Many orphanages encouraged relationships between children and their surviving parents and relatives, while others tried to limit those relationships as much as possible; the former became more typical as time passed. Some asylum managers saw children as innocents in need of protection, while others viewed their children as in need of strict discipline (although presenting those two views as mutually contradictory is itself a simplification).

What did asylum managers want their children to learn, and to become? Some sent their children to public schools, while others schooled their children within the asylums where they could keep more control. Some taught a very specific religious belief, others a vaguer moral code (usually broadly Protestant). In most orphanages, moral education and character training were considered as important as, or more important than, academic training. Many asylums simply hoped to help their children prepare to become useful, well-behaved servants or wives (for girls) or manual workers or farmers (for boys). But others expected their children to *become* middle-class as well as to adopt "middle-class values" of hard work, sobriety, and faith. Placing older children in high school classes, and even occasionally sending them off to college, became a fairly regular occurrence in some orphanages around the turn of the century. While orphanages were much more a refuge for needy children than a ladder for upward mobility, in some instances they tried very hard to be both.

The institutions varied on a number of other fronts as well. Men managed some, while women ran others; some were managed by churches, others by secular groups or individuals. Some placed children out in homes whenever possible; others considered institutional care preferable for all. Some asylums accepted only children of a specific ethnicity or race, while others took in anyone in need so long as there was room; asylums that mixed white and black children were rare, but they did exist, particularly among public and Catholic orphanages. Many asylums avoided babies and infants, while others specialized in the care of young children. Some were funded completely by private charity, but many received important but limited public money; some existed largely on the public purse, while others depended heavily on parental contributions for room and board to make ends meet.

A few asylums kept many of their children for year after year, while others saw most of their children off within months of their arrival; most asylums provided short-term care to many and long-term care to those with nowhere else to go. A few would take in children with severe behavioral problems, but many would not. Many were coed, but others, particularly Catholic homes, accepted only boys or only girls. Some asylums were governed by people very different from the children within them, such as orphanages for African-American children that were managed by whites. Others were managed by people who had a great deal in common with the children in their care. Some asylums were tiny, consisting simply of a house; others were huge institutions with many hundreds of children, where superintendents were hard-pressed to know the names of every child.[7]

Most of these qualities could be found in a number of orphanages at any time between the 1830s and the 1930s; others were more matters of time, with orphanages in 1850 being predominantly one way, and orphanages in 1920 predominantly another. For example, far more orphanages accepted children with two living parents by the 1910s than they had in the 1840s. And in the mid-nineteenth century most asylums schooled their own children, whereas by the twentieth century most sent their children to public schools. Like many changes that asylums underwent, this occurred partly because of changing perceptions of how (or if) children should interact with the outside world, and were partly due to changes in the outside world. Public school systems were much more common and much more likely to have space for orphanage children after the turn of the century than they had been fifty years earlier.

These points are meant to keep us from extrapolating too easily from *an* orphanage to orphanages in general. There was tremendous variety among institutions for dependent children—as much, perhaps, as there is among families today. I do not, however, mean to downplay the important similarities that existed among the vast majority of orphanages. Orphanages of all types and sizes took in children they saw as being in need. They were founded and run for basically charitable reasons. They provided a home of sorts for the children within their walls, for days, months, or years. Moreover, orphanage managers were all very concerned with their institutions truly being a *home* for children, though they varied in how well they succeeded (and in how well they thought they were succeeding). But when we speak of orphanages as a historical entity, and wonder about the lessons to be learned from them, we need to remember that individual orphanages varied tremendously in many, many ways. Later I will discuss some of the lessons I believe we can take from orphanages. But they will by and large be lessons from an era when institutions formed the centerpiece of care for orphans and other dependent children—lessons from the disorganized *system* of private and public care of children in institutions designed for that purpose by local groups, rather than lessons drawn from individual orphanages.

The Decline of Orphanages

The number of orphanages dropped dramatically between the 1930s and the 1960s, and by the 1960s and 1970s the orphanages that did still exist were serving children who needed different kinds of aid than their predecessors had. Scholars have developed a number of arguments about why orphanages went out of style in the middle of the twentieth century. Some focus on the specific reasons individual orphanages changed their nature or closed, while others try to explain the relationship between the decline of orphanage care and other changes in American society in the middle of the twentieth century. Kenneth Cmiel has traced the forces that led the Chapin Hall Center for Children of Chicago to shift from caring for dependent children to treating emotionally disturbed children in the late 1940s and 1950s. Pressure from the professional welfare community played a central role in this change, as did the drastically reduced number of "half-orphans" and orphans needing care—the very clientele the institution had been formed to aid nearly a century before. In addition, Chapin Hall was under serious financial pressure—which could be dealt with by accepting children with more severe problems, and the public funding available to care for those children.[8]

Nurith Zmora's study of orphanages in Baltimore traces several of the interrelated reasons that different kinds of orphanages there closed down or changed focus. Criticisms of orphanages and constant pressure to offer more and better services helped orphanages become better homes, but also played a role in ending orphanages' existence. Financial strains arose from a variety of factors, including this need to offer more extensive and costly services, and the large numbers of children seeking entrance, numbers far beyond institutional capacity. The Dolan Home, the Catholic asylum Zmora studies, carried on long after the individual Jewish and Protestant institutions she describes had closed or changed focus.[9]

Marshall Jones has examined a number of orphanages

in Pennsylvania and points to the important long-term effects of the Great Depression on institutions for children. The Depression strained the finances of most asylums to (or past) the breaking point, and as a result orphanages often found themselves forced to use up part or all of their endowments to survive. The creation of Aid to Dependent Children in the 1935 Social Security Act meant that many of the children orphanages had traditionally cared for, such as half-orphans with living mothers, would be able to stay in their own homes, both during and after the Depression. On top of that, people would be paying taxes to help other people's children, which would not help orphanages in their future fundraising efforts.[10]

There is obviously some overlap among these views, but they differ on a number of points, particularly about what mattered most in moving child welfare away from privately managed institutional care. I do not believe this is because some views are right while others are wrong; instead, this variety represents what actually happened in different locations. Some scholars have looked at individual institutions and discovered very specific reasons why that *particular* institution closed or changed its nature. Other scholars have examined a group of orphanages, either in one location or of one type, and focused on why those orphanages eventually changed or closed. Matthew Crenson's work, which makes arguments about why orphanages *as a loosely based national system* declined and virtually vanished, portrays a complex interaction of forces and decisions; my work elsewhere, with similar goals, does so as well.[11] Partly because we look at different actors and different asylums, our arguments overlap quite a bit but differ in a number of ways, from each other's and from what scholars such as those mentioned briefly above have found. These differences probably stem as much or more from the specific sources and institutions and individuals we studied as from anything else. Based on my own research and the work of these and other scholars, I believe there are a number of issues that deserve emphasis, particularly when we are thinking about the rise, nature, and decline of orphanages, to help us think about modern child welfare options.

Asylums could only flourish so long as they had popular support. Asylum care had been challenged in the second half of the nineteenth century by Charles Loring Brace and other "expert" advocates of placing children in families, but even child-placing advocates usually saw a meaningful role for orphanages (and, for that matter, orphanages themselves did quite a bit of child-placing). More importantly, if there was an accepted "best" approach to helping orphans and other children without a home prior to 1900, it was orphanages, not placement in homes or aid to poor parents to allow them to keep children at home. Communities built orphanages for their own, and took great pride in them as institutions and as proof that their communities were successful and charitable.

But between 1900 and 1930 there was a decisive shift away from the belief that orphanages were "good" places to raise children. As social work rose to prominence, it increased the number of highly visible "experts" on child welfare. And with increasing frequency these experts saw orphanages as the least desirable option, inferior both to placing children in homes and to supporting them in their own families. By the 1910s, advocates of mothers' pensions and many other observers argued that the best place for a child was in his or her own home. (That mothers' pensions were less expensive than institutional care was a point that was made again and again in opposition to orphanages, right alongside the idea that children should be kept with their mothers whenever possible.)[12] Placement in someone else's home—what we now know as foster care—was the next best option; orphanages were third, in effect the last resort in the eyes of many prominent child welfare experts.

Local orphanages were often able to ignore this ideological shift, for a few years or even a few decades. As long as a community believed in its orphanage, and was willing and able to support it, and there were no more desirable options easily or widely available to parents, orphanages continued to thrive; "expert" opinion did not matter much to local communities that believed they knew better. In fact, the growth of social work enhanced a number of changes orphanages had been undergoing before 1900 that made them better places for their children: increased access to the outside world, more support for ongoing relationships with surviving parents, and better schooling, to name a few. The most prominent early blow against orphanages came at the 1909 White House Conference on Dependent Children, yet the number of orphanages rose from under 1,000 in 1910 to over 1,300 in 1923, then basically stabilized until the early or mid-1930s. One group—fraternal organizations such as the Odd Fellows—built *most* of their orphanages in the 1910s, going from just eighteen in 1910 to eighty by 1923; the number of Jewish orphanages doubled during the same period, reflecting in large part the sizable Jewish immigration to America since the 1890s.[13] Expert condemnation helped push orphanages to improve how they cared for children, but they did not directly drive orphanages out of business or into caring for a different clientele. That would require both an economic collapse and the creation of new state and federal approaches to the problems of extremely impoverished families.

Depressions always affected orphanages negatively in two different ways. First, they limited the ability of most orphanages to receive donations from the community members who supported them (and could reduce government aid, where it was available at all). Second, they greatly increased the number of families that sought help. Asylums that only accepted full orphans may not have been much affected by this, but those that accepted half-orphans, and especially those that would accept children with two living parents, were flooded with more admission requests than they could approve. The Great Depression of the 1930s was a watershed event in how the United States deals with poverty, not only because it saw the birth of New Deal programs but also because of its impact on private charities, most definitely including orphanages. Dorothy Brown and

Elizabeth McKeown sum up the change when they write about Catholic orphanages and Catholic charity more generally in New York: "By the end of the New Deal, Catholics in financial need were assisted primarily through public agencies."[14]

By far the most significant of the public programs created during the 1930s concerning the care of dependent children was Aid to Dependent Children (ADC), later changed to Aid to Families with Dependent Children (AFDC). (It became TANF in the 1990s.) The creation of ADC was hardly inevitable, but in retrospect it is reasonable to see it as the culmination of a decades-long shift in thinking about the proper role of the government in addressing the poverty of women and children. State governments had some involvement with child welfare in the late nineteenth century, especially by visiting private and public orphanages to inspect them. They became more involved in the early twentieth century, though how closely varied greatly from place to place. And in some places, as has already been noted, states paid orphanages on a per capita basis for the children within them, believing that such care was a public responsibility. In the 1910s the movement for mothers' (or widows') pensions swept across the nation; by 1920 most states had such a program, though how well funded and how accessible it was to most needy women varied enormously. When the New Deal created its second major wave of programs in 1935, it was hardly surprising that ADC was created, and patterned on mothers' pension programs.[15] From 1935 on, a federal program existed to help many of the children who might otherwise need to turn to the local orphanage for shelter. For mothers in desperate situations, there might be a stigma attached to receiving welfare, but that was almost always going to be preferable to giving up a child to a local institution.

Another change that weakened orphanages was that the kind of community that had supported most asylums—of relatively homogenous ethnicity and religion, but with working-class, middle-class, and more prosperous members—was giving way in most urban areas to a more class-segregated setting. Suburbanization enhanced this shift as middle- and upper-middle-class families moved out of cities altogether in increasing numbers. Strict limits placed on immigration before and after World War I ended the huge flow of immigrants that had played a crucial role in establishing (and inhabiting) orphanages. Finally, ethnic and religiously-based communities were undercut by the increasing development of a national culture transmitted through media such as radio and movies.[16] While the effects of these developments on orphanages were not as immediate as that of the Depression or the creation of ADC, over time they changed the landscape that had supported orphanages.

As has also been mentioned above, the specific needs of children arriving at orphanages began to change in the early twentieth century. In part, it was a matter of definition rather than substance, as social work developed and advocated for new ways of thinking about children's needs. But this shift became far more important for orphanage managers as mothers' pensions and then Aid to Dependent Children allowed many women to keep their children at home, whereas in an earlier age they might have been forced to turn to an orphanage. Just as the number of children who were seen as needing extensive—and expensive—emotional or psychological aid and treatment was growing, the number of children arriving at orphanages needing help largely or solely due to the poverty of their surviving parent diminished. After World War II, comparatively few healthy but desperately poor children would need to come to an institution for help. The clientele that orphanages had tended to was less and less likely to need institutional care. It was a perfectly logical move on the part of many asylums to shift their approach and begin caring for the newly available clientele. In fact, given that orphanages had always struggled to get by financially and that there was now significant public money available to care for this new clientele, it was a change that was almost unavoidable.

Bellefaire, which had been the Cleveland Jewish Orphan

Asylum until 1929, shifted purpose completely between 1940 and 1954. In 1940 it began serving Jewish children with severe emotional problems, who required a therapeutic residence and could not properly be helped in a foster home; in 1943, those became the only kind of children it would accept. In 1954, it dropped its focus on Jewish children, instead deciding to accept children from any racial or religious background who needed extensive treatment for emotional problems.[17] Like the Chapin Hall Center for Children, Bellefaire adjusted by becoming a residential treatment center within the growing foster care system. Other asylums extended their placing-out practices and gradually abandoned institutional care, becoming foster care agencies. Still others simply closed their doors. Of course, a number of orphanages continued on, much as they had in earlier years, into the 1960s and even beyond, but the total number of such institutions had dropped drastically, and their place within the child welfare system was now at the margins. Catholic orphanages may have been more likely to continue for a few more years than most other religious asylums for children. And southern orphanages probably resisted these changes longer (on average). The South had been slower to adopt public schools in the nineteenth century than had the rest of the nation, and most southern states were relatively resistant to adopting federal welfare programs such as ADC. The need for traditional orphanages may have lasted a decade or two longer in most Southern states than elsewhere, but in the end the same forces that changed child welfare in the rest of the country came to the South. Foster care expanded, ADC/AFDC became reasonably available, and orphanages could either change or close.

Some Lessons from the Historical Record

Over the past two decades, there have been repeated calls for a shift back toward private charity to address an array of social problems. These calls have had positive and negative aspects, certainly, but their sense of history has been weak at best. In the 1980s they were often based on a nostalgic look back toward a time when charity had cared for all who truly needed help. This supposed past has been contrasted to the "welfare state" that is claimed to have created (or at least furthered) poverty, particularly the transmission of poverty and certain attitudes that some people associate with poverty from one generation to the next.

But the historical record is very clear on this: Private charity was never able to provide for all those in need. It is no coincidence that the two states where institutional care of dependent children was most widespread, California and New York, were states where the government paid private institutions for the care of children, because those states saw such care as a vital public interest. It is impossible to say with certainty, but it is reasonable to guess that if no public money had ever been made available for orphanages, instead of the 1,300 that existed in the 1920s and early 1930s, there might have been only two-thirds as many. It is more certain that without public aid, orphanages would have helped far fewer children, and provided less for many of the children they did manage to take in. The impetus for orphanages in the United States came from private citizens and private groups, and they provided the backbone of the loose orphanage system that dominated child welfare from the 1840s to the 1920s. But institutional care was a private-public venture in fundamental ways, and would have been far less widespread without aid from local and state governments. Perhaps the most important thing about that private-public venture was that it was initiated and centered on the decisions and actions of private citizens; public agencies provided crucial support in specific ways, and some oversight concerning quality, but little else.

One of the most telling lessons from the history of orphanages in the United States is that it shows the likelihood that any system of care for needy children will expand to care for children with a much broader array of needs than the system was originally developed to address. Orphanages were initially created to care for *orphans*—children with no parents and no other family to care for them. But from the start some orphanage managers could see there were other children with as much need for help as orphans. This was most clearly true of many half-orphans, who had a surviving parent unable to provide them with any sort of home, at least temporarily. As a result, throughout the course of the nineteenth century, an increasing percentage of asylums took in half-orphans as well as full orphans. More telling was the shift by one asylum after another to take in children with two living parents, labeled as "destitute" or "dependent" or "neglected" children by orphanage managers. By the end of the nineteenth century, many orphanage populations were made up largely of these "dependent" children and half-orphans, with full orphans only in a small minority. Any new approach to child welfare, including a new take on an old approach such as orphanages, will need to think carefully about just who it intends to help, whom it will exclude, and whether that distinction is appropriate and feasible.

Another important lesson to take from the history of orphanages is that limited funding severely curtailed what could be done for children. Staffs were often poorly trained, and in far too many cases transitory. The prevalence of Catholics among orphanage managers and clientele was not simply due to the large numbers of needy Catholics; it was also made possible by the availability of relatively well-trained and inexpensive orphanage staff in the form of nuns (and, to a lesser extent, male Catholic orders). The resources required for appropriate institutional care now are far greater. Given the attacks on welfare over the last two decades, and the funding problems that plague foster care across the nation, finding adequate funding is one of the most difficult and important tasks for anyone considering any sort of private provision for dependent children, institutional or otherwise. The "private" group homes that I know of tend to spend a great deal of energy seeking private donations, *and* receive sizable amounts of government funding.

We also need to consider the issue of sexual abuse of children in orphanages. There is simply no way to know how often children were abused within orphanages, just as there is no way to get at how common sexual abuse was in people's own homes in the decades before and after 1900. The historical data does not exist to give a firm national comparison on this issue, and to the extent that we know about abuse that did occur, it does not give definitive answers because there is no way of knowing who was abused but never reported it. To whatever extent it did occur in orphanages, the poorly paid and poorly trained staff members that cared for children in most asylums are a probable source (that, in turn, is related to the funding problems mentioned above). Another possible source of abuse is the older children within the same institution. While it is impossible to know the extent to which this occurred, there is no question that it did, just as there is no question that abuse happened in some households. How widespread it may have been in orphanages, or in society, is not a historical question that can be definitively answered.

Both of these problems, poorly paid and trained staff and sexual abuse of children, have emerged in other forms of care for dependent children; they are not unique to the history of orphanages. The foster care system has suffered from both problems, and still does. Many of the residential institutions currently used by state, local, and private foster care officials to care for children deemed to need an institutional setting have had problems with sexual abuse at one time or another. From what I know of the system, the problems that become public knowledge are the tip of an appallingly large iceberg. For that matter, it is not unusual for children in family foster care to be abused, whether by an older child in the same home, by a foster parent, or by another adult with access to the home. Guarding against this problem is something that is, unfortunately, beyond the ability of many foster care agencies; any return to more extensive use of orphanages—group homes, in modern parlance

—will need to find better answers to this problem than did orphanage managers of the past, just as parents today are far more aware of sexual abuse.

Another lesson to be learned comes from what orphanage managers themselves saw as the appropriate role of institutions (to the extent this generalization can be made). Many orphanages did not accept babies, and those that did usually tried to place them out in homes, not seeing institutional care as appropriate. (The high mortality rate of babies in most asylums that did accept them would tend to make the point more strongly.)[18] In addition, many asylums placed young children who did not have parents to return to in families, seeing that as preferable to institutional care. Most orphanages were not catch-all institutions that served all children equally well, and we need to remember that.

But there were children who were better served by orphanages than they could have been by the other forms of child welfare available before the 1910s, especially in terms of keeping their families together in the long run. The other available options for children, such as adoption, placing out in homes, and orphan trains, all aimed to split families apart, as some orphanages had intended to do, particularly before the Civil War.[19] The majority of children who entered orphanages left within a year or two, almost always to return to their own families once their parent or parents were back on their feet financially, in better health, remarried, or otherwise once again able to care for their children. In effect, the family was temporarily broken up, but allowed to reunite in the long run because of the care provided in the short term by orphanages. Sibling groups also benefited from orphanage care, through which they were allowed to stay together under one (sometimes quite large) roof. Orphanage managers were very conscious, and proud, of the fact that they were able to keep five, six, or more brothers and sisters together, which was—and is—virtually impossible when children are placed out in families.

Conclusion

There is a distinction between child welfare, addressing issues of poverty, and child protection, addressing issues of abuse and neglect. It is easy to make too much of this distinction, seeing welfare in its current fragmented state as child welfare and state foster care agencies as child protection. There is in practice considerable overlap between the two, especially given that poverty is sometimes mistaken for neglect and that poverty certainly increases the forces that can lead parents to be abusive and/or neglectful. This is not the proper place for a lengthy discussion of these two related problems, but it is appropriate to ask where orphanages fit in.

Historically, nineteenth-century orphanages formed the centerpiece of American child welfare, caring for children whose fundamental problem was poverty. Now, however, many residential homes and orphanages (though not necessarily all of them) are part of the child *protection* system, taking in children who have been abused or seriously neglected. Discussions of reviving orphanages, such as that of the mid-1990s led by Charles Murray and Newt Gingrich, have generally envisioned the new orphanages as once again being part of child welfare. But it is not at all clear in most discussions exactly what kinds of children new institutions would care for, or for how long, or how they would be funded. These were all fundamental questions each orphanage manager had to address in the past; they would be no less crucial now.

Contributors

David T. Beito is a professor of history at the University of Alabama and the author of *Taxpayers in Revolt: Tax Resistance During the Great Depression* (University of North Carolina Press, 1989), *From Mutual Aid to the Welfare State: Fraternal Societies and Social Services, 1890–1967* (University of North Carolina Press, 2002), *The Voluntary City* (University of Michigan Press, 2003), and *Black Maverick: T. R. M. Howard's Fight for Civil Rights and Economic Power* (University of Illinois Press, 2008).

Kenneth Cmiel, the author of *A Home of Another Kind: One Chicago Orphanage and the Tangle of Child Welfare* (University of Chicago Press, 1995), was a professor of history and American Studies at the University of Iowa in Iowa City. He died suddenly in 2006 and his manuscript was edited by his wife, **Anne Duggan**, who is a writer and editor. At the time of his death, Professor Cmiel was the director of the University of Iowa Center for Human Rights and was writing two books, one on the composition of the Universal Declaration of Human Rights and the other on the uses of information and knowledge.

Anne Duggan is the director of publications for the Office of Health Science Relations at the University of Iowa. She is a graduate of the University of California, Berkeley, and lives in Iowa City, Iowa.

Timothy A. Hacsi has been a postdoctoral fellow on children's policy issues at the University of Chicago and on evaluation methods at Harvard University. He currently teaches in the history department at the University of Massachusetts, Boston. He is the author of *Second Home: Orphan Asylums and Poor Families in America* (Harvard University Press, 1998) and *Children as Pawns: The Politics of Educational Reform* (Harvard University Press, 2003). He is currently working on a history of state universities and access to higher education.

Marilyn Irvin Holt has been an adjunct professor at the University of Kansas and Emporia State University. She has written for academic journals, and served as a research consultant for PBS documentaries. Her book publications include *The Orphan Trains: Placing Out in America* (University of Nebraska Press, 1992), *Indian Orphanages* (University Press of Kansas, 2001), and *Children of the Western Plains: The Nineteenth-Century Experience* (Ivan R. Dee, 2003). Material for her chapter was drawn largely from previous research used in writing *The Orphan Trains* and is being published herein with the permission of the University of Nebraska Press.

Duncan Lindsey is a professor at the UCLA School of Public Affairs. He serves as Editor-in-Chief of *Children and Youth Services Review*, the premier research journal in the child welfare field. He is the author of *The Welfare of Children*, 2nd ed. (Oxford University Press, 2004) and the editor of *Child Welfare Research* (Oxford University Press, 2008). His most recent book is Child Poverty and Inequality (Oxford University Press, 2009). Professor Lindsey is the 2003 winner of the *ProHumanitate* Medal for his research in child welfare.

Anne E. C. McCants is the Margaret MacVicar Faculty Fellow and Chair of the Department of History at the Massachusetts Institute of Technology, where she teaches European economic and social history and Women's Studies. She is the author of *Civic Charity in a Golden Age: Orphan Care in Early Modern Amsterdam* (University of Illinois Press, 1997) and numerous articles on historical demography, material culture, and the standard of living in the Dutch Republic.

Richard B. McKenzie is the Walter B. Gerken Professor of Enterprise and Society in the Paul Merage School of Business at the University of California, Irvine. In addition to writing widely on economics and management issues, he has written *The Home: A Memoir of Growing Up in an Orphanage* (Basic Books, 1996; Dickens Press, 2006). He has edited *Rethinking Orphanages for the Twenty-First Century* (Sage Publications, 1998), and he has produced a documentary film, *Homecoming: The Forgotten World of America's Orphanages* (HomeFront Productions, 2006), which has aired on PBS television stations across the country.

Timothy S. Miller is a professor of history at Salisbury University and the author of *The Orphans of Byzantium* (Catholic University of America Press, 2003). Before studying orphanages, he wrote a monograph on the origins of medical hospitals in the Byzantine Empire, *The Birth of the Hospital in the Byzantine Empire* (Johns Hopkins University Press, 1985; reissued in 1997 in paperback with a new introduction).

Marian J. Morton is an emeritus professor of history at John Carroll University in University Heights, Ohio. Her recent publications include "Surviving the Great Depression: Orphanages and Orphans in Cleveland," *Journal of Urban History* (May 2000); "Institutionalizing Inequalities: Black Children and Child Welfare in Cleveland, 1854–1998," *Journal of Social History* (September 2000); "The Suburban Ideal and Suburban Realities: Cleveland Heights, Ohio

1860–2001," *Journal of Urban History,* (September 2002); and *Cleveland Heights: The Making of an Urban Suburb* (Arcadia Publishing, 2002).

John E. Murray is a professor of economics at the University of Toledo. His publications include *Origins of American Health Insurance* (Yale University Press, 2007) and articles in the *Journal of Economic History, Bulletin of the History of Medicine,* and *Demography.* He has co-edited the volume *Children Bound to Labor in Early America* with Ruth Wallis Herndon (forthcoming from Cornell University Press). His essay with Herndon entitled "Markets for Children in Early America" (*Journal of Economic History,* 2002) won the Program in Early American Economy and Society Prize. He is currently writing a history of the children, families, and management of the Charleston Orphan House. His chapter was originally published in the *Journal of Interdisciplinary History* and is being reprinted here with the permission of that journal.

Paul H. Stuart is a professor in the Robert Stempel College of Public Health and Social Work at Florida International University, where he also serves as Director of the School of Social Work and Coordinator of the Ph.D. Program in Social Welfare. A specialist in social welfare history, he is a former president of the Social Welfare History Group and a former Chairperson of the Group for the Advancement of Doctoral Education, an organization of social work doctoral programs in the United States and Canada. He is co-editor of the *Encyclopedia of Social Welfare History in North America* (Sage Publications 2005) and of books and articles on Indian-white relations, settlement houses, and the history of the social work profession.

Nurith Zmora is a professor of history at Hamline University and the author of *Orphanages Reconsidered: Child Care Institutions in Progressive Era Baltimore* (Temple University Press, 1994). She is currently working on a history of foster care in the United States. In the past six years, she directed a project in which Israeli, Palestinian, Jordanian, and Lebanese high school teachers, with the assistance of Hamline professors, wrote a textbook in civic education for high school students and piloted it in the region. The project aims at bringing reconciliation through education to the Middle East.

Notes

Preface

1. See Gingrich (1994). Representative Gingrich's orphanage proposal became embedded in the Personal Responsibility Act of 1995 (H.R. 4. 1995). The Act allowed states to use any savings from reducing teen pregnancy and unmarried teens' welfare benefits to set up orphanages. The Republican sponsors of the bill eventually replaced the word "orphanage" with "group facilities" in the Personal Responsibility Act of 1995, most likely because of the stinging criticisms heard in the orphanage debate of 1994. According to the Congressional Research Service, however, "nothing in H.R. 4, as passed by the House, would limit the ability of the states to use [welfare] funds to support foster children in residential or group facilities, which are the modern equivalent of orphanages" (Spar 1995).

2. For academic reviews of journalistic reports on the orphanage issue, see Fineman (1995) and London (1998).

3. See, for example, *Newsweek*'s cover and story on orphanages in late 1994 (Morganthau 1994).

4. Goodman (1994).

5. As quoted in Purdum (1994).

6. Dean of Columbia University's School of Social Work Ronald Feldman's exact words in 1994 were, "Children raised in custodial care [i.e., orphanages] are more likely to have serious problems adjusting to society when they leave. Children reared in supportive, family-like environments [i.e., foster care] will become better adults, parents, and taxpayers—all things that Mr. Gingrich says we want" (Feldman 1994). Given the problems with the foster care system, which have received continual media attention since 1994, we must wonder if the choice Dean Feldman suggested in

1994 was not a false one. Mary Ford and Joe Kroll, writing for the North American Council on Adoptable Children during the orphanage debate, also found in their review of the historical and child welfare literature nothing but negative outcomes from orphanage care: "Institutionalized children are denied the opportunity to form a consistent relationship with a caregiver in their early years and are at serious risk for developmental problems and long-term personal disorders....Many insecurely institutionalized children lack empathy, seek behavior in negative ways, exhibit poor self-confidence, show indiscriminate affection toward adults, are prone to noncompliance, and are more aggressive than their non-institutionalized counterparts" (Ford and Kroll 1995).

7. As reported by *Washington Post* columnist Mary McGrory (1994).

8. McKenzie (1994).

9. McKenzie (1995 and 2006).

10. McKenzie (1997 and 2003). In both journal articles, I lay out the *potential* upward biases in my generally positive findings. I did, however, have a response rate in excess of 60 percent (an extraordinary response rate for a survey instrument that was nine pages long). If conventional orphanage wisdom is to be believed, I should not have been able to find anywhere near as many alumni with positive outcomes as I did.

11. McKenzie (1998).

12. *Homecoming* (2006). The film can be purchased through the sponsoring PBS station, KVIE in Sacramento, California (www.KVIE.org).

Chapter 1: Orphanages in History and the Modern Child Welfare Setting

1. Bremner 1971, vol. II, 365.

2. An Act for the Relief of the Poor 1601, V.

3. Lindert 2004.

4. Lindert 2004.

5. An Act for the Amendment and better Administration of the Laws relating to the Poor in England and Wales.

6. Rothman 1971.

7. Dix 1850.

8. Downs and Sherraden 1983.

9. Stuart 1979.

10. Pratt 1892.

11. "Outing Rules" 1907.

12. See, for example, Sanborn, 1890.

13. Rothman 1980.

14. Burson 2001.

15. Neher 1984; Sallee 2004.

16. Clopper 1921, 154.

17. Kelso 1923

18. Wolins and Piliavin 1964.

19. Mass and Engler 1959, p. iii.

20. Ferguson, Dwight H. (1961). Children in need of parents: Implications of the Child Welfare League Study. *Child Welfare 40:*1–6.

21. Ibid., 2.

22. Maas and Engler 1959.

23. Jeter 1962.

24. Wolins 1969; Wolins and Wozner 1978; Wolins, Wozner, and Slye 1980.

25. Ibid.

26. Harlow 1958 1961; Harlow and Zimmerman 1959.

27. Bowlby 1958.

28. Bowlby 1969.

29. Goldstein, Freud, and Solnit 1973; Johnson and Fein 1991.

30. Maas and Engler 1959, 1.

31. Norris and Wallace 1965.

32. Fanshel and Eugene Shinn 1978.

33. Fanshel and Shinn 1978, p. 476.

34. See Goldstein, Freud, and Solnit 1973.

35. Antler and Antler 1979; Kamerman and Kahn 1990; Kadushin and Martin 1990; and Lindsey 1994.

36. Antler and Antler 1979, 201.

37. Kempe, et al. 1962.

38. McCurdy and Daro 1993.

39. Kamerman and Kahn 1990, 7–8.

40. Pringle 1969, 5.

41. Wolins and Piliavin 1964.

42. Maas and Engler 1959.

43. Kamerman and Kahn 1990, 121.

44. Lindsey 1994, 13.

45. Kamerman and Kahn 1990.

46. Thurston 1930, as quoted by Kadushin and Martin 1990, 348.

47. Bliss 1905.

Chapter 2: The Early History of Orphanages

1. Miller 1994, 83–104.
2. Miller 2003, 182–88.
3. Miller 2003, 223–41.
4. Jolowicz 1947, 82–90.
5. Nani 1943–44, 60–63.
6. Miller 2003, 24–25.
7. Cohn 1919–20, 435–37.
8. Josephus 1968, 2:369.
9. *Shepherd* 2003, 192–93.
10. *Didascalia* 1905, 218–19.
11. Sokrates 1995, 137–38.
12. Basil 1857–66, 951–58.
13. Basil 1961, 4:390.
14. Miller 2003, 116–17.
15. Dagron 1970, 229–76.
16. Miller 1997, 74–88..
17. Miller 2003, 268–74.
18. Gregory 1971, 232–33.
19. *Vita Euthymii* 1939, 8–11, 32.
20. *Vita Clementis* 1857–66, 815–25.
21. *Vita Petri* 1888, 1–17.
22. Apokaukos 1971–72, 85–86, 150–52.
23. Apokaukos 1971–72, 151.
24. Apokaukos 1971–72, 151.
25. "The symbol of education is the rod." Byzantine writers attributed this saying to Philo of Alexandria, the famous Jewish philosopher and biblical scholar. This saying was included in a collection of standard expressions supposedly assembled by Leontios of Byzantium. See PG [86 (part 2): 2073–74].
26. Komnena 1937–45, 3:217–18.
27. Zachariah 1899, 80.
28. *De cerimoniis* 1935–39, 1:140, 153, 69.
29. *Kletorologion* 1972, 186–87.
30. *Vita Antonii* 1907, 211–12.
31. Miller 2003, 214–18.

32. Patala 1996, 512–30.
33. Apokaukos 1971–72, 151–52.
34. Komnena 1937–45, 3:217–18.
35. Miller 2003, 227–32.
36. Miller 2003, 228–29, 243–45.
37. Theodore 1992, 333–34.
38. Boswell 1988, 228–55.
39. Boswell 1988, passim.
40. Miller 1978, 709.
41. Kedar 1999, 24–26.
42. Miller 1978, 720.
43. Luttrell 1994, 77.
44. Hunecke 1992, 123–53.
45. Gregory 1971, 232–33.
46. Hunecke 1992, 131.
47. Schiavoni 1991, 1031–38.
48. Porter 1997, 174.
49. Corsini 1991, 93.
50. Di Giacomo 1928, passim.
51. Pincherle 1957, 15–38.

Chapter 3: Christian Charity and the Politics of Orphan Care in the Dutch Republic

1. Temple 1932, 104.
2. van der Vlis 2002, 18–19.
3. van Leeuwen 1994, 589.
4. van Leeuwen 1982, 119.
5. Bossy 1985, 144.
6. Geremek 1994, 25.
7. McCants 1997 and 2007, and van der Vlis 2002.
8. Kossmann 1992, 31.
9. 't Hart 1993, 150.
10. Rowen 1990, 107.
11. Rowen 1990, 126.
12. This struggle for power between the House of Orange
and the Regent (mercantile) oligarchs of the urban western
provinces in particular played out on the charitable arena
as well. Linda Stone-Ferrier, a seventeenth century Dutch
art historian, has done some very interesting work on the
pictorial representations of charity and the patrons of charitable

institutions. She finds that there were significant differences in the representational strategies of those who support Regent-dominated charity versus those who saw the House of Orange as the true protector of the weak and disenfranchised. Indeed, for the latter, the merchant elite was a far cry from being the body that could offer protection to widows and orphans. To the contrary, it was from their avarice that widows and orphans most needed protection (Stone-Ferrier 2000, 233).

13. Kalff does not report the year of this citation. It appears to date from the early seventeenth century. The Regents of the *Burgerweeshuis* presented this request on account of the overcrowding in the orphanage, which would be consistent with such a date. The institution saw its peak occupancy rates in the decade of the late 1620s and 1630s and again in the third quarter of the seventeenth century (McCants 1997, Appendix A, quoted in Kalff 1899, 6).

14. quoted in Dankers 1991, 14.

15. quoted in Dankers 1991, 51.

16. All of the summary information about the standard of care in the Amsterdam Municipal Orphanage is taken from McCants 1997.

17. McCants 1992, 84–87.

18. McCants 1995, 204.

19. McCants 1995, 205.

20. McCants 1997, 64–69.

21. McCants 1997, 194.

22. McCants 1997, 195.

Chapter 4: Mooseheart

1. U.S. President's Research Committee on Social Trends 1933, 935; U.S. Department of Commerce, 1975, 21; Beito 2000, 14.

2. U.S. Department of Commerce, Bureau of the Census 1913, 44, 63–125; Areson and Hopkirk 1925, 87.

3. U.S. Department of Commerce, Bureau of the Census 1910, 44.

4. U.S. Department of Commerce, Bureau of the Census 1933, 63–125.

5. Olivier 1952, 48–51.

6. Loyal Order of Moose 1912, 27, 57, 59; Olivier 1952, 118–19.

7. Olivier 1952, 48–51.

8. Fuller 1918, 15–17; Davis 1922, 246–47.

9. Olivier 1952, 122.

10. Olivier 1952, 137.

11. Olivier 1952, 135–36; Mooseheart necessities, *Mooseheart Magazine* 1919, 1.

12. New Arrivals, *Mooseheart Weekly* 1919, 2.

13. Hart to Ford, 7 May 1923, Hart Papers.

14. Olivier 1948, 32. Before 1915, the Board of Governors had admitted a few elderly members to Mooseheart, but the experiment did not work. In 1922, the Supreme Lodge opened a separate old folks' home in Orange Park, Florida. Olivier 1952, 175–79. Dubbed Moosehaven, it had 203 residents by 1930 (twenty-nine women and 174 men). Loyal Order of Moose, *Proceedings* 1930, 292.

15. Mooseheart, *Mooseheart Magazine* 1923, 1; Binder 1934, 30; Loyal Order of Moose, *Mooseheart Year Book* 1919–1920, 47, 150; Reymert and Hinton 1940, 258; What we find at Mooseheart: The school that trains for life, *Mooseheart Weekly* 1919, 1.

16. Davis, 1922, 249–50; Reymert 1941, 88; Binder 1934, 153; Loyal Order of Moose, *Mooseheart Year Book* 1918–1919, 134; Mooseheart, Superintendent, Report, 12 January 1923, Hart Papers.

17. Olivier 1952, 78.

18. *Mooseheart High School Senior's Book* 1925, 112.

19. From the Philadelphia Record, *Mooseheart Magazine* 1920, 15.

20. Reymert to Spearman, 4 November 1930, Reymert papers.

21. Reymert 1941, 80–81, 92–95; Stumpf 1996.

22. Loyal Order of Moose, *Mooseheart Year Book* 1918–1919, 38–40.

23. An Achievement of the Common Man, *Moose Docket* 1932, 47.

24. Meister 1996.

25. Deardoff 1924, 47.

26. Loyal Order of Moose, *Mooseheart Year Book* 1918–19, 22.

27. Holloran 1989, 171; Friedman 1994, 162–63; Zmora 1994, 69.

28. Mooseheart, Board of Governors: Correspondence and Reports 1922–1924, Folders 1–2, Box 14, Hart Papers.

29. Loyal Order of Moose, *Proceedings* 1930, 13.

30. Loyal Order of Moose, *Mooseheart Year Book* 1918–1919, 21.

31. Mooseheart, Board of Governors: Correspondence and Reports, 1922–1924, Folder 1 and 2, Box 14, Hart Papers.

32. Loyal Order of Moose, *Mooseheart Year Book* 1918–1919, 21.

33. Mooseheart, Board of Governors: Correspondence and Reports 1922–1924, Folder 1 and 2, Box 14, Hart Papers; Koepp 1996.

34. Loyal Order of Moose, *Mooseheart Year Book* 1918–1919, 21; Mooseheart, Superintendent, Report 29 March 1924, Hart Papers.

35. Loyal Order of Moose, *Proceedings* 1929, 21.

36. Loyal Order of Moose, *Proceedings* 1947, 247; Cottingham 1996; Meister 1996; Kelly 1996; Koepp 1996.

37. Binder 1934, 151; Deardorff 1924, 47.

38. Reymert 1941, 83; Meister 1996; Stumpf 1996.

39. Deardorff 1924, 47.

40. Hart to Davis, 19 September 1924, Hart Papers.

41. Loyal Order of Moose, *Minutes* 1925, 15.

42. Loyal Order of Moose, *Minutes* 1925, 15, 93–95.

43. Olivier 1952, 79–80.

44. "Impressive Figures With Which Every Lodge Officer Should Be Familiar," *Moose Docket* 1932, 85; Loyal Order of Moose, *Proceedings* 1929, 21, 240.

45. Henning, "First, learn all the facts, then if you must—criticize," *Moose Docket* 1933, 65–66. Complete information is not available for mothers' pensions in California and New Jersey. U.S. Department of Labor, Children's Bureau 1933, 8–9, 28–29.

46. Olivier 1952, 79–80

47. Strengthen the Degree Staff, *Moose Docket* 1932, 32.

48. Loyal Order of Moose, *Proceedings* 1930, 13.

49. Olivier 1952, 233–36; Loyal Order of Moose, *Proceedings* 1929, 285–89.

50. Zmora 1994, 16.

51. The Loyal Order of Moose, *Minutes* 1925, 209A; Loyal Order of Moose, *Mooseheart Year Book* 1919–1920, 29; Loyal Order of Moose, *Proceedings* 1931, 289.

52. Harvison 1920, 11.

53. Loyal Order of Moose, *Mooseheart Year Book* 1919–1920, 31, 42–43; Loyal Order of Moose, *Minutes* 1925, 212A.

54. Kelly 1996; Reymert 1941, 76–77, 83.

55. Reymert 1941, 76; Binder 1934, 30.

56. Baylor 22 October 1923, Hart Papers; Koepp 1996.

57. Loyal Order of Moose, *Mooseheart Year Book* 1919–1920, 42, 46; Loyal Order of Moose, *Minutes* 1925, 212A.

58. Cottingham 1996; Kelly 1996.

59. Reymert 1941, 76.

60. Cottingham 1996; Stumpf 1996; Smejkal 1996.

61. Cottingham 1996.

62. Mooseheart, Superintendent, Report, 15 December 1922, Hart Papers.

63. Mooseheart, Superintendent, Report, 15 December 1922, Hart Papers; Morlock 1996; Cottingham 1996.

64. Adams 17 December 1921, 2.

65. Cottingham 1996; Kelly 1996; Smejkal 1996; Meister 1996.

66. Reymert and Hinton 1940, 257.

67. Burch 1996.

68. Morlock 1996.

69. Morlock 1996; Meister 1996.

70. Burch 1996.

71. Loyal Order of Moose, *Proceedings* 1932, 88–92; Whitcomb 1949, 23–24; Reymert 1938, 288–94; Olivier 1952, 139–50.

72. Meister 1996; Burch 1996; Kelly 1996.

73. Cottingham 1996.

74. Smejkal 1996.

75. Cottingham 1996.

76. Merryweather 1932, 398, 400–4; Kasser 1945, 131–36.

77. Burch 1996.

78. Meister 1996; Kelly 1996.

79. Binder 1934, 151; Mooseheart, Board of Governors, Minutes, 15 December 1923, Hart Papers.

80. Burch 1996; Meister 1996; Kelly 1996; Koepp 1996.

81. Mooseheart, Superintendent, Report, 29 March 1924, Hart Papers.

82. Mooseheart, Superintendent, Report, 29 March 1924; Meister 1996; Koepp 1996.

83. Mooseheart, Superintendent, Report, 29 March 1924; Meister 1996; Koepp 1996; Kelly 1996.

84. Koepp 1996; Burch 1996.

85. Adams 17 December 1921, 2; Loyal Order of Moose, *Minutes* 1925, 209A.

86. Binder 1934, 30; Chapple 1928, 237.

87. Fuller 1918, 55.

88. Binder 1934, 152; Adams 17 December 1921, 2.

89. Mooseheart, Superintendent, Progress Report, 23 January 1934, Hart Papers; Binder 1932, 856–57; *Mooseheart High School Seniors Book* 1925, 68, 76, 84, 88; Burch 1996; Meister 1996; Loyal Order of Moose, *Mooseheart Year Book* 1919–1920, 86.

90. Loyal Order of Moose, *Proceedings* 1934, 191.

91. Loyal Order of Moose, *Proceedings* 1940, 90–91; Loyal Order of Moose, *Proceedings* 1941, 258.

92. *Mooseheart High School Seniors Book* 1925, 134, 172, 178, 195.

93. Loyal Order of Moose, *Proceedings* 1932, 57; Rolfe and Wehrmeister 1992, 16–17.

94. Mooseheart, Board of Governors, *Minutes,* 29–30 March 1924, Hart Papers; Mooseheart, Superintendent, Report, 20 July 1924; Mooseheart, Board of Governors, *Minutes,* 27 July 1924, Hart Papers.

95. Kelly 1996; Morlock 1996.

96. Fuller 1918, 53; Reymert 1941, 91.

97. Mooseheart, Superintendent, Report 20 July 1924.

98. Cottingham 1996; Morlock 1996; Meister 1996; Stumpf 1996; Binder 1935, 322; Reymert 1941, 91.

99. Burch 1996; Smejkal 1996; Cottingham 1996; Meister 1996; Reymert 1941, 78–79.

100. Olivier 1948, 42.

101. Cottingham 1996.

102. Binder 1932, 855; Burch 1996; Smejkal 1996.

103. Mooseheart, Superintendent, Report 19 May 1923, Hart Papers.

104. Burch 1996.

105. Loyal Order of Moose, *Minutes* (1925), 219A.

106. Loyal Order of Moose, *Minutes* (1915), 65.

107. Olivier 1952, 152–58; *Mooseheart High School Seniors Book* 1925, 92; Protestant church services started at Mooseheart, *Mooseheart Weekly* 2 May 1919, 9.

108. Olivier 1952, 160–61; *Mooseheart Annual* 1930, 80.

109. Loyal Order of Moose, *Minutes* 1925, 218A.

110. Mooseheart, Superintendent, Report, 15 March 1923, 19 May 1923, Hart Papers.

111. Mooseheart, Board of Governors, Action Taken on the Superintendent's Docket by Executive Committee February 14–15, 1923, Hart Papers.

112. Holl 1971; Ashby 1984, 133–69.

113. Loyal Order of Moose, *Minutes* 1925, 214A-216A, 220A; Binder 1932, 856; Loyal Order of Moose, *Mooseheart Year Book* 1918–1919, 134.

114. Mooseheart, Superintendent, Report, 15 March 1923; Rules and regulations for use of savings fund, *Mooseheart Weekly* 1919, 3; Loyal Order of Moose, *Mooseheart Year Book* 1919–1920, 66–67.

115. Cottingham 1996.

116. Loyal Order of Moose, *Mooseheart Year Book* 1919–1920, 67.

117. "Self-sacrifice," *Mooseheart Weekly* September 4, 1920, 4.

118. About Mooseheart and the Loyal Order of Moose, *Mooseheart Magazine* June 1916, 8.

119. Kelly 1996.

120. Loyal Order of Moose, *Mooseheart Year Book* 1919–1920, 55–59.

121. Adams to Hart, 16 November 1923, Box 14, Hart Papers.

122. Loyal Order of Moose, *Mooseheart Year Book* 1919–1920, 59–60.

123. Merryweather 1932, 400; Meister 1996; Burch 1996; Hart to Adams, 1 October 1924, Hart Papers.

124. Havlik to Adams, 7 August 1922, Hart Papers.

125. Smejkal 1996.

126. Loyal Order of Moose, *Mooseheart Year Book* 1918–1919, 122–23; Mooseheart, Superintendent, Report, 15 March 1923.

127. Cottingham 1996.

128. Mooseheart, Superintendent, Report, 15 March 1923; Loyal Order of Moose, *Mooseheart Year Book* 1918–1919, 122–23.

129. Smejkal 1996; Meister 1996; Stumpf 1996.

130. Hart to Ford, 8 December 1923, Adams to Hart, 17 September 1924, Hart to Adams, 1 October 1924, Hart Papers.

131. Hart to Adams, 1 October 1924, Hart Papers.

132. New conduct rating plan for all halls now in effect, *Mooseheart Weekly* 31 July 1931, 1; Loyal Order of Moose, *Proceedings* 1930, 284.

133. Mooseheart Governors, Minutes 1922–1924, Hart Papers.

134. Burch 1996; Kelly 1996.

135. Smith 1995, 138.

136. Cottingham 1996; Kelly 1996; Burch 1996; Morlock 1996; Smejkal 1996; Stumpf 1996; Meister 1996. The publications of the Loyal Order of Moose also carried ads listing the job skills of individual graduates ("When a Feller Needs a Friend," *Moose Docket* 1933, 10–11). For the check-out procedure for graduates, see Superintendent, Report, 15 March 1923, Folder 2, Box 14, Hart Papers.

137. Loyal Order of Moose, *Mooseheart Year-Book and Annual* 1931, 145; Loyal Order of Moose, *Proceedings* 1931, 37–38.

138. Meister 1996.

139. Loyal Order of Moose, *Mooseheart Year-Book and Annual* 1931, 142–45; National Industrial Conference Board 1931, 6.

140. Because the median age of respondents was only twenty-two, these figures tended to understate the earnings potential of Mooseheart graduates. The source for the raw data on male and female college attendance (1929–1930 school year) is U.S. Department of the Interior, Office of Education 1935, 22 and for the numbers of Americans ages eighteen to twenty-four is U.S. Department of Commerce, Bureau of the Census 1933, 185.

141. Loyal Order of Moose, *Proceedings* 1932, 54–59; Loyal Order of Moose, *Proceedings* 1936, 190; Loyal Order of Moose, *Proceedings* 1941, 181; Olivier 1952, 87–8.

142. Mooseheart, Superintendent, Progress Report, 25 February 1933, Davis Papers; Loyal Order of Moose, *Proceedings* 1936, 58; Loyal Order of Moose, *Proceedings* 1946, 176.

143. Loyal Order of Moose, *Proceedings* 1942, 37; Olivier 1952, 92–96.

144. Giles 1934, 49; Kleemeier 1954, 347–49.

145. Loyal Order of Moose, *Proceedings* 1939, 123; Loyal Order of Moose, *Proceedings* 1942, 38; Loyal Order of Moose, *Proceedings* 1943, 256.

146. Mooseheart, the famed Moose "child city" http://www.mooseheart.org/childcity.asp (accessed 17 June 2007).

147. Reymert 1951, 4.

148. The history of Mooseheart child city and school http://www.mooseheart.org/history.asp (accessed 17 June 2007).

149. Sheets 2000, 1940.

150. Mooseheart, the famed Moose "child city" http://www.mooseheart.org/childcity.asp (accessed 17 June 2007).

151. McKenzie 1999, 103–26.

152. Beito 2000, 98–107.

153. Burch 1996; Meister 1996; Kelly 1996; Smejkal 1996; Stumpf 1996; Koepp 1996; Morlock 1996.

Chapter 5: A Home of Another Kind

1. For a parallel analysis that looks at the rise of private think tanks in Washington, D.C., during the 1960s and 1970s as, in part, a means of interpreting waves of statistical information that float through that city, see Ricci 1993.

2. The earliest accounts of the origin of the Half-Orphan Asylum date from the late 1880s. They differ on specifics. Some claim that the institution was started by Mrs. Samuel Howe in the winter of 1859, others say that Howe, Miss Catherine West, and Mrs. Elizabeth Blakie started the nursery in the spring of 1860. *Chicago Tribune*, 21 April 1857.

3. Chapin Hall Collection 1868.

4. Bremner 1980.

5. For the best discussions of nineteenth-century environmentalism as applied to child welfare, see Brenzel 1983.

6. Bremner 1970.

7. Bremner 1971.

8. Houghteling Reynolds.

9. Palmer 1932.

10. *Chicago Nursery Annual Report, 1869*, 10–12.

11. From the ragged school on the sands, the asylum moved to 151 North Market Street in the fall of 1860. The next spring, "owing to the increase in applicants," the institution moved to a home on Ohio Street. In 1862, a large building on Michigan and Pine was rented. Finally, in 1865, another house, on Wisconsin and Clark, was rented. This remained the home of the asylum until 1871. *Chicago Nursery Annual Report, 1869*, 10.

12. The length of stay could be determined for 521 children between 1865 and 1890. The averages do not change appreciably in those twenty-five years.

Length of stay in asylum, 1865–90

Time in months	N Children	%
Under 3	201	38.6
3–6	99	19.0
6–9	55	10.6
9–12	24	4.6
15–18	18	3.5
18–21	9	1.7
21–24	8	1.5
Over 24	75	14.4

Chapin Hall Collection, Box 11, Folder 1.

13. *Chicago Tribune*, 5 August 1883.

14. *Chicago Nursery Annual Report, 1874*, 5.

15. To take some obvious examples, the working poor are least likely to have health insurance but are ineligible for Medicaid. And the absence of a coherent family policy means that the unemployed are eligible for AFDC but the working poor are not.

16. *Lakeside Annual Directory*, 1885, 1900, 1910.

17. *Chicago Nursery Annual Report, 1891*, 53–55.

18. Most general histories of welfare acknowledge in some way the persistence of pre-progressive habits in the delivery of welfare services after 1890. But because these histories are organized around national leaders and new public policy instead of how services were actually delivered, they have not demonstrated that tensions between the old and new were central to progressive-era welfare. Most historians simply portray a progressive elite ousting a Victorian elite. I offer instead the image of progressives as a "counter-establishment." Before historians think about the failures of progressives, they might ponder how long and trying a task it was for progressives to take control of urban welfare systems. With this in mind, looking at a conservative institution like the Half-Orphan Asylum is particularly instructive, as it affords us a hint of just how strong the established charities were and how they interacted with the new reformers. Standard histories of American welfare that paint a picture of a progressive takeover after 1890 include: Leiby 1978, 136–62; Katz 1986, 113–45; Tiffin 1982; Ashby 1984.

19. Katz 1986, 118–21; Leiby 1978, 144–46,150–51; Platt 1977, 61–66.

20. Skocpol 1992, 424–79.

21. Addams 1902, 13–70.

22. *Chicago Nursery Annual Report, 1916*, 28–29; Richmond 1930, 43.

23. Pierce 3: 320–23.

24. Palmer 1932, 85–86; *Chicago Nursery Annual Report, 1910*, 13. The same report states of the lower north district: "Here is the problem of congestion in the highest degree known to Chicago. . . . There is unusual need of prompt giving in food, fuel, and medical care."

25. Chapin Hall, Minutes of Meetings of the Board of Managers, Meetings of 4 May 1897; 15 February 1898; 2 January 1900; 16 October 1900.

26. *Chicago Nursery Annual Report, 1906*, 19; *Chicago Nursery Annual Report, 1908*, 21; *Chicago Nursery Annual Report, 1910*, 22.

27. *Chicago Nursery Annual Report, 1899*, 20; *Chicago Nursery Annual Report, 1905*, 18.

28. *Chicago Nursery Annual Report, 1911*, 19.

29. To be precise, between 1910 and 1916, the number of children averaged 142 and the number of staff people living in the building averaged twenty-six. The figures are taken from Chapin Hall's annual reports.

30. Henderson 1908, 109.

31. Good citizenship was a common progressive theme. For examples of how Chicago progressives applied this theme to child welfare, see the essays published by the Chicago School of Civics and Philanthropy, 1912.

32. Dunn 1912. Dunn and her brother, William Dunn, were prominent crusaders against the court. This pamphlet is filled with stories about greedy social workers, bad judicial decisions, the collapse of legal rights of both children and parents, and examples of how the court wantonly made children wards of the state.

33. For the story of how the Chicago Erring Women's Refuge was changed by becoming dependent on the city for admissions, see Linehan 1991, 76–94.

34. Chapin Hall, Minutes of Meetings of the Board of Managers, Meetings of 15 February 1898; 17 July 1898; 6 May 1902; 25 March 1903; 25 March 1904; 25 March 1905.

35. Chapin Hall, Minutes of Meetings of the Board of Managers, Meetings of 18 June 1901; 2 July 1901; 19 May 1903, 1 November 1904.

36. Martin 1906.

37. *Chicago Nursery Annual Report, 1914*, 20–21; *Chicago Nursery Annual Report, 1915*, 20.

38. The women realized that the Half-Orphan Asylum was not as well-known as it had been twenty years prior, but they did little to changes the situation. In 1904, for example, the annual report noted that the long-standing policy of no public entertainments had "kept us from being well-known in the community." *Chicago Nursery Annual Report, 1904*, 18. Public entertainments were ended in 1880 because they raised no substantial funding. By 1904, the managers saw such events not in terms of the income they would bring in directly but in terms of the publicity they would generate. The managers did nothing to follow up on this in these years, but the thought laid the groundwork for the annual fashion shows that began after World War II.

39. Green 1914. Chapin Hall, Minutes of Meetings of the Board of Managers, 27 September 1915.

40. *Chicago Nursery Annual Report, 1913*, 21; *Special Report, 1913*, 16–17.

41. *Chicago Nursery Annual Report, 1918*, 12.

42. *Chicago Nursery Annual Report, 1925*, 24.

43. Tyson 1925, 27–28.

44. Niemeyer.

45. Chapin Hall, Minutes of Meetings of the Board of Managers, Meeting of October 1, 1929.

46. Chapin Hall, Minutes of Meetings of the Board of Managers, Meeting of September 3, 1929; *Chicago Nursery Annual Report, 1932*, 15.

47. Camp n.d.; *Seventy-Eighth Annual Report of the Chicago Home for the Friendless*, 6; Irvine n.d.; Horwich 1977, 41–44; *Caritas Christi* 1981, 813–14.

48. Devine 1935, 29.

49. McCarthy 1982, 137.

50. Chapin Hall, Minutes of Meetings of the Board of Managers, Meetings of 18 November 1924; 7 December 1926; 18 January 1927.

51. For example, in 1932, of the 132 children in the asylum,

only fifteen had been placed by the Juvenile Court. Illinois Department of Public Welfare 1931, 27.

52. Stehno 1985, 156–57.

53. Welfare Council of Metropolitan Chicago 1923.

54. Camp n.d., 98; Irvine n.d., 29; Report of St. Mary's 1941–1942–1943, 3; Fifty Years of Boy Building, 27–28; Horwich 1977, 37.

55. Chicago Council of Social Service Agencies 1930.

56. Between 1934 and 1948, the highest average number of children in the institution was 136 (in 1937) and the lowest was 126 (in 1942). Secretary's Reports, 1934–1948.

57. **Illinois Dependent Children**

Year	In Institutions	Under Foster Care
1923	11,264	2,339
1933	10,301	5,151

Children Under Institutional Care 1923, 18.
Children Under Institutional Care and in Foster Homes 1933, 72.

58. Between 1934 and 1936, 462 children entered Chapin Hall; 241 of them (52.1 percent) were from parents who were either divorced, separated, or deserted. Between 1946 and 1968, of the 530 children who lived in Chapin Hall, 320 (60.3 percent) came from such homes. Before 1937, illegitimate children were generally included in other categories. Yet they were accepted into Chapin Hall from the late 1920s. The 1931 annual report noted that in 1930, the Half-Orphan Asylum housed eleven children born out of wedlock. *Chicago Nursery Annual Report, 1931*, 13–14.

59. *Social Security Bulletin* 1955. In 1920 there were estimated to be 750,000 full orphans. In 1930, only 450,000, and by 1954, only 60,000.

60. *Chicago Nursery Annual Report, 1925*, 23; *Chicago Nursery Annual Report, 1926*, 13.

61. Jones 1989, 613–29.

62. In 1929, the manager Julia Thompson noted that about two-fifths of the children stayed less than a year, "proving that we are attaining our object of helping many people temporarily over hard times." In the 1879s and 1880s, however, 74 percent of children left Chapin Hall within a year. The 40 percent figure

cited by Thompson did not indicate traditional standards of temporary care as she suggested. It rather indicated just the opposite. *Chicago Nursery Annual Report, 1926*, 13; *Chicago Nursery Annual Report, 1925*, 24; *Chicago Nursery Annyal Report, 1926*, 17.

63. *Chicago Nursery Annual Report, 1920*; *Chicago Nursery Annual Report, 1924*; *Chicago Nursery Annual Report, 1928*.

64. Chapin Hall, Minutes of Meetings of the Board of Managers, Meetings of 17 February 1931; 5 May 1931; 18 April 1933; 15 October 1935.

65. Chapin Hall, Minutes of Meetings of the Board of Managers, Meeting of 2 June 1931.

66. *Chicago Nursery Annual Report, 1932*, 14.

67. Devine, 91; *Chicago Nursery Annual Report, 1933*, 17; Chapin Hall, Minutes of Meetings of the Board of Managers, Meeting of 17 November 1931; *Chicago Nursery Annual Report, 1932*, 15.

68. In 1928, donations added up to $12,451.21. By 1940, they were $7,787. *Chicago Nursery Annual Report, 1928*, 19, 24; *Chicago Nursery Annual Report, 1940*.

69. In 1928, parental board payments totaled $23,964. In 1932, they added up to $10,823.59. *Chicago Nursery Annual Report, 1929*, 19, 24; *Chicago Nursery Annual Report, 1933*, 21.

70. Secretary's Report 1935.

71. Loomis 19–20.

72. Chapin Hall, Minutes of Meetings of the Board of Managers, Meeting of 4 August 1931.

73. Chapin Hall, Minutes of Meetings of the Board of Managers, Meetings of 19 May 1931; 2 June 1931; 16 June 1931; 4 August 1931.

74. Chapin Hall, Minutes of Meetings of the Board of Managers, Meetings of 18 August 1931; 17 November 1931.

75. Chapin Hall, Minutes of Meetings of the Board of Managers, Meeting of 19 May 1931.

76. Devine, 25; *Chicago Nursery Annual Report, 1934*, 16; Chapin Hall, Minutes of Meetings of the Board of Managers, Meeting of 20 March 1934; *Chicago Nursery Annual Report, 1937*, 19.

77. Chapin Hall, Minutes of Meetings of the Board of Managers, Meeting of 3 December 1940.

78. *Chicago Nursery Annual Report, 1937*, 19.

79. Council of Social Agencies 1935.

80. Annual Report 1941; Annual Report 1948.

81. Council of Social Agencies 1937, 30.

82. Griffith 1930, 354.

83. Thompson, a leader from the Progressive Era and one of the women who led the effort to alter the direction of the asylum in the 1920s, also had her suspicions about the new professionalism. In 1923, she wrote, "In the steady pursuit of better material conditions, however, we must endeavor to emulate the truly charitable purpose which animated the labours of the early workers in this particular field." *Chicago Nursery Annual Report, 1923*, 22. After she led the battle to hire the first social worker and to have the agency keep more extensive case records, Thompson again pointed out the ambiguous nature of the gains. *Chicago Nursery Annual Report, 1929*, 16–17.

84. Goddard 1948.

85. DelliQuardi 1948. The 15 percent figure is based on the 1947 budget. The budget is attached to Goddard 1948.

86. Chapin Hall, Minutes of Meetings of the Board of Managers, Meeting of 16 August 1949.

87. Welfare Council of Metropolitan Chicago 1962, 2.

88. Polsky 1991, 179–80.

89. Headley 1974, 3; Headley 1975, 3–4; Annual Report, President of the Board of Managers.

90.Jay Buck interview, May 1987. Personal diary Buck kept of the closing years of Chapin Hall.

91. Buck 1987; Newman 1989.

92. Richman 1983.

Chapter 6: Fates of Orphans

1. John Murray is a professor of economics at the University of Toledo and co-editor of *Children bound to labor in early America* (Cornell University Press, forthcoming). This contribution has been reprinted from *The Journal of Interdisciplinary History*, XXXIII (2003), 519–545, with the permission of the editors of *The Journal of Interdisciplinary History* and The MIT Press, Cambridge, Massachusetts. © 2003 by the Massachusetts Institute of Technology and The Journal of Interdisciplinary History, Inc

2. Degler 1980; Wall 2000.

3. Demos 1970.

4. Greven.1977.

5. Smith 1977–78.

6. Main 2001.

7. Degler 1980, 73–98.

8. Cott 1977.

9. Tocqueville 2000, 558–567.

10. Johnson and Roark 1984; Wikramanayake 1973.

11. Schwartz 2000.

12. Lewis 1983, Censer 1984, Jabour 1998, Glover 2000.

13. Glover 2000.

14. Weir 1997, 235, quoting Bernard Bailyn.

15. Cecil-Fronsman 1992.

16. Bolton 1994, 1.

17. Lebsock 1984.

18. Bylaws 1861.

19. Rutman and Rutman 1994, 195.

20. Censer 1984, 20.

21. Murray and Herndon 2002.

22. Whitman, forthcoming.

23. Murray, forthcoming.

24. Fraser 1989, 235.

25. Charleston City Council 1861, 10.

26. *Minutes*, 26 January 1797.

27. Charleston City Council 1861, 8.

28. *Minutes*, 7 August 1809.

29. Murray 2004.

30. Weir 1969.

31. Houer to Commissioners, 6 January 1859, "Rejected Indentures"; Hunter to Commissioners, 18 October 1843, "Indentures"; *Minutes*, 7 November 1803, 20 June 1805.

32. House painting: *Minutes*, 30 June 1808 and indenture of Charles Reyer, "Indenture Book"; Moles to Commissioners, 7 January 1815, "Indentures"; one of many examples of rejected applications by apothecaries: *Minutes*, 27 September 1800, 9 May 1793, 4 October 1832.

33. J.R. Cook to Commissioners, 5 May 1859, "Indentures"; David, Samuel, and William Cook, "Indenture Book."

34. Murray, forthcoming.

35. *Minutes*, 28 February 1805, 1 and 9 November 1832.

36. Hamilton 1995, 556.

37. *Minutes*, 14 December 1794, 26 June 1817.

38. DeBow 1854.

39. Steckel 1986.

40. Waring 1964, 260–263.

41. Fraser 1989, 189–190, 217; "Report of Steward and Physician, 1809–1816," "Report of Steward and Physician, 1823–1830," and "Annual Report of the Physician, 1829–1853"; *Minutes*, 20 March 1806.

42. Adams, "Indenture Book."

43. Hacsi 1997, 129–133.

44. Hacsi 1997.

45. Courtney and Wong 1996; Vogel 1999.

46. Courtney and Wong 1996.

47. Murray 2004; Beckham to Commissioners, 19 May 1852, "Indentures."

48. Murray 1997.

49. Lockridge 1974, 33–34; Graff 1987, 381–390.

50. Becker 1975, 9.

51. Aram and Levin 2001; Murray 1997.

52. Courtney and Wong .1996.

Chapter 7: The Transformation of Catholic Orphanages

1. Gavin 1962, 1–3; Brown and McKeown 1997, 3.

2. Oates 1995, 20, 29.

3. O'Grady 1930, 71; Hacsi, 1997, 52–53.

4. O'Grady 1930, 77–82, 100, 157–159.

5. McTighe 1994, 17.

6. City of Cleveland 1856, 45.

7. O'Grady 1930, 73.

8. Houck 1903, 740–742.

9. Gavin 1955, 1–55.

10. Hacsi 1997, 143.

11. St. Vincent's Asylum1853–1881; Stanislaus, 40; St. Joseph's Admissions Book 1894–1942.

12. St. Joseph's Admissions 1868–1883.

13. Stanislaus, 40.

14. Religious Community Questionnaire; Stanislaus, 36.

15. Stanislaus, 35.

16. Stanislaus, 110.

17. Hynes 1953, 167.

18. Hynes 1953, 222; Houck 1903, 740, 744.

19. Marks 1973, 39; Crenson 1998, 72.

20. The Home 1898, 364; Crenson 1998, 206–208.

21. Gavin 1962, 1–3.

22. Gavin 1962, 105; Standards 1919, 170.

23. Care of Dependent Children 1910, 290, 292; Adjourned Meeting 1912, 245, 248.

24. Catholic Child-Caring 1923, 207.

25. Care of Dependent Children 1910, 291; Policy and Practice 1916, 171–180; The Future 1922, 145.

26. O'Grady 1930, 153, 158–159; O'Grady 1923, 141.

27. U.S. Bureau of the Census 1927, 107.

28. Brown and McKeown 1997, 6, 51–52; Oates 1995, 92–100.

29. Horstmann, 1901.

30. Orphans Fair Report; Hynes 1953, 279.

31. The Cleveland Community 1925, 25.

32. Sheete, 1927, 11.

33. Sheete 1927, 45–50.

34. Catholic Charities 1922, 242.

35. A New Cottage-Plan Institution 1922, 235.

36. O'Grady 1928, 175.

37. Cooper 1931, 498.

38. U.S. Bureau of the Census 1935, 4; Jones 1989, 627.

39. In Children's Agencies 1931, 154–155; Child Care Today 1933, 319; The Appeal 1934, 5

40. Present Problems 1928 .

41. Analysis of Financial Status.

42. Parmadale Financial Report, 1925–1934; Minutes, Advisory Board, 1933.

43. St. Joseph's Orphanage, 1933–1945; Cox, 1936.

44. Minutes, Advisory Board, 1934.

45. Report of the Study, 1933–45.

46. Shehan, 1943, 62–63.

47. Report of the Committee 1942.

48. Revitalizing St. Joseph 1933–45; Religious Community Questionnaire.

49. Type and Capacity 1947.

50. A Continuing Ideological 1946, 113; McGovern 1947, 121–125; McGovern, 1946, 177–179.

51. O'Grady 1941, 41–42.

52. Marstello 1955, 8–10.

53. Gavin 1962, 42.

54. Oates 1995, 20, 87.

55. In Praise of Institutions 1951, 84–85.

56. Kasprowicz 1965, 4–9; Casal l967, 11-12.

57. Beatrice, 1951.

58. Parmadale Reports 1947.

59. Child Welfare Division, 1950–1955.

60. Children Under Care, 1925–1950.

61. Minutes 1951; Minutes 1958.

62. Cuyahoga County Commissioners 1962.

63. Annual Reports 1955–1966; Program Inventory.

64. Minutes 1966; Residential Care Review 1968.

65. Dolan 1992, 437–438.

66. Closing 1967, 3.

67. Advisory Board 1970; Advisory Board 1969.

68. Dunkin 1972, 9.

69. Turner 1977, 1253.

70. Parmadale Cost Per Diem 1961; Self- Study Reports 1973–1975.

71. State of the Village 1981.

72. Comparative Study, 1967–1974.

73. State of the Village 1983.

74. Summary 1985–1986.

75. State of the Village, 1981; Statistical Update, 1985; State of the Village, 1983; Program Beneficiary, 1984–1985.

76. Brown and McKeown 1997, 9, 195.

77. Catholic Identity 1986, 10–13.

78. Program Diversification 1988, 18–29; Catholic Residential 1988, 4.

79. Summary of Service-Area, 1985.

80. Parmadale Board of Trustees 1991.

81. Parmadale Brochure, no date.

82. Woll 1996.

83. McKeown,1997, 242.

Chapter 8: Baltimore's Nineteenth-Century Orphanages

1. Cooks 1984, 156–162.

2. Other methods of caring for dependent children were placing them out in families or supporting them at home.

3. Franch 1984, Table 15.

4. Some of the orphanages merged with others or disappeared like the Dolan's Farm School for Boys founded in 1849. Department of Commerce, U.S. Bureau of the Census 1914, 108–109.

5. Blum 1910, 20.

6. Jewish Family and Children's Bureau 1956.

7. Aaronsohn 1946, 13; Levin 1960, 7 and 352; Matters 1874, 4; Howard 1889, 621.

8. B. 1988.

9. Aaronsohn 1973, 212; The Hebrew Orphan Asylum Minute Book, 1911–1916, 5.

10. Rayner 1873, 6 and 9.

11. Rayner 1873, 9.

12. Rayner 1873, 10–12.

13. Ashby 1984, 7; and Brenzel 1983, 137.

14. The collective description is based on biographies of these individuals. Blum 1910; 165, 169, 187, 237, 270, 407. Some are described in detail and some appear in the list of members of various social clubs and philanthropic organizations.

15. Blum 1910, 99, 165, 169, 187, 237, 270; Aaronsohn 1973, 23.

16. Blum 1910, 153, 203, 211, 253 (doctors), 261 (lawyers). A good example of this trend is Abraham Cohen, a graduate of the City College and a Ph.D. in mathematics from Johns Hopkins University, who became a professor of Mathematics at Johns Hopkins University and served on the Board of the HOA from 1898 (Blum 1910, 149).

17. For the standard of education in the orphanage during the 1870s, see Zmora (1988, 452–475). The standard of education in the HOA during the 1900s is discussed in Zmora (1994, chap. 4).

18. For example, returning children home or making decisions about their schooling. See the Superintendent's Reports 1893–1905, 26.

19. *The Jewish Comment* 1910, 1–2.

20. "All in A Happy House" 1894, 74.

21. In 1882 there were fifty-eight children in the HOA, seventy-eight in 1907, and ninety-two in 1909 (*The Eleventh Annual Report of the Hebrew Orphan Asylum.* 1883). For Freudenthal's suggestions for improvement see *S.R. (H.O.A.) 1893–1905*, 24, 83, 102.

22. *The Hebrew Orphan Asylum Minute Book,* 23 March 1911, 4; Aaronsohn 1973, 22, 27; a telephone interview with

Dr. Milton Reizenstein's son, Dr. Milton Reizenstein, 26 May 1988.

23. *The Hebrew Orphan Asylum Minute Book*, 16 April 1911, 5.

24. In 1908, the Federated Jewish Charities was established. It organized all charity organization of the German Jews in Baltimore under one roof.

25. Jeanette Rosner Wolman, interview with author, 22 June 1988.

26. Sharlitt 1959, 29–93.

27. Bess Hammet, the last secretary of the HOA, telephone interview with author, 15 March 1984.

28. Meginnis 1987, 12–18.

29. Burgess and Smoot 1973, 43, 111. .

30. Allan 1883, 7–25. The reference RG-S.R.S. is to the Samuel Ready School Collection in the Langsdale Library Special Collections in the University of Baltimore.

31. Meginnis 1987, 21–22. Miss Rowe's reports to the trustees from her trips during 1886/87 are in RG-S.R.S. Box 17; Rowe to Perine and from Perine to Rowe, letters 1886–1887, Box 17.

32. In The S.R.S. Board of Trustees Minute Book, 50 (1913), the trustees report a choice of a new trustee: "Mr. Hurst nominated Mr. George W. Corner Jr. of the firm of Rouse Hempstone J. Co. and son of Mr. George W. Corner, for 33 years a trustee and for 13 years a president of the Board, to fill the vacancy." Mr. Hurst himself was a second-generation trustee since his father John E. Hurst had been on the Board before him. E. Glenn Perine was the son of David M. Perine who wrote the charter of the Samuel Ready Orphan Asylum. E. Glenn Perine served on the board from 1864 to his death in 1922. Daniel C. Gilman and Charles H. Latrobe were trustees until their deaths.

33. The Samuel Ready School viewed itself as a fine boarding school, and demanded that the children work hard to be good scholars. Children had to win reappointment for each academic year in the orphanage. The S.R.S. Board of Trustess, *Prospectus of the Samuel Ready Asylum for Female Orphans*, 3–4. RG-SRS, Box 19

34. A good example of the role of the trustees in handling the institution's finances is the 1 February 1911 meeting of the Board, at which a raise of Miss Rowe's salary was discussed. The debate was extensive, but Miss Rowe ultimately received her raise. The S.R.S. Board of Trustees Minute Book, 1–16.

35. Eulogy on "Good Father Dolan" The Apostle of the Point 1970, 25–20.

36. Dolan 1870.

37. "Young Catholic's Friend Society" 1890, 5.

38. Dolan's will specifies what kind of orphanage he wanted in the item referring to the St. Patrick's orphanage: "[S]aid boys and girls to be kept at said asylum or school until of twelve years of age and no longer, and then to have said boys and girls bound or placed in some good Catholic families." The executors of the will applied these guidelines to the Dolan Children's Aid Society (Dolan 1870).

39. *Sisters of the Holy Cross Centenary 1859–1959.*

40. Dolan Children's Aid Society Minute Book, 165.

41. Dolan Children's Aid Society Minute Book, 1–241

42. Dolan Children's Aid Society Minute Book, 142, 121.

43. "Death of Dr. Chatard" 1900.

44. Crooks 1984, 176, 228 and 229.

45. William.S. Rayner, the Director of the HOA, served as one of the managers of the House of Refuge (City Council of Baltimore 1886/180, 3). Simon I. Kemp from the Dolan Home and Joseph Friedenwald, the former president of the HOA, were both trustees of the almshouse in 1886 (City Council of Baltimore RG 16/S1, 1886/180, in Baltimore City Archives). Dr. Chatard, for example, was involved with two orphanages: St. Mary's Orphan Asylum and the Dolan Home. His wife was among the officers of St. Elizabeth Orphan Asylum. The women of most of the directors of the HOA belonged to the Hebrew Orphan Ladies Aid Society, which helped supply the HOA with clothes and linens.

46. Meginnis 1987, 17; Annual Meeting of the Trustees 1911, 1–4.

47. In the Annual Report 1911 of the Kelso Home (in the M.H.S.), the sum spent on each of the forty-three girls in the Home was approximately $200 if we take only the direct expenditures for the girls. The Hebrew Orphan Asylum spent the same amount for each child. Both institutions used the public schools, and in both institutions doctors volunteered their services.

48. "Many are the advantages enjoyed by 'Ready' girls today to which we of 1887 were strangers." A Retrospect: Impressions of Three "Old Girls,"

49. *The Ready Record* 1892, 1. "The new building" has a description of the new school buildings and the new dormitory. *The Ready Record* (1895, 1) describes the new library. Both were trustees' donations. There were more donations by the trustees and their friends later. Meginnis, 1987, 34.

50. The Dolan Children's Aid Society Minute Book, introduction.

51. St. Patrick's School was the first parochial school in the United States, which started in 1815, and was free of charge supported by contributions (*Sisters of the Holy Cross Centenary 1859–1959, St. Patrick's Girls School and Orphanage*; The Dolan Children's Aid Society Minute Book 109, 123).

52. Annual Report of the Trustees 1890.]

53. These legacies and donations were listed under "sink fund account" in the annual reports of the HOA. In 1903, the list of members and annual contributors included more than 650 members who contributed between $5 and $100.

54. The Purim organization raised money only in the first years of HOA's existence (Blum.1910, 121); Hebrew Ladies Orphan Aid Society Minute Book, 1882–1901, manuscript in the Maryland Jewish Historical Society.

55. See Baltimore City Court, Equity Docket 1907, file 7336A: Equity Docket 1923, file 14043A, are examples of legacies left for the HOA.

56. Zmora 1994, 48–69.

57. Ibid., 71–82.

58. Ibid., 82–84.

59. Ibid., 84–92.

60. Ibid., 128–160.

61. Ibid., 93–125.

62. Ibid., 161–179.

63. The view of orphanages as isolating institutions was first introduced by David J. Rothman in the path-breaking research on childcare institutions in the early nineteenth century. "The asylum and the refuge were two more bricks in the wall that Americans built to confine and reform the dangerous classes" (Rothman, 1971, 210). Timothy Hacsi (1997, 101) contends that "[t]owards the end of the nineteenth century asylums shifted from being institutions that controlled virtually all aspects of their children's lives whether for isolating or protective reasons, towards being more integrative. Some female managers em-

braced this change, while others opposed it; the same was true of male orphan asylum managers."

64. "Change was introduced slowly and unevenly, especially in the larger institutions, where remnants of the old system, with all its shortcomings, could be found until well into the twentieth century" (Friedman 1994, 71).

65. Kenneth Cmiel in his research on Chicago warned that "historians need to be more attuned to the resistance that Progressives faced in the early years of the century, certainly in Chicago through 1910" (Cmiel 1995, 63). "Asylums like the Chicago Nursery and Half-Orphan Asylum had the financial independence needed to ignore calls for reform. Most of Chicago's orphanages and industrial schools proceeded in the same way" (Cmiel 1995, 63).

66. David R. Contosa (1997, 5) describes the Carson school as continuously flexible and adaptable to community needs: "In responding to real and changing issues of urban families, Carson continued to work within the spirit of progressive reform."

67. See also Marilyn Irvin Holt (2001, 106–108). Holt describes the response of the Cherokee Council to a report that detailed deficiencies in the orphanage, and to the pleas of the superintendent for improvements. The Council dedicated large sums of money to renovate the orphanage.

Chapter 9: The Orphan Trains as an Alternative to Orphanages

1. "Orphan Train Sisters" 1988, 5.
2. Hacsi 1997, 16; Rothman 1971, 119; Holliday 1985, 122–23.
3. Letchworth 1878, 913.
4. *Annual Reports* 1854/1971, 4, 6; *First Annual Report of the Children's Mission* 1850, 9.
5. Farge and Revel 1991, 30–31.
6. Holt 1992, 41–45; Langsam 1964, 117–118.
7. Brace 1894, 158.
8. *Annual Reports* 1854/1971, 9.
9. Askeland 2006, 8.
10. *Annual Reports* 1854/1971, 9; *Children's Aid Society of New York* 1893, 39–40.
11. Brace 1873, 330.

12. *Jacksonville Journal* 1860, 3.

13. Brace 1894, 201.

14. Brace 1880/1967, 242.

15. Kidder 2001, 115.

16. Kidder 2001, 62.

17. *Salina Daily Union* 1912, 3.

18. *Aberdeen Daily American* 1914, 2.

19. Odquist 1950, 9.

20. "Orphan Train Rider in Kansas" 1994, 117–120.

21. Brace 1880/1967, 40.

22. Holt 1992, 69–71.

23. Brace 1880/1967, 249, 272.

24. *Children Aid Society of New York* 1893, 40.

25. Holt 1992, 64–66; Holt 2006, 17–29.

26. Kidder 2006, 268–269.

27. *First Annual Report of the Children's Mission* 1850, 8–9; *Ninth Annual Report of the Executive Committee* 1858, 3–5, 12, 16.

28. Holt 1992, 88–90; Rothman 1971, 214, 234–235; *New York Juvenile Asylum* 1856, 25.

29. Bremner 1980, 85–86.

30. "Report of the Commissioner of Education" 1878, 182–208.

31. Holt 2001, 97 and 120.

32. Brace 1880/1967, 242; Brace 1894, 258; Holt 1992, 99–103.

33. Holt 1992, 99–103.

34. Hirshson 1989, 5, 11; Bremner 1980, 87; Abbott 1927, 219.

35. "Plan of Work" 1890, 1, 39; Hirshson 1989, 14, 16, 36–37.

36. Holt 1992, 107–110.

37. *Ellis Co. News* 1948, 3.

38. Holt 1992, 113.

39. *White Hall Orphan's Home Society* 1907, 2.

40. Holt 1992, 116; "Children's Home of Cincinnati, Ohio" 1987, 1; White 1893, 220.

41. Kidder 2001, 91.

42. Langsam 1964, 25, 56–57.

43. Holt 1992, 137.

44. Langsam 1964, 60, 62–63.

45. Stanley Correspondence 1902.

46. "Report of Miss A. L. Hill" 1924.

47. O'Connor 2001, 177–193; Holt 1992, 125–126.

48. Kidder 2001, 175–176.

49. Holt 1992, 148–151; Holt 2006, 26; U.S. Children's Bureau Publication 1924.

50. Lundberg 1928, 435.

51. Reeder 1925, 285.

52. Hacsi 1997, 41; Pleck 1987, 79, 131.

53. *Fifty-first Annual Report* 1900, 6–8; *Children's Mission to the Children* 1925, 3; Holt 1992, 162.

54. Holt 2006, 26–27.

Chapter 10: Orphanages as a National Institution

1. Katz 1986; Gittens 1994.

2. Nasaw 1979, 44–84.

3. Cmiel 1995, 8–10; Roth 1934; Polster 1990, 4–6; Bellows 1993, 121; King 1984, 1.

4. Gittens 1994, 24–27.

5. Hacsi 1997.

6. Hacsi 1997, 89–103.

7. Hacsi 1997.

8. Cmiel 1995, 122–132.

9. Zmora 1994, 181–195.

10. Jones 1989, 624–626.

11. Crenson 1998.

12. Gittens 1994, 52–56.

13. Hacsi 1997, 53.

14. Brown and McKeown 1997, 194.

15. Skocpol 1992; Gordon 1994.

16. Zunz 1982; Cohen 1990.

17. Polster 1990, 196.

18. Hacsi 1997, 152–153.

19. Hacsi 1997, 54–68.

Bibliography for All Chapters

A Continuing Ideological Battle. 1946. *Catholic Charities Review (CCR)* 30: 113.

A New Cottage-Plan Institution. 1922. *CCR* 6: 234–236.

Aaronsohn, Michael. 1946. *Broken Lights*. Cincinnati: Johnson and Hardin p. 13.

Aaronsohn, Michael. 1973. *That the Living May Know*. Cincinnati: Johnson and Hardin, p. 212.

Abbott, Edith. 1927. "The Civil War and the Crime Wave of 1865–70." *Social Service Review* 1 (June): 219.

Aberdeen (SD) Daily American. March 4, 1914.

Adams, Matthew P. 1921. The home atmosphere at Mooseheart. Part 1. *Mooseheart Weekly*. December 10, 2–3.

Adams, Matthew P. 1921. The home atmosphere at Mooseheart. Part 2. *Mooseheart Weekly*. December 17, 1–3.

Addams, Jane. 1902. *Democracy and Social Ethics*. New York: Macmillan Co.

Adjourned Meeting of the Committee on Dependent Children. 1912. National Conference on Catholic Charities *Proceedings* 2: 245–256.

Advisory Board of Parmadale, Minutes. September 14, 1966, FCCS\CCC, Box 21, Parmadale Reports, CCDA.

Advisory Board of Parmadale, Minutes. February 12, 1969, FCCS\CCC Records, Box 21, Parmadale Reports, CCDA.

Advisory Board of Parmadale, Minutes. September 9, 1970, FCCS\CCC Records, Box 21, Parmadale Reports, CCDA.

"All in A Happy House" in the *Baltimore American*. May 20, 1894. Interview with Simon. Z., January 18, 1988.

Allan, William. 1883. *The Organization of the Samuel Ready Asylum for Female Orphans—A Letter from Col. William*

Allan, Principal of McDonogh School, To the Trustees. Baltimore. pp. 7–25. In letters 1886–1887, box 17.

An Act for the Amendment and better Administration of the Laws relating to the Poor in England and Wales. 1834. 45 George IV. The Workhouse. http://www.workhouses.org.uk/ (September 15, 2007).

An Act for the Relief of the Poor. 1601. 43 Elizabeth. The Workhouse. http://www.workhouses.org.uk/ (September 15, 2007).

Analysis of Financial Status, Children's Services, MSS 4020, container 4, folder 56, Western Reserve Historical Society (WRHS).

Annual Meeting of the Trustees, February, 1, 1911, in The S.R.S. Board of Trustees Minute Book, pp. 1–4.

Annual Report 1911 of the Kelso Home (in the M.H.S.).

Annual Report, President of the Board of Managers, vol. I.

Annual Report to the State Department of Public Welfare for the year ending Dec. 31, 1940.

Annual Report to the State Department of Public Welfare for the year ending Dec. 31, 1941.

Annual Report to the State Department of Public Welfare for the year ending Dec. 31. 1948.

Annual Report of the Trustees, December 31, 1890, RG-S.R.S. Box 17.

Annual Report of the United Charities, 1910, 13.

Annual Reports of the Children's Aid Society, Nos. 1–10, Feb. 1854–Feb. 1863. 1971. New York: Arno Press and the New York Times.

Annual Reports, Parmadale - Statistics (1955–1966 Annual Report). Richfield Archives.

Antler, Jane, and Stephen Antler. 1979. From child rescue to family protection: The evolution of the child protection movement in the United States. *Children and Youth Services Review* 1:177–204.

Apokaukos, Joannes. 1971–72. Unedierte Schriftstücke aus der Kanzlei des Joannes Apokaukos. Edited by N. A. Bees. In *Byzantinische neugriechische Jahrbücher* 21: 55–247 (pages are numbered separately from the articles in an appendix entitled "Aus dem Nachlasse von N. A. Bees"). There are no translations of these letters into English, French, or German.

Aram, Dorit and Iris Levin. 2001. Mother-child joint writing in low SES: Sociocultural factors, maternal mediation, and emergent literacy. *Cognitive Development* 16: 831–852.

Areson, C. W. and Hopkirk, H. W. 1925. Child welfare programs of churches and fraternal orders. *Annals of the American Academy of Political and Social Science* 71 (September): 85–95.

Ashby, LeRoy. 1984. *Saving the Waifs: Reformers and Dependent Children.* Philadelphia: Temple Univ. Press.

Ashby, LeRoy. 1997. *Endangered Children: Dependency, Neglect, and Abuse in American History.* New York: Twayne.

Askeland, Lori. 2006. "Informal Adoption, Apprentices, and Indentured Children in the Colonial Era, and the New Republic, 1605–1850." In *Children and Youth in Adoption, Orphanages and Foster Care: A Historical Handbook and Guide.* Edited by Lori Askeland. Westport, CT: Greenwood Press.

B., Ilene. June 28, 1988. Interview with author, and Mr. Benjamin, July 20, 1988. Interview with author (the names of the interviewees were changed to protect their identities).

Basil of Cappadocia. 1857–66. Interrogatio XV. *Regulae fusius tractatae.* Greek text in PG, 31: 951–58. English translation by W. K. Lowther Clarke. 1925. *The Ascetic Works of Saint Basil.* London: Society for Promoting Christian Knowledge.

Basil of Cappadocia. 1961. *Letters.* Edited and translated by Roy D. Deferrari and Martin R. McGuire. The Loeb Classical Library. 4 vols. Cambridge, MA: Harvard University Press.

Beatrice, Sr. Mary. Container Parmadale, Archives of the Sisters of Charity of St. Augustine, Richfield, Ohio.

Becker, Gary. 1975. *Human capital: A theoretical and empirical analysis with special reference to education.* Chicago: University of Chicago Press.

Beito, David T. 2001. *From mutual aid to the welfare state: Fraternal societies and social services, 1890–1967.* Chapel Hill: Univ. of North Carolina Press.

Bellows, Barbara L. 1993. *Benevolence Among Slaveholders: Assisting the Poor in Charleston, 1670–1860.* Baton Rouge: Louisiana State University Press, 1993.

Binder, Rudolph M. 1932. Mooseheart: A socio-pedagogical experiment. *School and Society* 35(913): 852–57.

Binder, Rudolph M. 1934. Education at Mooseheart. *Education* 55(3): 150–55.

Binder, Rudolph M. 1934. Mooseheart's aim is education for life. *Literary Digest*, July 14, 30.

Binder, Rudolph M. 1935. Mooseheart: A model community. *Sociology and Social Research* 19 (March-April): 314–23.

Bliss, H. L. 1905. Census statistics of child labor. *Journal of Political Economy 13*, 2, 245–257.

Blum, Isidor. 1910. *The Jews of Baltimore*. Baltimore: Historical review Publishing Co. p.20.

Bogen, Hyman 1992. *The Luckiest Orphans: A History of the Hebrew Orphan Asylum*. Urbana and Chicago: University of Illinois Press.

Bolton, Charles C. *Poor whites of the antebellum South: Tenants and laborers in central North Carolina and northeast Mississippi*. Durham: Duke University Press.

Bossy, John. 1985. *Christianity in the West, 1400–1700*. Oxford: Oxford University Press.

Boswell, John. 1988. *The Kindness of Strangers: The Abandonment of Children in Western Europe from Late Antiquity to the Renaissance*. New York: Pantheon Books.

Bowlby, John. 1958. The nature of the child's tie to his mother. *International Journal of Psychoanalysis 39*:350–373.

Bowlby, J. 1969. *Attachment and loss. Vol. 1. Attachment*. New York: Basic Books.

Brace, Charles Loring. 1859. *The best method of disposing of pauper and vagrant children*. New York: Wyncoop and Hallenbeck.

Brace, Charles Loring. 1872. *The Dangerous Classes of New York and Twenty Years' Work Among Them*. New York: Wynkoop & Hallenbeck; reprint, Montclair, NJ: Patterson Smith, 1967.

Brace, Charles Loring. 1873. The Little Laborers of New York City. *Harper's New Monthly Magazine* 47 (August): 330.

Brace, Emma, ed. 1894. *The Life of Charles Loring Brace, Chiefly Told in His Own Letters*. New York: Scribner's Sons.

Bremner, Robert, ed. 1970. *Children and Youth in America: A Documentary History, vol. 1, 1600–1865*. Cambridge, Mass.: Harvard University Press, 655.

Bremner, Robert, ed. 1971. *Children and Youth in America: A Documentary History, vol. 2, 1866–1932*. Cambridge, Mass.: Harvard University Press, 269.

Bremner, Robert. 1980. *The Public Good: Philanthropy and Welfare in the Civil War Era*. New York: Alfred A. Knopf, 85–87.

Brenzel, Barbara. 1983. *Daughters of the State: A Social Portrait*

of the First Reform School for Girls in North America, 1956–
1905. Cambridge, Mass.: MIT Press.

Brown, Dorothy M. and Elizabeth McKeown, 1997. The Poor
Belong To Us: Catholic Charities and American Welfare. Cambridge, Mass.: Harvard University Press.

Buck, Jay. 1987. Interview, May. Personal diary Buck kept of
the closing years of Chapin Hall.

Burch, Leonard. 1996. Telephone interview with David T. Beito,
April 29.

Burgess, Hugh F. Jr. and Robert C. Smoot III. 1973. McDonogh
School: An Interpretive Chronology. Columbus, Ohio: Charles
F. Merril, pp. 43, 111.

Burson, Ike. 2001. Alabama's Mother's Pension Statute: Identification and Analysis of Institutional Determinants. Ph.D. Dissertation, University of Alabama.

By-laws of the Orphan House of Charleston, South Carolina,1861 version, quoting 1790 city ordinance. Electronic edition at http://docsouth.unc.edu/imls/orphan/menu.html

Camp, Orton Ruth. n.d. Chicago Orphan Asylum, 1849–1949.
Privately Printed.

Care of Dependent Children. 1910. Conference of Catholic Charities. Proceedings. 1:284–296.

Caritas Christi Urget Nos: A History of the Offices, Agencies and
Institutions of the Archdiocese of Chicago, vol. 2. 1981. 813–
14. Chicago: Archdiocese of Chicago.

Casal, Lourdes. 1867. Sources of Tension in Children's Institutions. 1967. CCR 51: 11–17.

Catholic Charities Drive in Cleveland. 1922. CCR 6: 242.

Catholic Child-Caring Standards Now Ready, 1923, CCR 7:
170–174.

Catholic Identity in Residential Child Care. 1986. Charities USA
13: 10–14.

Catholic Residential Care Mission Statement. 1988. Charities
USA 15: 4.

Cecil-Fronsman, Bill. 1992. Common whites: Class and culture
in antebellum North Carolina. Lexington: University Press of
Kentucky.

Censer, Jane Turner. 1984. North Carolina planters and their
children, 1800–1860. Baton Rouge: Louisiana State University Press.

Chapin Hall Collection at the Chicago Historical Society, Minutes of Meetings of the Board of Managers, 15 February 1868, 25 February 1898, 17 July 1898, 18 June 1901, 2 July 1901, 6 May 1902, 25 March 1903, 19 May 1903, 15 March 1904, 1 Nov. 1904, 25 March 1905, 27 September 1915, 18 Nov. 1924, 7 Dec. 1926, 18 Jan. 1927, 1 Oct. 1929, 17 Feb. 1931, 5 May 1931, 19 May 1931, 2 June 1931, 16 June 1931, 4 August 1931, 18 August 1931, 17 Nov. 1931, 18 April 1933, 20 March 1934, 15 Oct. 1935, 3 Dec. 1940, 16 August 1949.

Chapple, Joe Mitchell. 1928. *"Our Jim": A biography*. Boston: Chapple Publishing.

Charleston City Council. 1861. *Circular of the city council on retrenchment, and report of the Commissioners of the Orphan House*. Charleston: Evans and Cogswell.

Chicago Council of Social Service Agencies. *1930 Social Services Directory*.

Chicago Nursery and Half-Orphan Annual Reports, 1869, 1874, 1891, 1899, 1904, 1905, 1906, 1908, 1910, 1911, 1913, 1914, 1915, 1916, 1918, 1920, 1923, 1924, 1925, 1926, 1928, 1929, 1931, 1932, 1933, 1934, 1937.

Chicago School of Civics and Philanthropy. 1912. *The Child in the City*. Chicago: Manz Engraving Co., The Hollister Press.

Chicago Tribune, April 21, 1857.

Child Care Today. 1933. *CCR* 17: 319.

Child Welfare Division of the Cuyahoga County Welfare Department. 1950, 1952, 1953, 1954, and 1955. Annual Reports. Child Welfare Collection, WRHS.

Children under Care, 1925–1950. Parmadale Papers, Richfield Archives.

Children under Institutional Care. 1923.

Children under Institutional Care and in Foster Homes. 1933.

The Children's Aid Society of New York: Its History, Plan and Results. 1893. New York: Wynkoop & Hallenbeck.

Children's Council, Welfare Federation, Analysis of Total Income by Agencies, Federation for Community Planning, MSS 3788, container 44, folder 1072, WRHS.

"The Children's Home of Cincinnati, Ohio." 1987. *Crossroads* 1 (fall): 1.

City Council of Baltimore 1886/180, p. 3.

City Council of Baltimore RG 16/S1, 1886/180, in Baltimore City Archives).

City of Cleveland *Annual Report*, 1856. Cleveland: City of Cleveland.

The Cleveland Community Drive. 1925. *CCR* 9: 25.

Clopper, Edward N. 1921. The Development of the Children's Code. *Annals of the American Academy of Political and Social Science* 98, 154–159.

Closing After 94 Years. 1967. *CCR 51:* 3.

Cmiel, Kenneth. 1995. *A Home of Another Kind: One Chicago Orphanage and the Tangle of Child Welfare*. Chicago and London: University of Chicago Press.

Cohen, Lizabeth. 1990. *Making a New Deal: Industrial Workers in Chicago, 1919–1939*. New York: Cambridge University Press.

Cohn, Marcus. 1919–20. Jüdisches Waisenrecht. *Zeitschrift für vergleichende Rechtswissenschaft, einschliesslich der ethnologischen Rechtsforschung* 37: 419–45.

Comparative Study of the Population of Parmadale Children's Village, 1967–1974. Parmadale Report (Periodicals) FCCS\ CCC, Box 22, CCDA.

Contosa, David R. 1997. *Philadelphia's Progressive Orphanage, The Carson Valley School*. (University Park, PA: Pennsylvania State University Press).

Cooper, John M. 1931. *Children's Institutions: A Study of Programs and Policies in Catholic Children's Institutions in the United States*. Philadelphia: The Dolphin Press.

Corsini, Carlo A. 1991. "Era piovuto dal cielo e la terra l'aveva raccolto": Il destino del trovatello. In *Enfance*, 81–119.

Cott, Nancy A. 1977. *The bonds of womanhood: "Woman's sphere" in New England, 1780–1835*. New Haven: Yale University Press.

Cottingham, Vivienne. 1996. Telephone interview with David T. Beito, June 27.

Council of Social Agencies 1935. *Social Services Year Book*.

Council of Social Agencies. 1937. *Study of Child Care Agencies*. Unpublished manuscript.

Courtney, Mark E. and Yin-Ling Irene Wong. 1996. Comparing the timing of exits from substitute care. *Children and Youth Services Review* 18: 307–334.

Cox, Mary M. Letter to Rev. Michael L. Moriarty, January 18, 1936, FCCS\CCC, Box 26, St. Joseph's, 1933-1945, Cleveland Catholic Diocesan Archives (CCDA).

Crenson, Mathew A. 1998. *Building the Invisible Orphanage.* Cambridge, Mass.: Harvard University Press.

Crooks, James. B. 1984. *Politics and Progress: the Rise of Urban Progressivism in Baltimore 1895 to 1911,* Baton Rouge: Louisiana State University Press, pp 156–162.

Cuyahoga County Commissioners. April 19, l962, Resolution. Cuyahoga County Archives, Cleveland, Ohio.

Dagron, Gilbert. 1970. Les moines et la ville: La monachisme à Constantinople jusqu' au Concile de Calcedoine (451). *Traveaux et Mémoires* 4: 229–76.

Dankers, J.J. and J. Verheul. 1991. *Als een Groot particulier Huisgezin: Opvoeden in het Utrechtse Burgerweeshuis tussen Caritas en Staatszorg, 1813–1991.* Zutphen: Walburg.

Davis, James J. 1922. *The iron puddler: My life in the rolling mills and what came of it.* New York: Grosset and Dunlap.

De cerimoniis. 1935–39. *Les livre des cérémonies.* 2 vols. Edited by A. Vogt. Paris: Les Belles Lettres.

Deardoff, Neva R. 1924. The new pied pipers. *Survey Graphic* 52 (1 April 1): 31–47.

"Death of Dr. Chatard, well known Catholic physician passed away," *The Catholic Mirror*, September 1, 1900. Michael A. Mullin, 19 Bar Association Report 1914, in: Dilenan Hayward File, Maryland Historical Society (M.H.S.)

DeBow, J.D.B. 1854. *Statistical view of the United States.* Washington: A.O.P. Nicholson.

Degler, Carl N. 1980. *At Odds: Women and the Family in America from the Revolution to the Present.* New York: Oxford University Press.

DelliQuardi, Fred. 1948. Letter to Mrs. Victor C. [Kay] Milliken, 4 August.

Demos, John P. 1970. *A little commonwealth: Family life in Plymouth Colony.* New York: Oxford University Press.

Department of Commerce, U.S. Bureau of the Census, June 1914. *Benevolent Institutions 1910*, (2nd edition), Washington D.C: Government Printing Office, pp. 108–109.

Devine, Isabel M. 1935. Report of Study of the Chicago Nursery and Half-Orphan Asylum. Unpublished report for the Chicago Council of Social Agencies.

Di Giacomo, Salvatore. 1928. *Il Conservatorio dei poveri di Gesù Cristo e quello di S. M. di Loreto.* Collezione settecentesca, 27. Naples: Sandron.

Didascalia. 1905. F. X. Funk (ed.), *Didascalia et Constitutiones Apostolorum.* Paderborn: Fernandi Scheoningh. English translation by R. H. Connolly, 1929. *Didascalia Apostolorum: The Syriac Version Translated and Accompanied by the Verona Latin Fragments.* Oxford: The Clarendon Press. The original Greek text of the *Didascalia Apostolorum* does not survive. It must be reconstructed from a later Greek text called the *Constitutiones Apostolorum* and from Latin and Syriac translations of the original Greek text of the third century.

Dix, Dorthea L. 1850. Memorial of Miss D. L. Dix to the Senate and House of Representatives of the United States http:// www.disabilitymuseum.org/lib/docs/1239.htm?page=20. Disability History Museum, www.disabilitymuseum.org (September 15, 2007).

Dolan Children's Aid Society Minute Book, p. 165, in the Children's Bureau Archives, Baltimore Associated Catholic Charities.

Dolan, Jay P., 1992. *The American Catholic Tradition: A History from Colonial Times to the Present.* Notre Dame and London: Notre Dame University Press.

Dolan, Rev. James. Last will and testament, Register of Wills, 1870, Book 36, Folio 26/27/28.

Downs, Susan Whitlaw, and Michael Sherraden. 1983. The Orphan Asylum in the Nineteenth Century. *Social Service Review* 17, 272–290.

Dunkin, George E. 1972. Crisis in Child-Caring Institutions. *CCR* 56: 9–12.

Dunn, Harriette N. 1912. *Infamous Juvenile Law.* Chicago: H.Dunn.

Eleventh Annual Report of the Hebrew Orphan Asylum. 1883, Baltimore. The Second, Third and Ninth Joint Report of the Federated Jewish Charities, 1907, 1909, 1915. Baltimore in Maryland Jewish Historical Society.

Ellis County (KS) News. August 12, 1948.

Enfance. 1991. *Enfance abandonnée et société en Europe, XIVe – XXe siécle.* Collection de l'École Française de Rome, 140. Rome: École Française de Rome.

Eulogy on "Good Father Dolan" The Apostle of the Point, delivered at the Request of the Young Catholic's Friend Society, at the Maryland Institute November 20, 1870 by William P.

Preston Esq., 1870. Baltimore. pp. 25–30. In the Associated
Catholic Charities Archives, Baltimore.

Fanshel, David, and Eugene Shinn. 1978. *Children in foster
care: A longitudinal investigation.* New York: Columbia University Press.

Farge, Arlette, and Jacque Revel. 1991. *The Vanishing Children
of Paris: Rumor and Politics before the French Revolution.*
Translated by Claudia Mieville. Cambridge, MA: Harvard
University Press.

Ferguson, Dwight H. 1961. Children in need of parents: Implications of the Child Welfare League Study. *Child Welfare*
40:1–6.

Fineman, Martha L. A. 1995. Masking dependency: The political
role of family rhetoric. *Virginia Law Review* 81(8, November):
2181–2215, as accessed July 27, 2007 at http://www.jstor.org/
cgi-bin/jstor/printpage/00426601/ap030636/03a00060/0.pdf?ba
ckcontext=page&dowhat=Acrobat&config=jstor&userID=80c8
23ae@uci.edu/01cce440610050bc2df&0.pdf.

Feldman, Ronald A. 1994. What you can't learn from "Boys
Town." *New York Times*, December 13, p. A19.

*Fifty-first Annual Report: The Children's Mission to the Children
of the Destitute.* 1900. Boston: Children's Mission.

*First Annual Report of the Children's Mission to the Children of
the Destitute.* 1850. Boston: Benjamin H. Greene.

Ford, Mary and Joe Kroll. 1995. *Countering the call for return to
orphanages: There Is a Better way: Family-Based Alternatives
to Institutional Care.* St. Paul, Minn.: National Council on
Adoptable Children, March, as accessed on July 27, 2007 at
http://www.casanet.org/library/foster-care/countret.htm.

Franch, Michael S. 1984. Congregation and Community in Baltimore, 1840–1860. *Ph.D. University of Maryland,* Table 15.

Fraser, Walter J. Jr. 1989. *Charleston! Charleston! The history
of a southern city.* Columbia: University of South Carolina
Press.

Friedman, Reena Sigman. 1994. *These are Our Children: Jewish
Orphanages in the United States, 1880–1925.* Hanover, N.H.:
Univ. Press of New England for Brandies Univ. Press.

Fuller, Guy H., ed., 1918. *Loyal Order of Moose and Mooseheart.*
Mooseheart, IL: Loyal Order of Moose.

The Future of Our Child-Caring Institutions. 1922. *NCCC Proceedings 8:* 144–160.

Gavin, Donald P. 1955. *In All Things Charity: History of the Sisters of Charity of St. Augustine, Cleveland, Ohio, 1851–1954.* Milwaukee: Bruce Press.

Gavin, Donald P. 1962. *The National Conference of Catholic Charities, 1910–1960.* Milwaukee: Catholic Life Publications.

The Gazette, October 23, 1876, p. 4,

GCS Die griechischen christlichen Schriftsteller der ersten Jahrhunderte. Leipzig and Berlin: Akademie-Verlag.

Geremek, Bronislaw. 1994. *Poverty: a History.* Oxford: Blackwell.

Giles, Malcolm R. 1934. Three important committees. *Moose Docket* 3(7): 49–50.

Gingrich, Newt. 1994. Gingrich offers defense plan for orphanages. *New York Times,* December 5.

Gittens, Joan. 1994. *Poor Relations: The Children of the State in Illinois, 1818–1990.* Urbana: University of Illinois Press.

Glover, Lorri. 2000. *All our relations: Blood ties and emotional bonds among the early South Carolina gentry.* Baltimore: Johns Hopkins University Press.

Goddard, Elizabeth. 1948. Evaluation Report of Chicago Nursery and Half-Orphan Asylum. April 26.

Goldstein, Howard Goldstein. 1996. *The Home on Gorham Street and the Voices of Its Children.* Tuscaloosa and London: University of Alabama Press.

Goldstein, Joseph, Anna Freud, and Albert Solnit. 1973. *Beyond the best interests of the child.* New York: Free Press.

Goldstein, Joseph, Anna Freud, and Albert Solnit. 1998. *The best interests of the child: The least detrimental alternative.* New York: Simon and Schuster.

Goodman, Ellen. 1994. If welfare is a nasty word, is orphanage high concept? *Los Angeles Times,* November 18, p. B11.

Gordon, Linda. 1994. *Pitied But Not Entitled: Single Mothers and the History of Welfare, 1890–1935.* New York: The Free Press.

Graff, Harvey. 1987. *The legacies of literacy: Continuities and contradictions in western culture and society.* Bloomington: Indiana University Press.

Green, William O. 1914. Letter to Mrs. Carroll H. Sudler, 11 November 1914, Chapin Hall Collection, Chicago Historical Society, Box 19, Folder 8.

Gregory of Nyssa. 1971. *Vita Macrinae.* Greek text with French translation, Grégoire de Nysse. *Vie de Sainte Macrine*. Edited and translated by Pierre Maraval, Sources Chrétiennes, 178. Paris: Les Éditions du Cerf.

Greven, Philip A. 1977. *The Protestant temperament: Patterns of child-rearing, religious experience, and the self in early America*. New York: Knopf.

Griffith et al. 1930. Receipts and expenditures of social agencies during the year 1928. *Social Service Review 4* (September).

Hacsi, Timothy A. 1997. *Second Home: Orphan Asylums and Poor Families in America*. Cambridge: Harvard University Press.

Hamilton, Gillian. 1995. Enforcement in apprenticeship contracts: Were runaways a serious problem? Evidence from Montreal. *Journal of Economic History* 55: 551–574.

Harlow, Harry. 1958. The nature of love. *American Psychologist 13:673–685*.

Harlow, Harry. 1961. The development of affection patterns in infant monkeys. In B.M. Foss, ed., *Determinants of infant behavior*, Vol. 1. London: Methuen.

Harlow, H.F., and R.R. Zimmerman. 1959. Affectional responses in the infant monkey. *Science* 130:421–432.

Harvison, Louis W. 1920. Mooseheart Service. *Mooseheart Magazine* 6(7–8): 11.

Headley, George. 1974. *Annual Report of the Executive Director for 1974*.

Headley, George. 1975. *Annual Report of the Executive Director for 1975*.

Henderson, Charles. 1908. *Introduction to the Study of the Dependent, Defective, and Delinquent Classes*. Ref. ed. Boston: D.C. Health & Co.

Henning, Edward J. 1933. First, learn all the facts, then if you must—criticize. *Moose Docket* 1(March): 65–66.

Hirshson, Roberta Star. 1989. *"There's Always Someone There": The History of the New England Home for Little Wanderers*. Boston: New England Home for Little Wanderers.

Hoffman, Frederick L. 1911. Fifty years of American life insurance progress. *American Statistical Association* 95 (September): 88.

Holl, Jack M. 1971. *Juvenile reform in the progressive era: William R. George and the Junior Republic Movement*. Ithaca: Cornell Univ. Press.

Holliday, J.S. 1985. "An Historian Reflects on Edgewood Children's Center." *California History* 4 (spring): 122–31.

Holloran, Peter C. 1989. *Boston's Wayward Children: Social Services for Homeless Children, 1830–1930*. Rutherford, NJ: Farleigh Dickinson Univ. Press.

Holt, Marilyn Irvin. 1992. *The Orphan Trains: Placing Out in America*. Lincoln: University of Nebraska Press.

_____. 2001. *Indian Orphanages*. Lawrence: University Press of Kansas.

_____. 2006. "Adoption Reform, Orphan Trains, and Child Saving, 1851–1929." In *Children and Youth in Adoption, Orphanages, and Foster Care: A Historical Handbook and Guide*. Edited by Lori Askeland. Westport, CT: Greenwood Press.

The Home or the Institution. *1898*. National Conference of Charities and Corrections. *Proceedings, 1:* 364 – 366.

Homecoming: The Forgotten World of America's Orphanages. 2006. Irvine, Calif.: HomeFront Productions, Inc. George Cawood, director; Sheila Moreland, film editor; Adam Hauck, producer; and Richard McKenzie and Gary Byrne, executive producers, with more information at www.homecomingmovie .org.

Horstmann, Ignatius. 1901. Letter, February 4, 1901, Farrelly Papers. Institutions: St. Joseph Orphanage, CCDA.

Horwich, Mitchell Alan. 1977. *Conflict and Child Care Policy in the Chicago Jewish Community, 1893–1942*. Chicago: Jewish Children's Bureau.

Houck, Rev. George F. 1903. *A History of Catholicity in Northern Ohio and in the Diocese of Cleveland*, Volume 1. Cleveland: Press of J.B. Savage.

Houghteling Reynolds, Laura L. Reminiscences of the War of the Rebellion. Unpublished manuscript, 2–3.

Howard, G.W. 1889. *The Monumental City*. Baltimore: J. D. Ehlers, p. 621.

HR 4. 1995. Personal Responsibility Act, 104th Congress, 1st Session, 1995.

Hunecke, Volker. 1992, Findelkinder und Findelhäuser in der Renaissance. *Quellen und Forschungen aus italienischen Archiven und Bibliotheken* 72: 123–53.

Hynes, Michael J. 1953. *History of the Diocese of Cleveland. Origin and Growth (1847-1952)*. Cleveland: Diocese of Cleveland.

Illinois Department of Public Welfare 1931. Inspection: Chicago Nursery and Half-Orphan Asylum, 15 August 1931, Welfare Council of Metropolitan Chicago; Devine.

In Children's Agencies. 1931. *National Conference of Catholic Charities*, Proceedings 17: 154–155.

In Praise of Institutions. 1951. *CCR* 35:84–85.

Irvine, William, n.d. *A Tradition of Caring: A History of Family Care Services of Metropolitan Chicago.* Privately Printed: Chicago Home for the Friendless.

Jabour, Anya. 1998. *Marriage in the early republic: Elizabeth and William Wirt and the companionate ideal.* Baltimore: Johns Hopkins University Press.

Jacksonville (IL) Journal. April 26, 1860.

Jenkins, Shirley, and Elaine Norman. 1972. *Filial deprivation.* New York: Columbia University Press.

Jenkins, Shirley, and Elaine Norman. 1975. *Beyond placement: Mothers view foster care.* New York: Columbia University Press.

Jeter, Helen R. 1960. *Children who receive services from public child welfare agencies.* Washington, DC: Children's Bureau.

Jeter, H. R. 1963. Children, problems and services in child welfare programs. Washington, DC: Children's Bureau.

The Jewish Comment. June 10, 1910. pp. 1, 2. In Maryland Jewish Historical Society.

Jewish Family and Children's Bureau. 1956. *A Century of Understanding, 1856–1956.* Baltimore: Associated Jewish Charities.

Johnson, Michael P. and James L. Roark. 1984. *No chariot let down: Charleston's free people of color on the eve of the Civil War.* Chapel Hill: University of North Carolina Press.

Jolowicz, Herbert F. 1947. The wicked guardian, *Journal of Roman Studies* 37: 82–90.

Jones, Marshall. 1989. Crisis of the American orphanage, 1931–1940. *Social Services Review 63.*

Josephus. 1968. *Bellum Judaicum (Jewish Wars).* Greek text with English translation by H. St. J. Thackaray. *Josephus,* vols. 2 and 3. Loeb Classical Library. Cambridge, MA: Harvard University Press.

Kadushin, A., and J.A. Martin. 1990. *Child welfare services. 4th Edition.* New York: Macmillan.

Kalff, S. 1899. *Het Amsterdamsche Burgerweeshuis.* Amsterdam.

Kamerman, S.B., and A.J. Kahn. 1990. Social services for children, youth and families in the United States. Special Issue of *Children and Youth Services Review* 12:1–184.

Kasprowicz, Alfred L. 1965. Implications of Change in Children's Institutions. 1965. *CCR 49:4–9.*

Kasser, Edmund. 1945. The growth and decline of a children's slang at Mooseheart, A self-contained community. *Journal of Genetic Psychology* 66: 129–37.

Katz, Michael B. 1986. *In the Shadow of the Poorhouse: A Social History of Welfare in America.* New York: Basic Books.

Kedar, Benjamin. 1999. A twelfth-century description of the Jerusalem Hospital. In H. Nicholson (ed.) *Military Orders. Vol. 2 (Welfare and Warfare):* 3–26. Aldershot, UK: Ashgate.

Kelly, Suzanne. Telephone interview with David T. Beito. June 26, 1996.

Kelso, Robert W. 1923. The Transition from Charities and Correction to Public Welfare. *Annals of the American Academy of Political and Social Science,* 105, 21–25.

Kempe, C. Henry, F. Silverman, B. Steele, W. Droegmueller, and H. Silver. 1962. "The battered-child syndrome." *Journal of the American Medical Association* 181:17–24.

Kidder, Clark. 2001. *Orphan Trains and Their Precious Cargo: The Life's Work of Rev. H.D. Clarke.* Bowie, MD: Heritage Books.

King, Susan L. 1984. *History and Records of the Charleston Orphan House, 1790–1860.* Easley, S.C.: Southern Historical Press, Inc.

Kleemeier, Robert W. 1954. Moosehaven: Congregate living in a community of the retired. *The American Journal of Sociology* 59(4): 347–49.

Kletorologion of Philotheos. 1972. In N. Oikonomides(ed.) *Les listes de préséance byzantines des IXe et Xe siècles: Introduction, texte, traduction et commentaire,* 67–235. Paris: Éditions du Centre National de la Recherche Scientifique.

Koepp, Helen. 1996. Telephone interview with David T. Beito. June 28.

Komnena, Anna. 1937–45. *Alexiade.* 3 vols. Edited by Bernard Leib. Paris: Les Belles Lettres. Translated into English by E. R. Sewter, 1969, *The Alexiad of Anna Comnena.* Baltimore: Penguin Books.

Kossmann, E. H. 1992. The Dutch Republic in the Eighteenth

Century. In *The Dutch Republic in the Eighteenth Century: Decline, Enlightenment, and Revolution,* eds. Margaret Jacob and Wijnand Mijnhardt, 19–31. Ithaca: Cornell University Press.

Lakeside Annual Directory of the City of Chicago, 1885–86. 1885. Chicago Directory Co., 33.

Lakeside Annual Directory of the City of Chicago, 1900–1901. 1900. Chicago: The Chicago Directory Co., 16–17.

Lakeside Annual Directory of the City of Chicago, 1910–11. 1910. Chicago: The Chicago Directory Co., 56–67.

Langsam, Miriam Z. 1964. *Children West: A History of the New York Children's Aid Society, 1853–1890.* Madison: State Historical Society of Wisconsin.

Lebsock, Suzanne, *The free women of Petersburg: Status and culture in a southern town, 1784–1860.* New York: W.W. Norton.

Leiby, James. 1978. *A History of Social Welfare and Social Work in the United States.* New York: Columbia University Press.

Letchworth, W.P. 1878. "Dependent and Delinquent Children: Institutions in New York in 1877." *American Journal of Education* 28: 913.

Levin, Alexandra Lee. 1960. *The Szolds of Lombard Street: A Baltimore Family, 1859–1909.* Philadelphia: Jewish Publication Society of America, pp. 7, 352.

Lewis, Jan. 1983. *The pursuit of happiness: Family and values in Jefferson's Virginia.* New York: Cambridge University Press.

Lindert, Peter H. 2004. Growing Public: Social Spending and Economic Growth since the Eighteenth century, 2 vols. New York: Cambridge University Press.

Lindsey, Duncan. 1994. *The welfare of children.* New York: Oxford University Press.

Linehan, Mary. 1991. "Vicious Circle: Prostitution, Reform, and Public Policy in Chicago, 1830–1930." PhD diss., University of Notre Dame.

Local Matters. *The Baltimore Sun,* November 13, 1874.

Lockridge, Kenneth A. 1974. *Literacy in colonial New England: An enquiry into the social context of literacy in the early modern west.* New York: W.W. Norton.

London, Ross, D. 1998. The 1994 orphanage debate: A study in the politics of annihilation. *Rethinking Orphanages for the 21st Century,* edited by Richard B. McKenzie. Thousand Oaks, Calif.: Sage Publications.

Loyal Order of Moose. 1912. *Historical souvenir of the Loyal Order of Moose*. Chicago: Loyal Order of Moose.

Loyal Order of Moose. 1915. 1925. *Minutes*.

Loyal Order of Moose. 1927–1946. *Proceedings*.

Loyal Order of Moose. Board of Governors. 1918–1919. *Mooseheart Year Book*.

Loyal Order of Moose. Board of Governors. 1918–1919. *Mooseheart Year-Book and Annual*.

Lundberg, Emma Octavia. 1928. "Progress of Mother's Aid Administration." *Social Service Review* 2 (September): 435.

Luttrell, Anthony. 1994. The Hospitallers' medical tradition, 1291–1530. In M. Barber (ed.) *The Military Orders: Fighting for the Faith and Caring for the Sick*, 64–81. Aldershot, UK: Variorum.

Maas, Henry S., and Richard E. Engler Jr. 1959. *Children in need of parents*. New York: Columbia University Press.

Main, Gloria L. 2001. *Peoples of a spacious land: Families and cultures in colonial New England*. Cambridge: Harvard University Press.

Marks, Rachel B. 1973. Institutions for Dependent and Delinquent Children: Histories, Nineteenth-Century Statistics, and Recurrent Goals, in Donnell M. Pappenfort *et al*, editors, *Child-Caring: Social Policy and the Institution*. Chicago: Aldine Publishing Co.

Marstello, Joseph. 1955. Program of Psychiatric Services for Child-Caring Homes. *CCR* 39: 8-10.

Martin, Florence. 1906. Letter to Azel Hatch, 27 September 1906, Chapin Hall Collection, Chicago Historical Society, Box 21, Folder 8.14.

McCants, Anne. 1992. Monotonous but not meager: the diet of burgher orphans in early modern Amsterdam. *Research in Economic History* 14: 69–116.

McCants, Anne. 1995. Meeting needs and suppressing desires: consumer choice models and historical data. *Journal of Interdisciplinary History* 26(2): 191–207.

McCants, Anne E. C. 1997. *Civic Charity in a Golden Age: Orphan Care in Early Modern Amsterdam*. Urbana, IL: University of Illinois Press.

McCants, Anne E. C. 2007. Inequality among the poor of eighteenth century Amsterdam. *Explorations in Economic History* 44(1): 1–21.

McCarthy Kathleen D. 1982. *Noblesse Oblige: Charity and Cultural Philanthropy in Chicago,* 1849–1929. Chicago: University of Chicago Press.

McCurdy, M. A., and D. Daro. 1993. *Current trends in child abuse reporting and fatalities: The results of the 1992 annual fifty state survey.* Chicago: National Committee for the Prevention of Child Abuse.

McGovern, Cecelia T. 1946. Some Problems of Group Management in Children's Institutions. *CCR* 30.

McGovern, Cecelia T. 1947. Children's Institutions as Social Agencies. *CCR* 31: 121–125.

McKenzie, Richard B. 1994. An orphan on orphanages. *Wall Street Journal,* November 29.

McKenzie, Richard. 1995 (hardback edition) and 2006 (paperback and expanded edition). *The Home: A Memoir of Growing Up in an Orphanage.* New York: Basic Books and Irvine, Calif.: Dickens Press.

_____. 1997. Orphanage alumni: How they have done and how they evaluate their experience. *Child and Youth Care Forum* (April): 87–111.

_____. 1998. *Rethinking Orphanages for the 21st Century.* Thousand Oaks, Calif.: Sage Publications.

_____. 2003. The impact of orphanages on the alumni's lives and assessments of their childhoods. *Children and Youth Services Review* (September 2003): 703–753.

McKeown, Elizabeth. 1997. Catholic Charities, in Michael Glazier and Thomas J. Shelley, eds., *The Encyclopedia of American Catholic History.* Collegeville, Minn.: Liturgical Press. 1997.

McTighe, Michael J. *A Measure of Success: Protestants and Public Culture in Antebellum Cleveland.* 1994. Albany: State University of New York Press.

Meginnis, Frances S. *Samuel ready . . . the Man and His Legacy.* 1987. Baltimore: University of Baltimore, pp. 12–18. The Langsdale Library Special Collections, University of Baltimore.

Meister, Ralph. Telephone interview with David T. Beito. April 24, 1996.

Merryweather, L.W. 1932. The argot of an orphans' home. *American Speech* 7(6): 398–4.

Miller, Timothy S. 1978. The knights of Saint John and the hospitals of the Latin West. *Speculum* 53: 709–33.

Miller, Timothy S. 1994. The Orphanotropheion of Constantinople. In E. A. Hanawalt and C. Lindberg (eds.) *Through the Eye of a Needle: Judeo-Christian Roots of Social Welfare*, 83–104. Kirksville, Missouri: The Thomas Jefferson University Press at Northeast Missouri State University.

Miller, Timothy S. 1997. *The Birth of the Hospital in the Byzantine Empire*. Paperback edition with new introduction. Baltimore and London: The Johns Hopkins University Press.

Miller, Timothy S. 2003. *The Orphans of Byzantium*. Washington, D.C.: The Catholic University of America Press.

Minutes, Advisory Board of Parmadale, September 8, 1933, Federation of Catholic Community Services\Catholic Charities Corporation (FCCS\CCC,) Box 21, Parmadale Reports, CCDA.

Minutes, Advisory Board of Parmadale, December 5, 1934, FCCS\CCC, Box 21, CCDA.

Minutes, Advisory Board of Parmadale, January 23, 1951, FCCS\CCC, Box 21, CCDA.

Minutes of Hebrew Orphan Asylum, March 19, 1911 to December 31, 1916, April 16, 1911. p. 5. The H.O.A. Minute Book, 1911–1916. The Maryland Jewish Historical society, M.J.H.S.

Minutes of the Monthly Meeting of Parmadale Board, November 12, 1958,FCCS\CCC Records, Parmadale Reports, History 1947-1975, CCDA.

Moose Docket. 1932–1933. Strengthen the degree staff. October, 32. 1932. Impressive figures with which every lodge officer should be familiar. October, 85.1932. An achievement of the common man. November, 47. 1933. When a feller needs a friend. June, 10–11.

Mooseheart Annual. 1930.

Mooseheart High School Seniors' Book. 1925.

Mooseheart Magazine

_____. 1916. About Mooseheart and the Loyal Order of Moose. June, 8.

_____. 1920. From the Philadelphia Record July 14. October, 15.

_____. 1920. Mooseheart necessities. September, 1.

_____. 1920. Mooseheart. June 1923, 1.

Mooseheart Weekly

_____. 1919. New arrivals. March 21, 2.

_____. 1919. Rules and regulations for use of savings fund, April 25, 3.

_____. 1919. Protestant church services started at Mooseheart, May 2, 9.

_____. 1919. What we find at Mooseheart: The school that trains for life. May 9, 1.

_____. 1920. Self-sacrifice. September 4, 4.

_____. 1931. New conduct rating plan for all halls now in effect. July 31, 1.

Morganthau, Tom. 1994. The orphanage (cover story). December 12, pp. 28–33.

Morlock, Kari. 1996. Telephone interview with David T. Beito. April 8.

Murphy, J. Prentice. 1922. Superficial Character of Child Caring Work, *National Conference on Social Work, 1922.* Chicago: University of Chicago Press.

Murray, John E. 1997. Generation(s) of human capital: Literacy in American families, 1830–1875. *Journal of Interdisciplinary History* 27: 413–435.

Murray, John E. 2004. Family, literacy, and skill training in the antebellum south: Historical-longitudinal evidence from Charleston. *Journal of Economic History* 64: 773–799.

Murray, John E. 2004. Literacy acquisition in an orphanage: A historical-longitudinal case study. *American Journal of Education* 110: 172–195.

Murray, John E. and Ruth Wallis Herndon. 2002. Markets for children in early America: A political economy of pauper apprenticeship. *Journal of Economic History* 62: 356–382.

Murray, John E. Forthcoming. Mothers and children in and out of the Charleston Orphan House," in Ruth Wallis Herndon and John E. Murray, editors, *Children bound to labor in early America* (Ithaca: Cornell University Press, forthcoming).

Nani, Teresa Giulia. 1943–44. Threptoi. *Epigraphica: Rivista italiana di epigrafia* 5–6: 45–84.

Nasaw, David. 1979. *Schooled to Order: A Social History of Public Schooling in the United States.* New York: Oxford University Press.

National Industrial Conference Board, February 28, 1931 *Service letter on industrial relations* (New Series) 74, 6.

Neher, Joanne Catherine. 1984. Interest Group Involvement

in Child Labor Legislative Policy in Missouri: 1915 to 1940.
Ph.D. Dissertation, St. Louis University.

New York Juvenile Asylum, Fourth Annual Report. 1856. New
York: New York Juvenile Asylum.

Newman, Bruce. 1989. Interview, July.

Niemeyer, Fred M. n.d. *A History of Angel Guardian Orphanage.*
Privately Printed.

*Ninth Annual Report of the Executive Committee of the Chil-
dren's Mission to the Children of the Destitute.* 1858. Boston:
John Wilson and Son.

Norris, M., and B. Wallace, eds. 1965. *The known and the unknown in child welfare research: An appraisal.* New York:
Child Welfare League of America.

Oates, Mary J. 1995. *The Catholic Philanthropic Tradition in
America.* Bloomington: O'Grady, John. 1941. Catholic Charities in 1941. *Catholic Charities Review (CCR)* 25: 36–42.

O'Connor, Stephen. 2001. *Orphan Trains: The Story of Charles
Loring Brace and the Children He Saved and Failed.* New
York: Houghton Mifflin.

Odquist, Maurice V. Ca. 1950. *The History of Graham.* New
York: Graham School.

O'Grady, John. 1923. A Preliminary Survey of Catholic
Child-Caring Work in the United States, *CCR* 7. 141–142.

O'Grady, John. 1928. Parmadale and Its Cottage Mothers. *CCR*
12: 175–177.

O'Grady, John. 1930. *Catholic Charities in the United States:
History and Problems.* Washington, D.C.: National Conference of Catholic Charities.

Olivier, Warner. 1948. City of children. *Saturday Evening Post.*
September 14, 32–33. "An Orphan Train Rider in Kansas:
Howard Dowell Interview." 1994. In *Model Ts, Pep Chapels,
and A Wolf at the Door: Kansas Teenagers, 1900–1941.* Edited
by Marilyn Irvin Holt. Lawrence: University of Kansas, Continuing Education.

Olivier, Warner. 1952. *Back of the dream: The story of the Loyal
Order of Moose.* New York: E.P. Dutton.

"Orphan Train Sisters Find Good Parents." 1988. *Crossroads* 4
(summer): 5.

The Orphans Fair Report, Farrelly Papers. Institutions: St. Joseph Orphanage, CCDA.

Outing Rules to Govern Carlisle Indian Students and Our Pa-

trons. 1907. http://home.epix.net/~landis/outing.html. Carlisle
Indian Industrial School (1879–1918), http://home.epix
.net/~landis/ (September 15, 2007).
Palmer, Vivian M. 1932. Study of the Development of Chicago's
Northside. Unpublished paper written for United Charities of
Chicago.
Parmadale Board of Trustees 1991, Minutes May 8, 1991,
FCCS\CCC Box 21, CCDA.
Parmadale brochure, no date, FCCS\CCC Box 21, CCDA.
Parmadale Cost Per Diem 1961–1971, FCCS\CCC, Box 22, Par-
madale Reports (Periodicals 1967–1974) CCDA.
Parmadale Financial Report, 1925–1934. Schrembs Papers (11)
Institutions: Parmadale: General,CCDA.
Parmadale Reports. 1947–1975. History. FCCS\CCC Records,
Box 22, CCDA.
Patala, Zoï. 1996. Les chants grecs du *Liber Politicus* du cha-
noine Benoît. *Byzantion* 66: 512–30.
Pelton, Leroy. 1989. *For reasons of poverty: A critical analysis
of the child welfare system in the United States.* New York:
Praeger.
PG. 1857–66. Patrologiae cursus completus. Series graeca. Ed-
ited by Jacques-Paul Migne. 161 vols. Paris: Migne.
Pierce, n.d. *A History of Chicago*, 3: 320–23.
Pincherle, Marc. 1957. *Vivaldi: Genius of the Baroque.*
Translated by Christopher Hatch. New York: Norton
Library.
"Plan of Work." 1890. *New England Home for Little Wanderers
Advocate and Report* 24 (January): 1–40.
Platt, Anthony. 1977. *The Child Savers: The Invention of Delin-
quency.* 2nd ed. Chicago: University of Chicago Press.
Pleck, Elizabeth. 1987. *Domestic Tyranny: The Making of Social
Policy Against Family Violence from Colonial Times to the
Present.* New York: Oxford University Press.
Policy and Practice of Catholic Institutions in Receiving, Caring
for and Discharging Children. 1916. National Conference on
Catholic Charities *Proceedings* 4: 171–180.
Polsky, Andrew. 1991. *The Rise of the Therapeutic State.* Prince-
ton: Princeton University Press.
Polster, Gary Edward. 1990. *Inside Looking Out: The Cleveland
Jewish Orphan Asylum, 1868–1924.* Kent, Ohio: Kent State
University Press.

Porter, Roy. 1997. *The Greatest Benefit to Mankind: A Medical History of Humanity.* New York and London: W. W. Norton and Company.

Pratt, Richard Henry. 1892. The Advantages of Mingling Indians with Whites. National Conference of Charities and Corrections, Proceedings, 19, pp. 45–59, National Conference on Social Welfare Proceedings (1874–1982), http://quod.lib.umich.edu/n/ncosw/ (September 15, 2007).

Present Problems of the Children's Agencies in Cleveland, November 2, 1928," Children's Services MSS 4020, container 4, folder 53, WRHS.

Pringle, M.L. Kelmer. 1969. *Studies in child development caring for children: A symposium on cooperation in child welfare.* Humanities Press: New York.

Program Beneficiary Statistics, Parmadale. 1984-1985, CCDA.

Program Diversification in Residential Child Care. 1988. *Charities USA* 15: 18–20.

Program Inventory Child-Caring Institutions. Federation for Community Planning MSS 3788, container 44, folder 1072, WRHS.

Purdam, Todd S. 1994. First lady v. orphanages. *Newsweek,* December 12, p. A11.

Rayner, William S., Esq. 1873. *Address Delivered Esq. at the Dedication of the Hebrew Orphan Asylum, May 8,* Baltimore: Deutch and Co., pp. 6, 9. The Enoch Pratt Free Library, Baltimore.

The Ready Record, v. 1, February 5, 1892, p. 1.

The Ready Record, v. 4, November 1, 1895, p. 1.

Reasons for A Catholic Child Care Agency. 1948. *CCR 32:* 121–124.

Reeder, R. R. 1925. "Our Orphaned Asylums." *Survey* 54 (June): 285.

Reid, Joseph H. 1959. Action called for—recommendation. In H. S. Maas and R. E. Engler, *Children in need of parents,* *378–397.* New York: Columbia University Press.

Religious Community Questionnaire, Daughters of the Heart of Mary, CCDA.

Religious Orders—Women—Sisters of Charity of St. Augustine —History, 40, CCDA.

Report of the Commissioner of Education for the Year 1877. 1878. *American Journal of Education* 28: 182–208.

Report of the Committee to Study the Shortage of Placement Facilities for Children, December 21, 1942. Committee on Child Placement Facilities, Wednesday June 2, 1943, Federation for Community Planning, MSS 3788, container 29, folder 719, WRHS. Report of the Study of St. Joseph's Orphanage, FCCS\CCC, Box 26, St. Joseph's, 1933–1945, CCDA.

Report of Miss A.L. Hill of an Inspection of All Children Placed Since 1911 in Family Homes in or near McPherson, Kansas. 1924. Orphan Train file. Library, Kansas State Historical Society, Topeka, KS.

Report of St. Mary's Home for Children, 1941–1942–1943, 3.

Reports, CCDA. May 8, 1991 Board of Trustees Minutes, FCCS\ CCC, Box 21.

Residential Care Review and Allocation Committee, September 12, 1968, Periodic Review of Parmadale, Parmadale, Historical Process, 1925–. Richfield Archives.

A Retrospect: Impressions of three "Old Girls," Twenty-Fifth Anniversary of the Samuel Ready, RG-S.R.S. Box 20.

Revitalizing St. Joseph's," FCCS\CCC, Box 26, St. Joseph's 1933–1945, CCDA. Self Study Report, Parmadale Reports, 1973–1975, FCCCS\CCC Records, Box 21, CCDA.

Reymert, Martin L. and Hinton Jr., Ralph T. The effect of a change to a relatively superior environment upon the IQ's of one hundred children. National Society for the Study of Education. *Thirty-Ninth Yearbook.* Bloomington, IL.: Public School Publishing, 1940, 255–68.

Reymert, Martin L. 1938. The Mooseheart graphic rating scale for housemothers and housefathers. *Journal of Applied Psychology* 22(3): 288–94.

Reymert, Martin L. 1941. The Mooseheart system of child guidance. *Nervous Child* 1(1): 75–97.

Ricci, David. 1993. *The Transformation of American Politics.* New Haven: Yale University Press.

Richman, Harold. 1983. "An Analysis of Options for Chapin Hall for Children." November.

Richmond, Mary E. 1930. *The Long View: Papers and Addresses.* New York: Russell Sage Foundation.

Rolfe, Lyle R. and Wehrmeister, Kurt. 1992. The amazing story of Mooseheart football. *Moose* 78(6): 14–17, 38–48.

Ross Legacy. 1897. Lyon's Hall: 1905.

Roth, Rev. Francis Xavier. 1934. *History of St. Vincent's Orphan Asylum, Tacony, Philadelphia: A Memoir of its Diamond Jubilee, 1855–1933*. Philadelphia: "Nord'Amerika" Press.

Rothman, David J. 1971. *The Discovery of the Asylum, Social Order and Disorder in the New Republic* Boston: Little, Brown.

Rothman, David J. 1981. *Conscience and Convenience: The Asylum and its Alternatives in Progressive America*. Boston: Little, Brown.

Rowen, Herbert. 1990. *The Princes of Orange: the Stadholders in the Dutch Republic*. Cambridge: Cambridge University Press.

Rutman, Darrett B. and Anita H. Rutman. 1994. *Small worlds, large questions: Explorations in early American social history, 1600–1850*. Charlottesville: University of Virginia Press.

Salina (KS) Daily Union. July 2, 1912.

Sallee, Shelley. 2004. *The Whiteness of Child Labor Reform in the Deep South*. Athens: University of Georgia Press.

Sanborn, F.B. 1890. Indoor and Outdoor Relief. National Conference of Charities and Correction, *Proceedings, 17*, pp. 71–80, National Conference on Social Welfare Proceedings (1874–1982), http://quod.lib.umich.edu/n/ncosw/ (September 15, 2007).

Schiavoni, Claudio. 1991. Gli infanti "Esposti" del Santo Spirito in Saxia di Roma tra '500 e'800: numero, ricevimento, allevamento e destino. In *Enfance*, 1017–63.

Schlossman, Steven L. 1977. *Love and the American Delinquent: The Theory and Practice of "Progressive" Juvenile Justice, 1825–1920*. Chicago: University of Chicago Press, 49–53.

Schwartz, Marie Jenkins. 2000. *Born in bondage: Growing up enslaved in the antebellum South*. Cambridge: Harvard University Press.

The Second Joint Report of the Federated Jewish Charities 1909. Baltimore, p. 74, in M.J.H.S.

Seventy-Eighth Annual Report of the Chicago Home for the Friendless for the Year Ending 1936.

Sharlitt, Michael. 1959. *As I Remember, the Home in My Heart*. Shaker Heights, Ohio: Belle Pair Jewish Children's Home, pp. 29–93.

Sheete, Mary Maher. 1927. *The Children's Bureau of Cleveland:*

A Study of the Care of Dependent Children in Cleveland, Ohio.
Washington, D.C.: Government Publishing Office.

Sheets, Tara E., 2000. *Encyclopedia of associations.* New York:
Gale Group.

Shehan, Lawrence J. Current Problems in Catholic Agencies.
1943. *CCR* 27: 60–61.

Shepherd of Hermas. 2003. Greek text with English translation
by Bart D. Ehrman, *The Apostolic Fathers,* vol. 2: 174–473.
Loeb Classical Library. Cambridge, Ma: Harvard University
Press.

*Sisters of the Holy Cross Centenary 1859–1959, St. Patrick's
Girls School and Orphanage.* In the Associated Catholic
Charities Archives, Baltimore.

*Sisters of the Holy Cross Centenary 1859–1959, St. Patrick's
Girls School and Orphanage.* The Dolan Home Minute Book,
pp.109, 123.

Skocpol, Theda. 1992. *Protecting Soldiers and Mothers: The
Political Origins of Social Policy in the United States.* Cambridge, Mass.: Harvard University Press.

Smejkal, Marie. 1996. Telephone interview with David T. Beito.
February 14.

Smith, Daniel Blake. 1977–78., Autonomy and affection: Parents and children in eighteenth century Chesapeake families.
Journal of Psychohistory 6: 32–51.

Smith, Eve P. 1995. Bring back the orphanages? What policymakers of today can learn from the past. *Child Welfare* 74(1):
115–41.

Social Security Bulletin 18. March 1955. Orphanhood—A Dimin-
ishing Problem.

Sokrates. 1995. *Kirchengeschichte.* Edited by Gunther Christian
Hansen. GCS, n.s. 1. Berlin: Akademie-Verlag.

Spar, Karen. 1995. *Welfare Reform: Implications of H.R. 4 for
Child Welfare Services.* Washington: D.C.: Congressional Research Service.

The S.R. (H.O.A.) 1893–1905, p. 24, p. 83, and p. 102.

St. Joseph's Admissions Book, 1868–1883, 1894–1942, CCDA.

St. Vincent's Asylum, Book A, 1853-1881, Cleveland Catholic
Diocese Archives (CCDA).

St. Joseph's Orphanage, FCCS\CCC, Box 26, St. Joseph's,
1933-1945, CCDA

Standards Relating to Children in Need of Special Care. 1919. *CCR* 3: 170–174.

Stanislaus, Sister. "History of the Congregation," Edward F. Hoban Papers (111).

Stanley Correspondence. 1902. G. Whiting Swayne to Gov. William Stanley. Archives, Kansas State Historical Society, Topeka, KS.

State of the Village, 1981.Annual Report. FCCS\CCC, Box 21, CCDA.

State of the Village, 1983. Annual Report. FCCS\CCC, Box 21, CCDA.

Steckel, Richard H. 1986. A dreadful childhood: The excess mortality of American slaves. *Social Science History* 10: 427–465.

Stehno, Sandra. 1985 "Foster Care for Dependent Black Children in Chicago, 1899–1934." Ph.D. diss., University of Chicago.

Stone-Ferrier, Linda. 2000. Metsu's *Justice Protecting Widows and Orphans*: Patron and Painter Relationships and their Involvement in the Social and Economic Plight of Widows and Orphans in Leiden. In *The Public and Private in Dutch Culture of the Golden Age*, eds. Arthur K. Wheelock, Jr. and Adele Seeff, 227–265. Newark: University of Delaware Press.

Stuart, Paul. 1979. *The Indian Office: Growth and Development of an American Institution, 1865–1900*. Ann Arbor, MI: UMI Research Press.

Stumpf, Leonara. 1996. Telephone interview with David T. Beito. April 5.

Summary of 1985-1986 Budget Information, FCCS\CCC Parmadale Reports, Statistics, CCDA.

Summary of Service-Area Directors' Three Year Plans, April 17, 1985. Parmadale

Superintendent's Reports 1893–1905 (the S.R. 1893–1905) p. 26, in the Hebrew Orphan Asylum Box 1, in Maryland Jewish Historical Society.

't Hart, Marjolein C. 1993. *The Making of a Bourgeois State: War, Politics and Finance during the Dutch Revolt*. Manchester: Manchester University Press.

Temple, William. 1932. *Observations upon the Netherlands*. Cambridge: Cambridge University Press.

Theodore of Stoudios. 1992. G. Fatouros (ed.) *Theodori Studitae Epistulae*. Corpus fontium historiae byzantinae, 31. Berlin and New York: Walter de Gruyter.

Thirty-Fourth Annual Report of the Chicago Relief and Aid Society, 1891, 53–55. *Chicago Charities Directory, 1906.* 1905. Chicago Charities Directory Association.

Tiffin, Susan. 1982. *In Whose Best Interest? Child Welfare Reform in the Progress Era.* Westport, Conn.: Greenwood Press.

Tocqueville, Alexis de (trans. and ed. Harvey C. Mansfield and Delba Winthrop). 2000. *Democracy in America.* Chicago: University of Chicago Press.

Turner, John B., editor. *1977. Encyclopedia of Social Work,* Volume 2. Washington, D.C.: National Association of Social Workers.

Type and Capacity of Children's Institutions. 1947. Microfilm Reel 27, Federation for Community Planning, MSS 3788, WRHS.

Tyson, Francis. 1925. Family protection through supplemental income. *Annals of the American Academy of Political and Social Science 121.* September.

U.S. Bureau of the Census. 1927. *Children Under Institutional Care, 1923.* Washington, D.C: Government Publishing Office.

U.S. Bureau of the Census. 1935. *Children Under Institutional Care and in Foster Homes, 1933,* Washington, D.C.: Government Publishing Office.

U.S. Children's Bureau Publication, no. 139. 1924. *Laws Relating to Interstate Placement of Dependent Children.* Washington, D.C.: Government Printing Office.

U.S. Department of Commerce. Bureau of the Census. 1913. *Benevolent institutions, 1910.* Washington, D.C.: Government Printing Office.

U.S. Department of Commerce. Bureau of the Census. 1933. *Abstract of the fifteenth census of the United States.* Washington, D.C.: Government Printing Office.

U.S. Department of Commerce. Bureau of the Census. 1935. *Children under institutional care and in foster homes.* Washington, D.C.: Government Printing Office.

U.S. Department of Commerce. 1975. *Historical statistics of the United States: Colonial times to 1970.* Washington, D.C.: Government Printing Office. pt. 1.

U.S. Department of the Interior. Office of Education. 1935. *Statistics of higher education. 1931–32.* Washington, D.C.: Government Printing Office.

U.S. Department of Labor. Children's Bureau. 1933. *Mothers' aid.* 1931. Washington, D.C.: Government Printing Office.

U.S. President's Research Committee on Social Trends. 1933. *Recent social trends in the United States: Report of the President's Research Committee on Social Trends.* New York: McGraw Hill. vol. 2.

van der Vlis, Ingrid. 2002. *Weeshuizen in Nederland: de Wisselende Gestalten van een Weldadig Instituut.* Zutphen: Walburg Pers.

van Leeuwen, Marco. 1982. *Bijstand in Amsterdam, ca. 1800–1850 : armenzorg als beheersings- en overlevingsstrategie.* Zwolle: Waanders.

van Leeuwen, Marco. 1994. Logic of charity: poor relief in pre-industrial Europe. *Journal of Interdisciplinary History* 24(4): 589–613.

Vita Antonii junioris. 1907. A. Papadopoulos-Kerameus (ed.) *Pravoslavnij Palestinskij Sbornik* 57: 186–216.

Vita Clementis. 1857–66. *Vita et certamen Sancti Clementis Ancyrani et sociorum.* In PG, 114: 815–94.

Vita Euthymii. 1939. E. Schwartz (ed.) *Kyrillos von Skythopolis: Leben des Euthymios.* In *Texte und Untersuchungen,* 49 (no. 2): 2–82.

Vita Petri. 1888. *Vita et conversatio Sancti Petri episcopi Argivorum.* In A. Mai (ed.) *Patrum nova bibliotheca,* vol. 9.3: 1–17. Rome.

Vogel, Cheri A. 1999. Using administrative databases to examine factors affecting length of stay in substitute care. *Children and Youth Services Review* 21: 677–680.

Wall, Helena M. 2000. Notes on life since *A little commonwealth*: Family and gender history since 1970. *William and Mary Quarterly* 57: 809–825.

Waring, Joseph I. 1964. *History of medicine in South Carolina, 1670–1825.* Columbia: South Carolina Medical Association.

Wehrmeister, Kurt. 1996. Telephone interview with David T. Beito, January 23.

Weir, Robert M. 1969. "The harmony we were famous for": An interpretation of pre-revolutionary South Carolina politics. *William and Mary Quarterly* 26: 473–501.

Weir, Robert M. 1997. *Colonial South Carolina: A History*. Columbia: University of South Carolina Press.

Weisman, Mary Lou. 1994. When Parents Are Not in the Best Interests of the Child, *The Atlantic Monthly*, July 1994: 43–63.

Welfare Council of Metropolitan Chicago. 1923. Minutes of the Meeting of the Children's Council, Meeting of 25 October 1923.

Welfare Council of Metropolitan Chicago. 1962. *Statistics 29*. (January-May).

Whitcomb, Mildred E. 1949. First grade—the school's last chance: An interview with Martin L. Reymert. *Nation's Schools* 43(3): 21–25.

White, Francis H. 1893. "Placing Out New York Children in the West." *Charities Review: A Journal of Practical Sociology* 2 (February): 216–25.

The White Hall Orphan's Home Society. Ca. 1907. Orphan File. Illinois State Historical Library, Springfield, IL.

Whitman, T. Stephen. Forthcoming. Orphans in city and countryside in nineteenth century Maryland. In *Children bound to labor in early America*, editors Ruth Wallis Herndon and John E. Murray. Ithaca: Cornell University Press.

Wikramanayake, Marina 1973. *A world in shadow: The free black in antebellum South Carolina*. Columbia: University of South Carolina Press.

Wolins, Martin, and Irvine Piliavin. 1964. *Institution or Foster Family: A Century of Debate*. New York: Child Welfare League of America.

Wolins, M. and Y. Wozner. 1978. Deinstitutionalization and the Benevolent Asylum. *Social Service Review* 51 (4), 601–623.

Wolins, Martin, Y. Wozner, and S. Slye. 1980. Rejuvenating the Asylum: A Field Study. 16 (1), *Social Work Research & Abstracts*, 17–25.

Woll, Thomas W. Interview, February 5, l996, in Parma, Ohio.

Young Catholic's Friend Society. *The Catholic Mirror*. April 26, 1890, p. 5.

Zachariah of Mitylene. 1899. *The Syriac Chronicle Known as That of Zachariah of Mitylene*. Translated by F. J. Hamilton and E. W. Brooks. London: Methuen.

Zmora, Nurith. 1988. A Rediscovery of the Asylum: The Hebrew

Orphan Asylum through the Lives of Its First Fifty Orphans. *American Jewish History*, v. 77 (March 1988): pp. 452–475.

Zmora, Nurith. 1994. *Orphanages reconsidered: Child care institutions in Progressive Era Baltimore*. Philadelphia: Temple Univ. Press.

Zunz, Olivier. 1982. *The Changing Face of Inequality: Urbanization, Industrial Development, and Immigrants in Detroit, 1880–1920*. Chicago: University of Chicago Press.

Bibliography for Chapter 4 (Beito)

Manuscript Collections

Adams, Matthew P. to Albert Bushnell Hart. November 16, 1923. Folder 2. Box 14. Albert Bushnell Hart Papers, Harvard Univ. Archives. Pusey Library. Harvard Univ.

Baylor, A.S. Memo. Visit to Mooseheart Vocational School. October 22, 1923. Folder 1. Box 14. Hart Papers.

Hart, Albert Bushnell to John W. Ford. May 7, 1923. Folder: Moose and Mooseheart vocational training, 1921–1925, Box 14. Hart Papers.

Hart, Albert Bushnell to James J. Davis. September 19, 1924. Folder 1. Box 14. Hart Papers.

Hart, Albert Bushnell to Mathew P. Adams. October 1, 1924. Folder: Moose and Mooseheart. Discipline. 1922–1924. Box 13. Hart Papers.

Havlik, Robert F. to Adams, August 7, 1922. Folder: Moose and Mooseheart. Discipline. 1922–1924. Box 13. Hart Papers.

Mooseheart. Board of Governors. Action taken on the superintendent's docket by executive committee. February 14 and 15, 1923. Folder 2. Box 14, Hart Papers.

Mooseheart. Board of Governors. Correspondence and Reports, 1922–1924. Folder 2. Box 14. Hart Papers.

Mooseheart. Board of Governors. Minutes. March 29–30, 1924. Folder 1 and 2. Box 14. Hart Papers.

Mooseheart. Board of Governors. Minutes. July 27, 1924. Folder 1. Box 13. Hart Papers.

Mooseheart. Superintendent. Report. December 15, 1922, January 12, March 15, May 19, 1923, March 29, July 20, 1924. Folder 2. Box 14. Hart Papers.

Mooseheart. Superintendent. Progress Report. February 25, 1933. James J. Davis Papers. The Library of Congress.

Reymert, Martin L. Report by the Director of the Mooseheart Laboratory for Child Research. January 12–13, 1951, p. 4. File: Conferences, etc. Box 3. Martin L. Reymert Papers. Archives of the History of American Psychology. Univ. of Akron.

Bibliography for Chapter 6 (Murray)

Manuscript sources

All are in Charleston Orphan House records, South Carolina Room, Charleston County Public Library.

Minutes of Commissioners' Meetings.
"Rejected Indentures"
"Indentures"
"Indenture Book"
"Report of Steward and Physician, 1809–1816"
"Report of Steward and Physician, 1823–1830"
"Annual Report of the Physician, 1829–1853"

Published sources

Aram, Dorit and Iris Levin. 2001. Mother-child joint writing in low SES: Sociocultural factors, maternal mediation, and emergent literacy. *Cognitive Development* 16: 831–852.

Becker, Gary. 1975. *Human capital: A theoretical and empirical analysis with special reference to education.* Chicago: University of Chicago Press.

Bolton, Charles C. *Poor whites of the antebellum South: Tenants and laborers in central North Carolina and northeast Mississippi.* Durham: Duke University Press.

*By-laws of the Orphan House of Charleston, South Carolina,*1861 version, quoting 1790 city ordinance. Electronic edition at http://docsouth.unc.edu/imls/orphan/menu.html

Cecil-Fronsman, Bill. 1992. *Common whites: Class and culture in antebellum North Carolina.* Lexington: University Press of Kentucky.

Censer, Jane Turner. 1984. *North Carolina planters and their children, 1800–1860.* Baton Rouge: Louisiana State University Press.

Charleston City Council. 1861. *Circular of the city council on retrenchment, and report of the Commissioners of the Orphan House.* Charleston: Evans and Cogswell.

Cott, Nancy A. 1977. *The bonds of womanhood: "Woman's sphere" in New England, 1780–1835*. New Haven: Yale University Press.

Courtney, Mark E. and Yin-Ling Irene Wong. 1996. Comparing the timing of exits from substitute care. *Children and Youth Services Review* 18: 307–334.

DeBow, J.D.B. 1854. *Statistical view of the United States*. Washington: A.O.P. Nicholson.

Degler, Carl N. 1980. *At Odds: Women and the Family in America from the Revolution to the Present*. New York: Oxford University Press.

Demos, John P. 1970. *A little commonwealth: Family life in Plymouth Colony*. New York: Oxford University Press.

Fraser, Walter J. Jr. 1989. *Charleston! Charleston! The history of a southern city*. Columbia: University of South Carolina Press.

Glover, Lorri. 2000. *All our relations: Blood ties and emotional bonds among the early South Carolina gentry*. Baltimore: Johns Hopkins University Press.

Graff, Harvey. 1987. *The legacies of literacy: Continuities and contradictions in western culture and society*. Bloomington: Indiana University Press.

Greven, Philip A. 1977. *The Protestant temperament: Patterns of child-rearing, religious experience, and the self in early America*. New York: Knopf.

Hacsi, Timothy A. 1997. *Second home: Orphan asylums and poor families in America*. Cambridge: Harvard University Press.

Hamilton, Gillian. 1995. Enforcement in apprenticeship contracts: Were runaways a serious problem? Evidence from Montreal. *Journal of Economic History* 55: 551–574.

Jabour, Anya. 1998. *Marriage in the early republic: Elizabeth and William Wirt and the companionate ideal*. Baltimore: Johns Hopkins University Press.

Johnson, Michael P. and James L. Roark. 1984. *No chariot let down: Charleston's free people of color on the eve of the Civil War*. Chapel Hill: University of North Carolina Press.

Lebsock, Suzanne, *The free women of Petersburg: Status and culture in a southern town, 1784–1860*. New York: W.W. Norton.

Lewis, Jan. 1983. *The pursuit of happiness: Family and values in Jefferson's Virginia*. New York: Cambridge University Press.

Lockridge, Kenneth A. 1974. *Literacy in colonial New England: An enquiry into the social context of literacy in the early modern west.* New York: W.W. Norton.

Main, Gloria L. 2001. *Peoples of a spacious land: Families and cultures in colonial New England.* Cambridge: Harvard University Press.

Murray, John E. 1997. Generation(s) of human capital: Literacy in American families, 1830–1875. *Journal of Interdisciplinary History* 27: 413–435.

Murray, John E. 2004. Family, literacy, and skill training in the antebellum south: Historical-longitudinal evidence from Charleston. *Journal of Economic History* 64: 773–799.

Murray, John E. 2004. Literacy acquisition in an orphanage: A historical-longitudinal case study. *American Journal of Education* 110: 172–195.

Murray, John E. and Ruth Wallis Herndon. 2002. Markets for children in early America: A political economy of pauper apprenticeship. *Journal of Economic History* 62: 356–382.

Murray, John E. Forthcoming. Mothers and children in and out of the Charleston Orphan House," in Ruth Wallis Herndon and John E. Murray, editors, *Children bound to labor in early America* (Ithaca: Cornell University Press, forthcoming).

Rutman, Darrett B. and Anita H. Rutman. 1994. *Small worlds, large questions: Explorations in early American social history, 1600–1850.* Charlottesville: University of Virginia Press.

Schwartz, Marie Jenkins. 2000. *Born in bondage: Growing up enslaved in the antebellum South.* Cambridge: Harvard University Press.

Smith, Daniel Blake. 1977–78., Autonomy and affection: Parents and children in eighteenth century Chesapeake families. *Journal of Psychohistory* 6: 32–51.

Steckel, Richard H. 1986. A dreadful childhood: The excess mortality of American slaves. *Social Science History* 10: 427–465.

Tocqueville, Alexis de (trans. and ed. Harvey C. Mansfield and Delba Winthrop). 2000. *Democracy in America.* Chicago: University of Chicago Press.

Vogel, Cheri A. 1999. Using administrative databases to examine factors affecting length of stay in substitute care. *Children and Youth Services Review* 21: 677–680.

Wall, Helena M. 2000. Notes on life since *A little commonwealth:*

Family and gender history since 1970. *William and Mary Quarterly* 57: 809–825.

Waring, Joseph I. 1964. *History of medicine in South Carolina, 1670–1825*. Columbia: South Carolina Medical Association.

Weir, Robert M. 1969. "The harmony we were famous for": An interpretation of pre-revolutionary South Carolina politics. *William and Mary Quarterly* 26: 473–501.

Weir, Robert M. 1997. *Colonial South Carolina: A History*. Columbia: University of South Carolina Press.

Whitman, T. Stephen. Forthcoming. Orphans in city and countryside in nineteenth century Maryland. In *Children bound to labor in early America*, editors Ruth Wallis Herndon and John E. Murray. Ithaca: Cornell University Press.

Wikramanayake, Marina 1973. *A world in shadow: The free black in antebellum South Carolina*. Columbia: University of South Carolina Press.

The documentary film *Homecoming: The Forgotten World of America's Orphanages,* directed by George Cawood and produced by Richard McKenzie and Gary Byrne, can be obtained directly from the sponsoring PBS station at www.kvie.org or from Richard McKenzie (mckenzie@uci.edu). A trailer on the film is available at http://homecomingmovie.org/.

Index

Page numbers followed by *t* indicate tables.
Page numbers followed by *f* indicate figures.

Dutch Republic, 43–62; charity care of "middling" citizens, 51–54, 58; ethical and religious nature of charity in, 43–46; "logic of charity" and, 46–49; political context of charity, 48–51; quality of municipal orphan care, 54–60

education and training: in *Burgerweeshuis*, 57–58; in Byzantine orphanages, 28–30, 31–32; at Chapin Hall, 98; at Charleston Orphan House, 131, 135; in general, 234–235, 236; at Hebrew Orphan Asylum, 184, 198; at Mooseheart, 66, 87–88; Progressive Era reforms and asylum idea, 1890–1910, 98–105; at Samuel Ready School, 188
Engler, Richard, 9–12, 13–14, 19
Essenes, 25–26
Euthymios, Saint, 29–30

Fanshel, David, 14–15
Farrelly, Bishop John, 161, 163, 175
Ferguson, Dwight, 9–10
Fields, Sarah, 137
foster care: in Baltimore, 203–204; criticisms of, 12–14; decline of orphanages and, 8, 239, 243, 246–247; Jewish organizations and, 110; role in child welfare setting, 1, 11*f*, 18–19, 21; studies of, 8–12, 14–16, 19
Fracastoro, Girolamo, 39
Frank, Bertha Rayner, 199
fraternal organizations, 63, 240. *See also* Mooseheart
Freemen's schools, 4–5
Freudenthal, Samuel, 185–186
Freudenthal family, 185

George, William R., 83
Gilman, Dr. Daniel C., 190
Gingrich, Newt, vii–viii, 248
Goddard, Elizabeth, 121

Goodman, Ellen, vii
Goudy, Helen, 95, 119, 120
Graham, W.L., 136–137
Great Depression: Cleveland orphanages in, 164–166, 175; decline of orphanages and, 238, 240–241
Greece, care of orphans in ancient, 23, 24–25
Greven, Philip, 128

Hacsi, Timothy A., 157
Haffner, Clarissa, 95, 120, 121, 122, 123
Half-Orphan Asylum. *See* Chapin Hall
Hamilton, Gillian, 138
Hampton Institute, 5
Harlow, Henry, 12–13
Hart, Albert Bushnell, 65, 70, 86
Hart, Hastings Hornell, 7, 220
Hartley, Robert M., 208
Hebrew Orphan Asylum (HOA), Baltimore, 181–187, 200; Board of Directors and financial management, 183–187, 197–199
Hebrew Orphan Asylum Ladies Aid Society, 198
Henderson, Charles, 103
Henning, Edward J., 4
Hill, Anna Laura, 221
Holy Ghost Greek Catholic Orphanage, Cleveland, 161, 176
Holy Ghost Roman Catholic Orphanage, Cleveland, 161, 176
Home of the Holy Family, Cleveland, 161, 163, 169, 176
Homecoming: The Forgotten World of America's Orphanages (film), xiii–xiv
Horstman, Bishop Ignatius, 161
Hospitallers, 36–37, 38
House of Orange, political context of Dutch charity and, 49–50, 61–62
Howard Mission and Home for Little Wanderers, 215